JOURNEYS OF COURAGE

Joy Carol's stories about the firefighters of New York City are just the stories we need after the tragedy and pain of 9/11. They are stories that will give us strength and courage for these times, and they will help us to heal. I highly recommend **Journeys of Courage** *for every person—and especially for all firefighters. I guarantee it will touch your heart and leave you feeling encouraged and filled with hope.*

   — **Jim Boyle**, retired president, **Uniformed Firefighters Association**

Joy Carol has done it again. Wide-ranging and wonderful, this is a unique guide to places and people that have much to teach us about how healing happens.

   —**Nina H. Frost**, author of *Soul Mapping*

These are the stories we need after 9/11, stories that can heal. With her sure sense of timing, Joy Carol has once again come forward to inspire us, to urge us on. Here her focus is on a larger context—community.

   —**China Galland**, author of **The Bond Between Women: A Journey to Fierce Compassion** and **Longing for Darkness: Tara and the Black Madonna**

Today, more than ever, we need community. The only question is "How do we heal the rupture that divides us?" Joy Carol explains the importance of communities coming together to both offer and receive support.

   —**Helen LaKelly Hunt and Harville Hendrix**, coauthors of **Getting the Love You Want**

Joy Carol tells stories of communities where evil has been confronted head on, where forgiveness and reconciliation have become possible through the courageous witness of ordinary saints. Her stories inspire, encourage, and challenge us.

   —**Leonora Tubbs Tisdale**, author of **Making Room at the Table**

Joy Carol comes from an inner place of truth, love, and integrity. Reading her books is a way to come back to our own reality . . . feeling safe and secure.

   —**Pat Pearson**, author of **Stop Self Sabotage**

Journeys of Courage *speaks to the ability of the human heart to survive the unthinkable. In the darkness of tragedy and loss, Ms. Carol has once again given voice to the many who have chosen to keep going.*

   —**Deirdre Felton**, **Bereavement Magazine**

We are all in need of healing, of stories such as these, to inspire and cheer us on against what often seem insurmountable odds. In struggle, we build community and find healing that gives hope and strength to create a different future.

   —**Mary Zepernick**, President, **Women's International League for Peace and Freedom**

JOURNEYS OF COURAGE

Remarkable Stories
of the Healing Power of Community

"A superbly crafted collection of moving
stories to inspire all of us!"
—**Archbishop Desmond Tutu**

JOY CAROL

 SORIN BOOKS™   Notre Dame, Indiana

Originally published as *Journeys of Courage* by Veritas Publications, 7-8 Lr Abbey Street, Dublin 1; Republic of Ireland (www.veritas.ie).

www.avemariapress.com

International Standard Book Number: 1-893732-79-7

Cover and text design by John Carson

Cover photo: Untitled (513/3) by Gerhard Richter ca. 1980 © Corbis. All Rights Reserved.

Printed and bound in the United States of America.

Library of Congress Cataloging-in-Publication Data
Carol, Joy, 1938-
  Journeys of courage : remarkable stories of the healing power of community / Joy Carol.
      p. cm.
  Includes bibliographical references.
  ISBN 1-893732-79-7 (pbk.)
  1. Helping behavior--United States--Case studies. 2. September 11 Terrorist Attacks, 2001. 3. Helping behavior--Ireland--Case studies. 4. Ireland--Social conditions--1973---Case studies. 5. Helping behavior--Religious aspects--Catholic Church--Case studies. 6. September 11 Terrorist Attacks, 2001--Religious aspects--Catholic Church--Case studies. 7. Church and social problems--Ireland--Case studies. I. Title.
BJ1474 .C37 2004
302'.14--dc22   2003021976

CONTENTS

ACKNOWLEDGMENTS 7

INTRODUCTION 9

THE UNITED STATES

Introduction 21

Community Gardening: *Tending Our Gardens* 25

The Firefighters
    Firehouse Engine 217: *Healing Around the Kitchen Table* 33
    A Firefighter's Family: *Discovering Our Hearts' Treasures* 48
    The Bagpipers: *Lifting Their Spirits* 63
    The Healing Trees: *Remembering Heroes* 71

The Department of Sanitation: *Clearing Sacred Ground* 77

St. Paul's Chapel: *Creating a Haven* 89

Our Children and "Ordinary People": *Touching Angels* 97

Contemporary Roman Catholics (CRC): *Running With God* 111

The Caregivers: *Caring for Our Souls* 123

THE REPUBLIC OF IRELAND

Introduction 133

The Church: *Facing the Truth* 137

Cuan Mhuire Addiction Center: *Finding a Way From Hell* 153

Mountjoy Prison's Dóchas Center: *Creating New Lives* 167

NORTHERN IRELAND

Introduction 185

Survivors of Trauma: *Yearning for Wholeness* 189

Political Prisoners in the Maze Prison:
    Embracing Our Mothers' Sons 205

The Corrymeela Community: *Welcoming to All* 215

Restoration Ministries: *Interlocking Our Journeys* 229

AFTERWORD 243

NOTES 250

*Dedicated with gratitude and admiration
to the communities who shared their inspiring and
courageous stories,
and to Wilson Julius Haupt, my loving and
courageous father.*

❖ ❖ ❖ ❖ ❖ ❖ ❖ ❖

*I live in times of great trial:
An age of change sits at my door.
Without a community with others I can so
easily lose the way. . . .*
— Edward Hays

ACKNOWLEDGMENTS AND GRATITUDE FOR HEALING COURAGE

This book has been blessed. It has taken me on a remarkable journey of courage with the most amazing people and communities. Behind this book are some special people who helped me find the courage to interview and write about communities that have been deeply traumatized, and whose stories will give us hope and confidence for the future. I thank each and every one of you; there is no greater gift that you could have given me than your support and belief in this book.

About two years ago, shortly after my beautiful mother, Alma Haupt, left this earth, I found myself amazed by the supportive community of people who gathered around my father, Wilson, and my family, to uphold and sustain us in our loss. I came to understand how powerful communities can be in the healing process. I am thankful for that revelation.

There are many people for whom I'm deeply grateful. First and foremost, I want to thank each one of the inspiring communities whom I interviewed in this book. They openly and courageously shared their healing and transforming stories—no matter how painful or difficult they might have been. By their examples, they have shown us how we, too, can live with hope and joy, even when we are in the midst of serious problems and deep distress.

I also give thanks to my family and friends, who are always there for me and whom I appreciate more than they can possibly know; my pal Gab McDonough, who lovingly read every word of every chapter at least twice—of this book and the last one; Dermod McCarthy, who introduced me to many wonderful communities in the Republic of Ireland and in Northern Ireland; Ellen Kirby, President of the American Community Gardening Association, who led me to the community gardeners in the first chapter; my friends who courageously worked in the ruins of the World Trade Center as recovery and rescue workers; my guardian angel Rosemary Weintraub, who continues to watch over me; and my friends Helen LaKelly Hunt and Harville Hendrix, who have showed endless enthusiasm for my books.

I feel particularly blessed to have had the extraordinary community of people at Sorin Books and Veritas Publications encouraging me to write this book filled with courage. I feel most appreciative of their leadership and support, as well as the invaluable assistance I've received from each one of them. I am pleased and honored to have had the privilege of working with them.

I give thanks to all of you.

INTRODUCTION

*We human beings cannot survive alone. If we were by
nature solitary, there would be no towns or cities. Our
own survival depends entirely on others. When we
consider the other as someone precious and respected,
it is natural that we will help them and share with
them an expression of our love.*
—*the Dalai Lama*

I grew up on a farm in the wide-open spaces of Nebraska in the heartland of America. As a child, I often climbed to the top of our rickety old windmill that stood near the barn. I loved to pretend that I was visiting friends in a tall apartment building in New York City. From the top, I could look for miles in every direction and not see another living soul. On those lonely, windswept plains I saw rolling hills filled with wheat, corn, oats, tumbleweeds, and occasionally cows and sheep, but it was almost impossible to see any discernible sign of a "community."

Yet, because I yearned to be connected, to feel included and involved in interacting with others, I created my own little "communities" without even knowing that was what I was doing. These special communities encompassed every aspect of my life on that Nebraska farm. Of course, I had my supportive family community: my parents, Wilson and Alma; my big sister, Shirley; and my grandparents, Edward and Johanna. I also had my loyal animal community: our pet dogs, Buddy and Brownie; our cats, Spot and Purr Mew; and my lambs, Blackie and Frisky. If for some reason these communities weren't available to me, I had my make-believe communities—the apartment building windmill and the "fence post people." On the way to the far pasture where I went to bring the cows home for their evening milking, I passed rusty wire fences strung between dead tree branches that served as fence posts. To me, each one of those fence posts was someone whom I could nurture, talk with and listen to. They played an important role in meeting my compelling human need to be part of the life of a community.

After those early days on the farm, my search for community continued throughout my life. I joined clubs, churches, choirs, support groups, centers. Later, as a professional, I worked for international community development organizations like the

Ford Foundation, Save the Children, and the Christian Children's Fund, whose major efforts were focused on strengthening communities throughout the world to become healthier and more self-reliant.

While working in some of the most impoverished areas in the world, I often witnessed people experiencing the benefits of what I call meaningful communities. In the slums of Karachi, Pakistan, for example, I saw destitution and diseases that I had never imagined could exist. Yet in the midst of what appeared to be miserable conditions, I experienced a great deal of camaraderie and joy within those communities. In more than 100-degree weather, families warmly welcomed me into their tiny mud-hut homes, surrounded by open sewers with flies and mosquitoes swarming around. Usually we sat on a dirt floor talking and laughing together. Often we shared a single cup of tea, respectfully passing it from person to person and drinking from it until it was empty. I confess I was astonished that these poorest of the poor had such a tangible sense of kinship and belonging in their lives. As I left their homes, I knew I had experienced the genuine gift of community spirit.

In these difficult and uncertain times in which we live, we may feel a foreboding sense of dread, anxiety, and gloom. We long to be a part of a healthy community where we will be safe and protected, where we can be restored and find peace, where we can be embraced for who we are. Sometimes we form new communities because we share common goals and feel a sense of belonging and security with them. Within the harbor of supportive communities, we can face our suffering and our fears, and we come to understand that we are not alone. It is then that we may find the courage to help others and the strength to resolve some of the problems that surround us in the world.

After the tragic events of September 11, 2001, those of us who lived in New York City soon realized how critical it was to be a part of a community, to join forces with others in order to lick our wounds, to grieve our losses, and to begin the process of recovery and healing. Without much thought or planning, we somehow were galvanized to pull together and to reach out to each other in our suffering and need. I'm certain the process of our "healing" from the horror of that day was enhanced because we felt a sense of fellowship—not only with each other in New York City but with people throughout the world who felt like an extension of our community too. An extraordinary, cooperative spirit emerged from this tragedy. Volunteers from all parts of the planet came forth from every culture, ethnic group, class, and profession. The poor worked with the wealthy; blue-collar workers gave their time alongside professionals. Everyone volunteered in some way by giving blood, searching for the missing, carrying buckets of water, handing out food and coffee, writing letters of encouragement, raising money for the victims.

Almost everyone was touched by the community spirit that seemed to take over New York City, a place that had often been called detached and impersonal. People felt free to cry and express their feelings in parks, in train stations, in churches, on the street. Strangers reached out and embraced one another in their pain. Every day hundreds of people stood along the streets and cheered the rescue workers as they entered and left the site of the ruins of the World Trade Center yelling, "We love you. We support you. Never give up." I saw a homeless beggar take money someone had given him and put it in a collection box for the victims. It brings tears to my eyes as I think about it. On the whole, people were kinder and gentler with each other. People willingly gave up their seats for others on buses and subways. We experienced a newfound respect and a feeling of compassion for all peoples. And we learned an important lesson: Although we could not change the terrible things that had happened to us, we could change how we responded to them.

The entire New York City community received volumes of encouragement from communities around the United States and the world. The outpouring of support and generosity was enormous. Children wrote letters, drew pictures, and sent candy bars with notes of love to the rescue workers. In spite of high security, visitors came to the city carrying empty suitcases. Their goal: to bolster New York City's shattered economy by purchasing things from stores that were faltering.

Community agencies, emergency and trauma services, hospitals, schools, and universities pooled their resources and worked as a team so things were done quickly and well to provide housing, financial assistance, emergency services, counseling, and food for the victims and to those who had been traumatized. Churches, synagogues, mosques, and temples learned what it meant to be genuine communities of service and turned themselves into houses of hospitality. Many opened their doors twenty-four hours a day. A firefighter told me, "Strangers have become a real community to each other because we have shared so much."

As time went on, I became aware of the fact that the number of people who died in the United States on September 11 in those 102 minutes of terrorism and violence was almost the same number as those who died in over thirty years of "the Troubles" in Northern Ireland. I was surprised to learn that more than 50 percent of the people who were killed in the World Trade Center in New York were of Irish descent. That information compelled me to begin thinking beyond the United States and about communities in Northern Ireland that have suffered severely during the Troubles and the kind of restoration process they were undertaking. Were there lessons that we too could benefit from? I was also conscious that the last two decades have brought enormous changes for communities in the Republic of Ireland. I wondered how people have coped with modifications they were forced to face and if there were things we could learn from them. Could all of these different communities in the United States, Ireland, and Northern Ireland teach us some useful lessons that would help break patterns of destruction and lead us to a healing process?

So I undertook the stimulating project of interviewing communities in these places that had experienced difficult and challenging situations that had caused them emotional, social, spiritual, or political problems. The outcome of my research is this book, which is filled with remarkable stories about communities that responded to their dilemmas by courageously facing them and changing their reactions to them. In the process, each community found courage, renewed joy, and meaning in life as they underwent some kind of transformation, some kind of healing process.

These stories touch on critical contemporary issues in today's world that affect many of our lives, such as our fears, losses, and griefs related to trauma, terrorism, and war; our disappointments in institutions that have failed us, such as our families, churches, schools; our addictions; our poverty of mind, body, and spirit; our vulnerabilities. The stories demonstrate the depth of human potential and the many acts of forgiveness and generosity that can be found within communities. They also teach us what helped communities to undertake a healing process and to reflect on new opportunities and options for ourselves.

In this book, "communities" are broadly defined to include families, children, community gardeners, firefighters, prisoners, addicts, victims of discrimination, churches, schools, neighborhoods. They range from people who were thrown together unexpectedly because of a traumatic incident to those who were in highly systematized and intentional organizations. They include people who were affected by the devastating losses of 9/11, to the survivors of trauma in Northern Ireland, to the victims of abuses within the church, to prisoners being integrated back into communities, to the people affected by addictions and poverty.

❖ ❖ ❖ ❖ ❖ ❖ ❖ ❖

Here we are, in the end, fellow beings on the journey. We come together or are brought together in so many ways. We are sharing the experience of unity. We are walking each other home.
                                                    —*Ram Dass*

Each one of the stories in this book is filled with remarkable lessons about the process of "healing." As I interviewed people in these communities, I was struck by the many different methods and ways that people united to undertake a healing process. It didn't take long to comprehend that the concept of the healing of communities is vast and extensive. As I did in my earlier book *Towers of Hope* (Forest of Peace, 2002), I expanded my definition of the healing process to be a rather broad and comprehensive one. Here are elements I now include in a definition of healing as it relates to communities.

Factors That Contribute to the Healing of Communities:

- **Becoming a more authentic community.** Healing is being clear about what we really value as a community, what our goals and purposes are, what we stand for and are willing to be counted for.

- **Connecting and reconnecting with others.** When we are connected to one another, we have a sense of interdependence; we are not isolated, nor are we autonomous. We share our humanity with each other. In that sharing, we may find a sense of purpose and a movement toward wholeness.

- **Being open to change and new possibilities** even when it may appear difficult, being willing to respond to problems and dilemmas by transforming the situation.

- **Accepting that problems, pain, and suffering are part of the life** of a community, of being in the world, that they are not isolated events and cannot be avoided. Such an acceptance enables our communities to approach problems and use painful and difficult events to learn to grow and mature.

- **Feeling accepted and acceptable, finding dignity and respect** in our work, in the roles we play, knowing what we have done is worthy and helpful even if we are not publicly commended or supported.

- **Valuing our "gifts"** so much that we want to share them with others who may be in need of them. It also means that we realize the importance of protecting ourselves, of taking special care of ourselves in order to avoid burnout or the dangers of an "empty tank" syndrome, especially when times are difficult.

- **Reaching out to others with our gifts** and, in like manner, receiving gifts from others with openness, generosity, appreciation, and thanksgiving.

- **Trusting and letting go of some of the control,** knowing that others have many capabilities and gifts, enjoying and appreciating that others can carry on without our close supervision.

- **Facing the truth,** releasing old images about our community that aren't true or genuine, understanding that the truth will free us and that we will be more real.

- **Accepting diversity and ending discriminatory actions** against those who are different from us, understanding that discrimination has the false effect of making us feel important, while putting down and harming others.

- **Treating all people with dignity, respect, and compassion—** ourselves included—even when people are regarded as inadequate, as unworthy, as addicts or criminals.

- **Being helpful to those who are hurting or are in pain** even when we ourselves are suffering and have more healing to undertake.

- **Doing something** when we feel helpless or powerless.

- **Listening and having the capacity to focus on others** who may need to be heard, who may want to tell their stories.

- **Being willing to share our stories** with others, understanding that our stories have healing power for ourselves and for others.

- **Being forgiving of our own dark sides, our problems and mistakes,** and being forgiven by others; giving others and ourselves the freedom to let go of rivalry, strife, anger, hatred, fear, and limitations.

- **Not giving up** when we know what we are doing is right— even when the times are tough and we feel we are going against the stream. Being willing to hang in for the long haul with patience and trust that things will eventually improve if we keep working at it.

- **Being loving and loved,** having a feeling of loving one's community and wanting to love and serve others, as well as being capable of receiving love. With loving comes an ability to trust one another and a feeling of greater participation in life.

❖ ❖ ❖ ❖ ❖ ❖ ❖ ❖ ❖

*Inclusion in a group is a human necessity; it is the
enduring cement that holds us to one another. . . .
Community is not a luxury. It's like air for us.*
                                    —*Kathleen A. Brehony*

We live in very turbulent and violent times. Many of our communities have been damaged or disconnected in some way. We yearn to feel more wholesome and peaceful, to find a reason for hope, to be more courageous. We may need and want to change our situation, but we are uncertain how to go about doing so. Through the examples found in stories, we can be helped to see various options for action. Stories have the ability to fill us with all kinds of possibilities. They can encourage us to move ahead by telling us truths about what has worked before, what has failed, what we can try ourselves, what we should avoid.

For centuries, storytelling has been used as a powerful and beneficial tool in the healing process. Healing stories can touch our hearts and help us understand that life is a series of challenges—not all good, not all bad. Healing stories can help us expand our consciousness so that we can see our lives and the world in new ways. Yes, telling and hearing stories can be powerful medicine.

Reading the moving accounts and challenges that these communities faced can help us put our own wounds, fears, and difficulties in a more meaningful and hopeful context. By sharing their choices and movements toward wholeness, these communities can become our guides and companions. They can show us how we can achieve transitions from suffering and pain to strength and courage. Their stories have the power to reach out to us and have a healing effect on us.

Every one of these stories contains powerful lessons that speak to some of our communities' needs in these times of change, fear, and uncertainty. The communities who tell their stories in this book faced many problems and found healing. These communities have been there, they have stumbled and fallen, they have learned, they have grown, and they have something to share with us. One of the most important lessons we can learn from them is that during times of crisis, such as that which occurred on September 11, 2001, we may feel paralyzed with fear and inertia. But if we work and act together as a team, we can be freed up from our inactivity and our numbness. Indeed, working in community during such difficult times can draw out the very best in us and can enhance our individual capacities. We may be surprised to find that our shared actions are more fruitful than we ever would have expected, that the whole is greater than the sum of the parts.

As you read these stories, you will see that transformation and positive change can take place that will make life on this planet more livable, more wholesome, more a *journey of courage*.

THE UNITED STATES

INTRODUCTION

*We must never forget that we may also find meaning
in life even when confronted with a hopeless situation,
when facing a fate that cannot be changed. For what
then matters is to bear witness to the uniquely human
potential at its best, which is to transform a personal
tragedy into a triumph, to turn one's predicament into
a human achievement.*

—Viktor Frankl

For more than two centuries, we who live in the United States
have not really understood or known what it means to live in
constant fear, to have armed military personnel with machine
guns patrolling our streets, to be troubled that we might be
exposed to anthrax, to worry about possible terrorist attacks, to
be on high alert. We were not forced to deal firsthand with such
frightening circumstances. We knew that they existed for people
in other parts of the world. But not in our country! Not in the
United States!

All of that changed on September 11, 2001, that pivotal day in
American history known as "9/11." Suddenly life seemed to chill
to our very bones and to shift entirely for us when terrorists
brutally attacked the World Trade Center and the Pentagon. As
the world watched in disbelief and shock, thousands of lives,
hopes, and dreams were destroyed in less than two hours. Since
then, it feels as though an invisible and indestructible line was
drawn in the sand, and we no longer have the luxury of returning
to our old ways of living. Whether we live in New York City, or
on a farm in Kansas, or in a suburb of Los Angeles, our style and
manner of existence has been forever altered. We are now forced
to live with high security in airports, a war on terrorism, and
confusing and frightening security announcements and alert
codes. Our carefree and unworried style of living has
disappeared, and we have lost some of our "innocence" and
certainly some of our naiveté. Today we talk about coping and
surviving. Perhaps for the first time in our history, we

understand what people in other parts of the world have lived with for decades.

Numerous books and articles have been written about the pain, suffering, trauma, and loss that took place on September 11. The tragic and desolate stories from that day have been told over and over. Sadly, there have been very few positive stories written about the communities that were able to undergo a healing process. Nor are there many stories about the communities that supported and assisted others.

If ever there has been a time when we have needed to hear some stories of "good news" from the United States, it is now. Healing stories have the power to give us hope and courage, to help us care for ourselves, our families, our communities, and our world. Ruth Patterson, a woman in Northern Ireland who has dedicated her life to restoring the spirit of communities in her violence-ravaged country, works tirelessly to help heal some of the horrible wounds caused by more than thirty years of "the Troubles." One day when I was visiting her in Belfast, she told me, "We can encourage the rest of the world if they hear our good stories, our stories of courage, of hope, of forgiveness, of coming together, of new life. I feel that healing stories need to be shouted from the rooftops."

In these chapters from the United States, we hear some very inspiring stories of communities that experienced loss, tragedy, disappointment, and deep wounds. They remind us that terrible things do happen to us, but that does not have to be the end of the story. I've been told that Helen Keller never cursed her fate. Rather, she attributed her accomplishments to what she learned from her hardships. She said, "Only through experience of trial and suffering can the soul be strengthened, vision cleared, ambition inspired and success achieved."

Certainly these communities were strengthened, had their vision cleared, their ambition inspired, and their success achieved. Each community transformed its own and others' anguish and troubles into joy, optimism, and wisdom. And each one made, or helped another community to make, a remarkable recovery.

These stories of courage, bravery, and compassion will give us hope because they confirm that the world is filled with people and communities who suffer but who are able to find dignity, meaning, and significance in life and who reach out to be connected, to be of assistance to others, to be part of a healing community. These moving stories, which have not been told before, deserve to be "shouted from the rooftops" to the entire world. They prove without a doubt that we can find treasures in the abyss of suffering. May these stories, which grew up out of ashes and pain, fill each of us with courage.

COMMUNITY GARDENING:
TENDING OUR GARDENS

As told by Community Gardeners in Seattle and New York City

It was gratifying and uplifting to see the Million Flower Compost from Seattle mixed with the soil of community gardens in New York City as a gift of our love and solidarity and as a living metaphor of hope and renewal. That day we felt so close to the renewal of New York City and of this small planet.
—Jon Rowley, Seattle

What the people from Seattle did for us gave us so much hope. We learned that there were people out there who didn't even know us, people who lived on the other side of the country, people who wanted to help us. . . . It was very healing to know that somebody cared about us and our gardens.
—Miriam Kimmelman, New York City

When our communities have been depleted, injured, and shattered, it is uplifting to have another community respond to us, to reach out to us in our pain. It gives us new hope and courage that we can be renewed to embark on our journey again, that we can make ourselves fresh and strong once more, that we can be restored.

On September 11, 2001, the Liberty Community Gardens in Battery Park City were almost destroyed when they were buried in the dust and ashes of the fallen Twin Towers of the World Trade Center. Later, the gardens were further damaged when they were used as a base for rescue and cleanup efforts at the site. The smashed fire trucks and cars from the site were temporarily stacked on one of the gardens. On another there were washing stations and changing rooms for the rescuers and workers from the site.

On the other side of the United States on September 11, shocked and heavy-hearted people in Seattle, Washington, responded almost instantaneously with their hearts and souls to the terrible tragedy. Nearly seventy-five thousand people expressed their concern by bringing more than a million flowers to the International Fountain in the Seattle Center. It was their way of honoring and supporting those who had suffered and died in a place nearly three thousand miles away. The P-Patch Community Gardening Program of Seattle, one of the strongest community greening programs in the country, decided to take matters into their own hands to help with the renewal and healing of the earth, of the gardens, of the City of New York—and ultimately of themselves.

❖ ❖ ❖ ❖ ❖ ❖ ❖ ❖

Jon Rowley, Community Gardener, Seattle

In Seattle, we have four thousand active gardeners in seventy P-Patch Community Gardens, which are managed through the city's Department of Neighborhoods. The Interbay P-Patch Garden, where I garden, has 130 gardeners and is the second largest and second oldest community garden in Seattle.

After 9/11, there was a spontaneous flower vigil at the large International Fountain at the Seattle Center. Tens of thousands of people came there just to stand, to pray or meditate, to cry, and to leave flowers at the fountain. Well over a million flowers were placed there as a collective expression of grief and loss.

When the flowers began to decay, several of our gardeners suggested that we compost them rather than allow them to be dumped. Hundreds of volunteers—Seattle P-Patch gardeners, firemen, police, schoolchildren, and residents—came together and patiently and deliberately separated the flowers from the plastic wrappings, the ribbons, the mementos, the wires, and the rubber bands. When they were finished, eighty cubic yards of flowers were delivered to our community garden. It was a huge pile! Then eighty volunteers chopped all those flowers by hand and mixed them up, pitchfork by pitchfork, wheelbarrow by wheelbarrow, with donated brown materials: leaves, pine needles, straw, rotted sawdust, and even pine-shaving bedding from circus elephants.

After 9/11 all of us needed to do something; we felt emotionally drained. It was impossible to get our minds around the tragedy and to comprehend what had happened. Making compost was a connection to the future. Compost is a metaphor for renewal, a part of the natural course of death and dying, of going through a process of decomposition, of returning to the earth, of getting new life. From new life we get hope. As we worked, we felt we were helping the earth, the gardens, our cities, and ourselves to be rejuvenated, to have new life. It provided healing for all of us.

As soon as we started the process of composting, one of the Interbay gardeners suggested that we commit some of the compost to the community garden closest to the World Trade Center site. This idea quickly met with approval. We contacted Ellen Kirby, the president of the American Community Gardening Association to get her help and she put us in touch with the Liberty Community Gardens in Battery Park City, which are only a block and a half away from the World Trade Center. We were astonished to learn that the gardens had been almost obliterated by debris after 9/11, that they were also used as a staging area by rescue and cleanup efforts at the site. Somehow that gave our small gesture more meaning. Getting some of the compost to gardens in New York City gave us a strong sense of purpose.

When we heard that gardeners from the Liberty Community Gardens were going to rededicate their ten-year-old gardens on September 28, 2002, we went into gear. Thirty-two clam and oyster boxes were each filled with forty to fifty pounds of the compost and flown to New York. Taylor Shellfish Farms donated the boxes and paid for the cost of the airfreight to New York, and UPS volunteered to bring the container from JFK Airport to the

Liberty Community Gardens. A delegation of eight community gardeners and Seattle City Council Members Richard Conlin and Judy Nicastro attended the rededication ceremony in New York. It was a real team effort in helping those composted memorial flowers make the cross-country journey to the community gardens near the World Trade Center.

The whole experience was very gratifying for us. We couldn't imagine what the people in the Battery Park neighborhood had been through, but we were happy to see plants growing and flourishing in their gardens again. We returned to Seattle with a meaningful and hopeful connection for ourselves and for the city of Seattle.

To put a small amount of compost in a garden is largely symbolic. But it was gratifying and uplifting to see the Million Flower Compost from Seattle mixed with the soil of community gardens in New York City as a gift of our love and solidarity and as a living metaphor of hope and renewal. That day we felt so close to the renewal of New York City and of this small planet. We believe Seattle became part of the regeneration of New York City that day.

John van Amerongen, Community Gardener and Musician/Songwriter, Seattle

In Seattle we had no concept of the horror of 9/11. We had heard many stories about people in the Towers making calls from cell phones, sending e-mails, leaving messages on answering machines for someone they loved. I wondered what it must have been like for the people who talked on the phone with a loved one before the Towers came down or who went home to find a light flashing on their message machine. Perhaps they thought: "Oh, they must be okay." Or maybe they just stared at the phone wondering if they had the courage to listen to the message. In the heart of those phone messages there was a lot about love. They probably had words like these: "I love you. I'm doing my best to get back to you. Do your best with the kids and give them a hug for me." That's the message we thought about in Seattle.

I knew I had to do something in response to 9/11, so I began writing a song. The weekend after I finished it, the Interbay P-Patch Garden started cutting up the flowers for the compost. I wanted to be with them, so I brought my guitar to the garden. I sang the song for the first time to the gardeners cutting up wilted flowers that would later become soil for the community gardens in New York City. A year later I sang it again at the rededication celebration of the Liberty Community Gardens. The message of love was at the core of the Seattle gardeners' involvement.

"Message from New York—Don't Forget to Say, 'I Love You' "[1] (final two verses)

Remember that I love you, remember that I care.
Remember I'm always with you, remember we all share
One heart as a family and the grace of God on high
No one can take that from us; that love can never die.

So don't forget them with the sunrise; don't forget them in the fall.
Don't forget their love and courage; take a lesson, one and all—
Don't forget to hug your children; don't forget those kiss goodbyes
Don't forget to say, "I love you." Build a love that never dies.

Miriam Kimmelman, Community Gardener, New York City

My husband, Richard Washburn, and I moved to Battery Park City ten years ago. What had attracted us to this place was the possibility that we might be able to have a small garden in the community gardens. I have dystonia, a neurological disability that affects my posture and my walking, but I have always managed to go to work and lead a fairly normal life. Richard was very anxious that I be outdoors and that I exercise more. He thought it would be therapeutic for me to get involved with gardening. He had a deep interest in gardening, and he loved doing composting. Richard and another gardener built the compost bins for the south garden; they are still standing even after the destruction of 9/11.

We worked together in our garden until the summer of 2000. Richard died in May of 2001. That whole summer after he died I continued to do a lot of gardening, and it made me feel that I was still working with him in the garden. Then came 9/11, and I was displaced from my home for several months. Although I didn't have a lot of damage in my apartment, I needed to live with friends in other locations until the air was a little cleaner.

When I came back in November, I met some of the Battery Park City gardeners, who told me I should not go near the gardens because my heart would be broken. The garden where Richard and I had done our gardening had been vacuumed level and looked as if it were completely destroyed. Finally, I went to look at it, and I saw a few early crocuses coming up. Even though I had lost a lot of plants, it was a positive sign for me. I thought maybe there was hope that other things would grow again in our garden. I dug up a few plants and took some of the dirt Richard had worked in and enriched with his compost. I was assigned a new plot in the south garden, and I put the soil and plants that I dug up into the new place. So I managed to save a little portion of the soil from my husband's garden.

In September 2002 I heard the marvelous news about the Seattle compost coming to our community gardens. On the day of the renewal of the gardens, I spent the whole day putting some of Seattle's compost in my new garden. I wanted to let my husband know that I was caring for "our garden" and caring for him. We all felt very grateful to the people of Seattle who had worked so hard to compost the flowers and to make this happen for us. Here was this wonderful renewing compost that had come all the way across the country to us in New York. What the people from Seattle did for us gave us so much hope. We learned that there were people out there who didn't even know us, people who lived on the other side of the country, people who wanted to help us. They were a real blessing to me and to so many community gardeners in New York City. It was very healing to know that somebody cared about us and our gardens.

Michael McCormack, Community Gardener, New York City

I first returned to my apartment in Battery Park City four days after 9/11. While there, I checked on the gardens and was astonished that so many plants were still alive. There was about four inches of World Trade Center dust and papers covering everything. A few of the taller, stronger plants were poking through all the debris, and there was what I call a "miracle marigold" that looked like it had grown right up through the dust, perfectly clean and pristine.

It was several weeks before I was allowed to move back into my apartment. I was relieved not to be homeless anymore. For the first months, I kept thinking things would return to normal in a few days. But every day as I went to my office, I had to walk by "the pile" on the site. The fires lasted until December, and there was no way to escape the horrible smell. Everything in my apartment had been completely covered with a "dust" that was gritty like fine sand and couldn't be easily wiped away. But I couldn't imagine leaving the area, because I really like the neighborhood and the gardens—it's my home. Now I understand better why people who live in flood zones or earthquake areas don't want to leave. Your home is your home. The period of January to March of 2002 was the hardest for me. Other people seemed to be moving on, but I was affected more than others around me because I worked and lived in the area. It seemed easier for people who just worked in the area, since they went home every night to places far from the site.

When things started getting back to "normal," I was amazed to see how many plants were still alive in our gardens. That gave us encouragement to start talking about the future of the gardens. When we were given some new space for the gardens, we wanted to hold a celebration to give thanks to the people who made it happen and to get the gardeners involved again.

The exchange with the Seattle community gardeners meant a lot to our community. The contribution of the Million Flower Compost to our community was a healing event that deeply moved us. It was much more than "just some dirt," It was wonderful to know that people so far away thought about us, that they cared so much about us that they were willing to share something of theirs with us. That's what community gardening is all about: it's not just about the community we live in; it's about the "bigger community."

❖   ❖   ❖   ❖   ❖   ❖   ❖   ❖

We must be the change we wish to see in the world.
To forget to dig the earth and tend the soil is to forget
ourselves.
—*Mahatma Gandhi*

This is a beautiful story about the healing of a community in New York City by another community thousands of miles away. As communities that are traumatized, damaged, or harmed during these volatile times, this story gives us confidence that seeds can sprout up out of ashes and ruins. Just when we feel that we have been devastated and possibly abandoned, another community thousands of miles away from us might respond to our needs with kindness and generosity, and we may find ourselves walking on fresh pathways of hope in a new garden.

When the people of Seattle started their caring actions, they were simply following their instincts and responding to another community's pain. They didn't plan to connect with them or to release them from their suffering. They didn't imagine that their efforts would dramatically help a New York City community in need. Out of the depths of their hearts, they were practicing what I call "soul compassion."

As a community, we may not know what our efforts, our tiny attempts to reach out, our little acts of kindness can do to help others. In fact, we might never know that what we tried to do had an enormously positive effect on another community that needed us to do just exactly what we did.

This healing story speaks volumes about getting together with others when trauma strikes, about joining forces to do the best we can to cope when times get really tough. It gives us a glimpse of why it's important to believe in the realm of possibilities and to keep a tiny spark of hope alive even when we are overwhelmed with our own and others' suffering and pain. We may be able to do something constructive and helpful when things seem out of our control and absolutely hopeless. It's encouraging to know that in the worst of times whenever we respond to others with "soul compassion," we make a difference in regenerating and restoring others and ourselves. I do believe that's true!

THE FIREFIGHTERS

FIREHOUSE ENGINE 217: HEALING AROUND THE KITCHEN TABLE

As told by Lieutenant Tom McGoff and Firefighters Danny White, Jim Hart, Frank Ardizzone, and John Byrne

We call what happens around the firehouse table the "healing process." . . . *There's a lot of stuff that goes on here, a lot of talking, crying, making fun of each other, laughing, healing.* . . . *Crying and laughing together have been important in our healing process.*
—Lieutenant Tom McGoff

Now we're crawling along. I'm not sure that we're really running yet, but we're getting better every day. That doesn't mean we won't fall down again. Not a day goes by when we don't think of our friends who were there who didn't return. Not a single day!
—Danny White

The tragic events of September 11, 2001, had an enormous impact on many communities in New York City, across the United States and throughout the world. One of the communities that suffered enormous losses was the Fire Department of New York City. The firefighters conscientiously and faithfully answered the alarm and without hesitation raced into the doomed Twin Towers of the World Trade Center. Many prayed on their rigs as they traveled toward the burning buildings. Their mission: to save as many people as possible. And they did. More than thirty-five thousand people were safely helped out of the buildings by these very compassionate and courageous firefighters. But the price was extremely high: 343 New York firefighters died in the line of duty on that dark day.

Many firehouses lost large numbers of men, while some lost only a few, and others lost none. But every firefighter lost friends, buddies, family members, companions. Each one of them felt the grief of a gaping hole in their hearts and in their lives. And they had the added burden of survivor's guilt: "Why not me? Why my brother, my friend?"

And if the disaster of 9/11 had not been enough anguish and sorrow for these bravest of the brave, almost every firefighter in New York City worked long shifts in the hellish pit at the site of the fallen Towers searching for the remains of bodies of their families, friends, and all who had died there. So posttraumatic stress didn't begin after 9/11 for them. They were still going through grief and raw agony as they attended funerals and carefully dug with their hands for their fallen comrades in the ashes and debris. When the Trade Center site was finally closed in May 2002, the firefighters had to face the next challenges: loss, grief, guilt, posttraumatic stress.

To heal from such pain and suffering is an enormous challenge— something neither easily nor quickly done. Under the best of circumstances it is a long and arduous task, and it is likely without real "closure." I chose to interview the firefighters at Engine 217 in Brooklyn, New York, the firehouse where Lieutenant Kenny Phelan worked before his death on September 11. The story of the healing of his family is written in this book's next section, "A Firefighter's Family."

There are twenty-nine firemen based at Engine 217. On a regular working day, six of them are present. On September 11, six gallant men headed to the World Trade Center with heavy hearts. Four of their beloved brothers died: Lieutenant Kenny Phelan, who was working in firehouse Engine 207 that day, and Firefighters Steve Coakley and Neal Leavy. Retired Firefighter Phil Hayes, who had worked for twenty years at Engine 217 and was the Fire Safety Director at the World Trade Center, also died.

On several occasions I spent hours sitting around a big kitchen table listening to the healing stories of this remarkable community: the firefighters of Engine 217.

❖ ❖ ❖ ❖ ❖ ❖ ❖ ❖

Lieutenant Tom McGoff

Sometimes when we look back at 9/11 and how that day developed, we realize that we really had no idea that events would unfold the way they did. At 8:45 in the morning the North Tower was hit, but we thought it was just an accident—a small airplane hitting the building. The fire companies near the World Trade Center area were told to go there immediately, so they needed to relocate other fire companies to that area to cover for them.

At 8:50 we were told to relocate to Manhattan, but soon after that we were told not to; when I told the guys we weren't going into Manhattan after all, they looked disappointed. It was such a beautiful day, and they wanted to get out of the firehouse. Then as we sat in front of the television, we saw the South Tower get hit. Suddenly it became an "Oh, shit" day. It was at that moment that we knew it wasn't a small plane and we understood that we were under attack. Two minutes later, the alarm came into the firehouse, and we were assigned to work in the South Tower. Suddenly, there was no excitement about going to Manhattan. As we drove in, we tried to select the best route and ended up going over the Brooklyn Bridge. I'm sure everybody was doing the same thing I was: looking up to the sky to see if there were any more kamikaze planes coming toward the bridge. As we drove toward the Trade Center, people were blessing themselves and praying. When we pulled up and took our hydrant, people hugged us. A cop told us that he had heard a third plane was coming, that we should be careful.

As we were heading toward the South Tower, Danny Suhr from Engine 216 was hit and killed by a person falling out of the building. So Jimmy Hart, Tommy Michel, and I helped Engine 216 carry him a block south, away from the other people falling from the Tower. Although we were certain he was already dead, we put him in an ambulance. While we were doing this, Steve Coakley and Neal Leavy, who were superb firemen from our firehouse, ran to the South Tower. Hundreds of people were walking out of the building, feeling relieved that they had escaped. But they were congregating right in front of the building in the zone where people were falling. Steve and Neal immediately tried to get them to move away and up the block. I'm certain they saved hundreds of lives that day by their actions.

After we put Danny Suhr in the ambulance, Jimmy, Tommy, and I started to walk toward the South Tower. It was then that I heard what sounded like a thousand freight trains. The building was collapsing. I looked up and yelled at the guys to run. You could hear the sound of each floor pounding on each floor as we ran. The concussion of the building blew us across the West Side Highway. I was certain I was going to die. I remember worrying about my wife and my kids, and I worried about the other guys. I'm not certain, but I don't think I lost consciousness. When I found I could still move, I couldn't believe I was still alive. It was very, very dark, and I heard things falling all around me. When the Tower fell, we were all within proximity of each other, but it was just the way the building fell or blew us that determined who lived and who died.

Danny Naughton, who was our chauffeur that day, had remained at the rig for a short time to hook it up to the hydrant. When he saw people falling out of the building, he too made a decision that he could save more lives by directing people to run up the block, away from the Towers. When the South Tower fell he was definitely in a dangerous area, very close to the building, and he suffered a serious back injury. He, too, saved a lot of lives that day. Jimmy, Tommy, Danny, and I tried to regroup as best we could. Tommy and Jimmy had found a *Daily News* photographer who was still alive, and they pulled him out of the rubble. They turned him over to some other firefighters before we went back to the rig, which we thought would be a good mustering point to meet Neal and Steve. The truck was scratched up, but it hadn't yet taken the beating that it took later when the North Tower came down.

We did a loop around the Trade Center site looking for Steve and Neal before we returned to the rig once more. We waited there for a few minutes hoping they would somehow show up. Then I went to a command post and reported that Steve and Neal were missing. We decided to do a full loop around the entire Trade Center lot, which encompassed all seven buildings in the system. We had just passed the North Tower when it came down. It sounded exactly like the first one collapsing—a thousand freight trains. I can hear that sound in my head to this day. We went through three collapses of buildings that day. We were all really banged up, but we kept searching for Steve and Neal; we couldn't stop looking for our brothers. Finally we decided to check out the place by the Hudson River just west of the site where they were loading injured people on boats to take them to hospitals across the river in New Jersey.

About 2:00 in the afternoon, we returned to the river and I sent my guys by boat to be treated at a hospital in Jersey City. I didn't leave the site until about 7:00 p.m., when they called off the immediate rescue. Then I went to a hospital in Hoboken, where I was treated for a broken rib and various lacerations. We all had bad abrasions of our eyes, and we were wheezing from the dust and other things in the air at the site. I was at a different hospital than the guys, so I wasn't in touch with them then.

The hospital staff wanted to keep me in the hospital overnight, but I really wanted to go home to my family. I was told that the city was locked down and they couldn't get me home. I had seen New York City police detectives at the hospital. So I asked the nurse to bring in one of the detectives. When a detective came, I broke down and started to cry. He told me they would get me home. The next thing I knew, two guys from the Hoboken Fire Department arrived and drove me home in the Chief's car. We were able to get over the Brooklyn Bridge because they were driving an emergency vehicle. I wish I could remember that detective's name so I could thank him. I don't think he will ever realize the huge favor he did for me by getting me home that night.

When I got home, I sat on the couch with my wife, Sandra, and my kids, and cried my eyes out. Then I saw the replay on TV of the Towers coming down. It looked very different from the way I had seen them fall, because I had been looking up at them from the ground. I couldn't believe the amount of area that the Towers covered when they fell. And I had been right in front of them as they came down. There was no reason why I should still be alive.

Like me, all the guys in our firehouse suffered physical injuries, but those are nothing compared to the injuries in our hearts and minds. We can easily deal with physical stuff, but the emotional stuff is really difficult. I can only recall about 80 percent of what happened that day. My mind hasn't released the other 20 percent yet. I don't know if it ever will.

If I was a regular fireman, I'd tell you that I was very, very lucky that day. But I'm not. I'm their lieutenant, and I lost two of my guys who were with me. I know I can't get them back. I know I can't change what happened that day. But I wish I could have five minutes with Stevie and Neal. I'd tell them I'm sorry. I'd tell them I'm proud of them. I'd give them a hug and say goodbye. That's the pain I wake up with every morning and go to sleep with every night. That's the tough part that I will have to live with all of my life.

The day after 9/11, some guys from 217 came by and picked me up and drove me to the firehouse. Then we all went to the site in a couple of pickup trucks to look for our guys. After that I was out on sick leave for nearly two-and-a-half weeks. When I first went to counseling for help, I saw five different counselors on five different days. So each time I had to start all over again. The first three times, I cried my eyes out. The fourth and fifth times, I went there and very unemotionally told my story. I didn't cry at all. I felt kind of happy that I made the counselors cry. Then I knew that wasn't helping me. So when I went back to the firehouse and the guys asked how counseling was going, I told them, "We're in a lot of trouble. They have no idea how to deal with us." Now I realize that the counselors were just as overwhelmed as we were. More recently, I went back to counseling again, and it's helped me a lot. I've worked with a woman who stayed with me for five sessions. With that continuity she helped clear up a lot of things for me.

Firefighting is a very dangerous business. It's not just an occupation, because thousands of people rely on us to take care of them. So regardless of how we might feel, we still have to go out and do our job well. After the World Trade Center came down on 9/11, most of the guys were anxious to go to a fire as soon as possible. It was like getting back up on a horse again after falling off and being injured.

We call what happens around the firehouse table the "healing process." This old kitchen table really helps us out. There's a lot of stuff that goes on here, a lot of talking, crying, making fun of each other, laughing, healing. Kenny and Stevie and Neal would want us to do it this way. We're a community, a family, and we try to be there for each other, to help each other out in various ways. One day we might be patting a guy on the back and then the next day dumping a bucket of water on his head. Crying and laughing together have been important in our healing process. Maybe that's what makes this occupation so special. There are many other occupations out there that don't have the luxury of being around a kitchen table, of having twenty-nine brothers growing up in a home together.

Danny White

Since September 11, there have been lots of days when we sat around this table and cried. Then, to break it up, somebody would say something really funny about somebody, and we would all start laughing about that. So we went from crying to laughing hysterically with each other. That might sound weird to an outsider, but it was the way we got through our pain. That's what helped us; it still does.

Jim Hart

Right after 9/11, this table was about the only place where we could come to talk about something else other than the tragedy at the Trade Center. Even when we picked up our kids at their school, people asked us how things were going at the site. But when we came into the firehouse, we were able to talk about someone buying a new car or how somebody screwed up on the meal or that somebody was late to work. It felt like this was the only place where we could talk about something other than 9/11.

Lieutenant Tom McGoff

But this was also the only place where we felt we could *really* talk about 9/11. Sometimes we didn't want to talk with civilians, because they didn't know what was going on. They didn't seem to understand.

In January of 2002 we hit rock bottom. It's a little like when you have a problem or a disease—especially something emotional— you sort of have to hit the bottom before you can bounce back up again. So the senior men of the company called everyone to a meeting, and we discussed a couple of ideas about what we should be doing, where we should be going. That meeting helped bring us together and got us back on our feet again. We basically decided to police each other to make sure none of us slipped and fell back down, because it had been a living hell in January. After that meeting, we started going back up and things seemed to get better. Now we're moving in the right direction, and we haven't stopped since.

The guys in this house are the greatest. Every person in this firehouse has a very special role, and everyone concentrates on doing what they're supposed to do. Nobody slacks off. People don't just do 100 percent; they all extend themselves. There isn't anybody in this firehouse that isn't performing at 125 percent. We've all been keeping at that same level of work, which is helping to pull us back up.

Danny White

Whenever we see someone feeling down or dwelling on things that are heavy on their hearts, we ask them what they're thinking about. Then we sit around as a group at lunch or dinner and talk about it. If someone says, "I can't believe this happened," then five guys might chime in that we did everything we could, that nobody did anything wrong, that we didn't set the building on fire, nor did we collapse the Towers. We all help each other along that way.

I was off on 9/11, so I came in from home. For those of us who weren't there, it's difficult because we have all the "why" questions: "Why am I still here? Why is he not? Why was I off that day?" All those guilty feelings. We've thought a lot and talked about this. If it was meant to be our turn, it would have hit on the day we were working. We can't change something that happened. It just happened that day. Some guys were working; some guys were off. We can't explain why Stevie worked overtime, why Kenny was over at Engine 207 that day. There are a lot of "whys" and there are no answers for them. It was just the way it happened. The guys who were at the World Trade Center and lived through everything—the sounds, the sights, the smells, the original hit—went through a lot more than those of us who weren't there. They need more support and understanding. Because we're a family here, problems that affect one guy touch all of us. If someone has a problem, they're not going to have to deal with it alone. We will likely hammer and harass them and help them get it out. In the big picture, it's probably for the good, because then we'll all get over it.

Now we're crawling along. I'm not sure that we're really running yet, but we're getting better every day. That doesn't mean we won't fall down again. Not a day goes by when we don't think of our friends who were there who didn't return. Not a single day!

Jim Hart

For those of us who were at the World Trade Center on 9/11, there's no rhyme or reason why we survived, how we missed those really big bullets. Because Danny Suhr from Engine 216 was hit by a person's body falling out of the South Tower and we stopped to put his body in an ambulance, we were delayed by a few minutes. If it had not been for him, we would have been in the building; if the building had come down a few minutes earlier or later, we would have been killed too.

Now we have our good days and our bad days. I've finally started to like coming into work again. Right after 9/11, for the first time ever, I didn't look forward to coming to the firehouse. But whenever I got here, it did me a world of good to be with the guys, to be with people who knew what Kenny and Steve and Neal meant to us. And what we meant to them. That's probably the biggest thing that got me through—just being here with the guys. There's a real sense of family here.

We all rely on each other so much as brothers. When we go to a fire and one of us doesn't have his head on okay, we won't do very well. So we had to come together. We had to make it work out or we couldn't do this job.

Lieutenant Tom McGoff

From the day the Towers fell until the day we closed the Trade Center site was like one long event. A lot of people thought we were going through posttraumatic stress around January or February, but we weren't. A counselor who worked with Vietnam vets explained to me that we weren't going through it yet, because it was all one incident. We were still trying to dig out our guys. When we finally closed the site in May 2002, that's when the posttraumatic stress began for us.

At the site, we were assigned thirty-day details, which meant that each division sent someone who was to dig for thirty days. During that time, he was taken off the work chart at the firehouse. Then after thirty days, he returned to the firehouse to resume his normal duties. We also had guys who volunteered to work at the site on their own time. I, myself, found it very rewarding, because it felt like I was doing my penance for 9/11, and for what had happened to my men.

Whenever we found a body, we tried to carefully dig each person out with delicacy and dignity and we tried to keep as much of the body intact as possible. We knew if we could keep the jawbone connected to the body, that person could be identified within two days. If it wasn't, it could take six or seven months. So we worked with great care, so as to spare the families unnecessary delays in identification. Every time a body was dug out, we covered it with the flag and took it up the ramp with an honor guard. Everything in that area of the city stopped: the machines, the torches. Even the ironworkers and the sanitation workers removed their helmets and held them over their hearts. The firemen and cops lined up along the ramp, and if it was a firefighter or cop, their company came down to carry the person up the ramp. We did the same for everyone, even the civilians. We took them out of the site with honor. It was always a very emotional time. Then we went right back to work digging again. We did that from September 11 until the end of May 2002.

We were especially grateful for what the ironworkers, operating engineers, construction workers, and sanitation workers did. They were some of the most important people on the site, and they deserve a lot of credit for everything they did. Without them, none of the heavy steel could have been moved. They had the equipment and the torches to move things so we could get to the bodies. If it wasn't for them, we would still be there now.

We recovered Neal and Steve's bodies outside the South Tower building on a sidewalk near Liberty Street. Neal was recovered almost right away. The day before Christmas Eve, Johnny Senese found Stevie. We always knew who the firemen were, because their gear was durable.

On Holy Saturday, I found Phil Hayes's name tag, and I said to Greg Seminara from Ladder 111, "We got Philly." He knew I had been looking for him, because Phil had worked for twenty years in our firehouse. Another guy standing next to me from 120 Truck, whose mother is best friends with Phil Hayes's wife, said, "I'm looking for Philly." And then a Port Authority cop asked, "Who said Philly Hayes?" He told me that he was looking for him too. To have spent all that time at the site and to have been involved in actually finding that person we were looking for was mind-boggling. Being a part of the team that recovered Philly Hayes was very healing to me, so I think God waited until we were all there. He knew I would recognize the name tag and give it to the guy from 120 Truck, who went home that night and gave it to his mother, who gave it to Philly's wife.

The Port Authority cop told us that Philly was like everybody's grandfather. He was a very caring guy. In fact his nickname was "Mother Hayes." On 9/11, he went to the daycare center in Building Five with shopping carts to evacuate the children. Making a game out of it, he said, "Come on, kids, we're going shopping to a supermarket." Not one child cried; they had no idea they were in any kind of danger. Once he got the kids out safely, he called his wife, Virginia, on his cell phone, told her he loved her and that he was going back into the building to make more announcements as Fire Safety Director. That's when the building came down.

All of us got kind of close after that—it was like a little community bonding together as we worked.

Danny White

It wasn't a happy time to be at the Trade Center site, because we were digging for body parts. I only found pieces of bodies—never the whole body. Whenever I found someone, I thought about what they had gone through; I wondered if they knew what was happening. I tried to figure out if they were married, if they had kids, where they had been in the building. Those were some of the things that went through my mind. Sometimes it really got to me—especially when I thought about how they felt as their life ended.

Frank Ardizzone

Whenever we found someone's body, we knew a family or a person was going to get a phone call, and the uncertainty would be over for them. It felt like we were bringing someone home. We hoped that recovering the remains of their loved one would give them some peace, that it would help them move toward "closure." They could now have a place where they could bring flowers and pray.

John Byrne

Before 9/11, when people died in the line of duty, we were always able to bring their bodies home. Not being able to recover all the bodies of our brothers at the Trade Center was really painful. That had never before happened, so it was very difficult for us.

Lieutenant Tom McGoff

About two months before the last steel beam was taken down, Johnny Senese from our firehouse was doing his thirty-day detail and he found a rock and scratched on the beam: "Always in our thoughts: Kenny, Steve, Neal, Philly." Before the Trade Center site was closed, the last beam was scheduled to be removed. As a company, we went to the site the day before with a can of spray paint. We put one name on the beam for our battalion. We put as many pictures of the guys on the beam as possible. When we started painting the number "217" on the beam, we saw what Johnny had written—right where we were painting the "7." It was almost unbelievable.

The day the site closed, we felt a kind of void. It had been therapeutic for us to work there, but on the other hand it was time to leave. We had done the best we could, and that was it. It was kind of bittersweet. We still feel that void, because we had a purpose as we worked together. And there was such a sense of accomplishment whenever we found someone—whether it was a civilian or a firefighter or a cop. It was a wonderful feeling to bring somebody home.

For thirteen months we went to memorials, wakes, funerals, the closing ceremony at the Trade Center, the 9/11 anniversary. We were constantly pulled here and pushed there. Don't get me wrong, it was an honor for us to attend those functions. But after the final memorial service on October 12, 2002, there was a sense of relief that we could truly start to heal.

Of course, it's a double-edged sword. We see something about 9/11 every day in the newspapers and on television. People talk about it all the time. Sometimes we wish it would go away, but if it did, I'm sure we would be upset, because we'd think everybody had just forgotten about the people who died. Obviously, we have very mixed feelings.

When we brought the rig back from the Trade Center the first time, it had a broken windshield, it was filthy, and it was totally stripped. So about twenty of us guys just stood in the back of the rig and polished up the numbers on it. We're very proud of our number. We would never do anything to disgrace it.

When we drove the rig through Bedford-Stuyvesant, the neighborhood where the firehouse is located, people were out on the streets clapping, cheering for us, and blessing us. At the corner near the firehouse, a youth gang called "the Bloods" came out with their red bandannas on, and they stopped the rig. They "high-fived" and hugged every one of us. That was very touching, and it made us cry. We needed their support and we needed to cry because we had so much dust in our eyes and sadness in our hearts from working the whole day at the Trade Center site.

This group of guys is a real community, and they really look out for each other and help each other to heal. After the 9/11 tragedy, the guys took this old, dirty, brown firehouse and cleaned and painted it. Then they built a beautiful memorial to honor the families and the four heroes we lost on 9/11. It was created by every person in the house, and it has four glass lockers with the bunker coats and helmets of the four guys who died.

As with everything we do as a firehouse, everyone helped with the memorial—from the newest member right up to the senior guys. It was very therapeutic and healing for us. I know that this company will do just fine and that we will always shine.

The Firefighters from Engine 217
Who Died at the World Trade Center on 9/11

Lieutenant Kenny Phelan

Firefighter Steve Coakley

Firefighter Neal Leavy

Retired Firefighter Phil Hayes

❖ ❖ ❖ ❖ ❖ ❖ ❖ ❖

*Life rushes us along and few people are strong enough
to stop on their own. Most often, something unforeseen
stops us and it is only then we have the time to take a
seat at life's kitchen table. To know our own story and
tell it. To listen to other people's stories.*
                                                    —Rachel Naomi Remen

As I listened to the firefighters talk around the kitchen table about their stories of sadness, pain, and healing, I realized how important it is for all "communities" to have such a place to share our stories, to have a chance to be heard, and to feel the support of others. Certainly, the telling of our stories can serve as a piece of our healing process. It can empower us to bring our anguish and our suffering out of the dark corners of our minds where they can fester and do us harm.

Perhaps the most impressive part of this story is that the people talking about this gentle form of healing are strong, brawny firefighters. These are guys you would never imagine talking about their feelings or crying about their terrible losses. After all, don't most Western cultures teach little boys that they should grow up to be tough, rugged, and powerful? That they would be wimps or sissies if they cried?

Years ago, families and friends often sat around their kitchen tables and told stories to each other. They learned so much from those experiences. They had the opportunity to laugh at their mistakes, to cry over their losses and pain, to celebrate their successes. And at that table, they probably gained wisdom from their elders, mastered the "real" rules of life, and found some kind of healing.

Today we don't seem to find enough time anymore to sit around a kitchen table and listen to each other's stories. We've been completely immersed in our frantic lifestyles—fast foods, busy work schedules.

Perhaps the luxury of sitting around a table has disappeared for us. Yet for the firefighters, the real healing takes place around the firehouse kitchen table. The table helps them to talk, cry, laugh, heal, and build a community that they know will be there for them. Maybe we too can make the time to gather together our "community," to slide our feet under life's kitchen table and tell our stories.

A Firefighter's Family:
Discovering Our Hearts' Treasures

As told by Danny and Helene Phelan

> *Although some things have been taken away from us,*
> *we think God has given us so much. . . . We will never*
> *know why things happened the way they did; we'll*
> *never have the answers. But whenever we get really*
> *down, our faith helps us back up again.*
> *—Helene Phelan*

> *It hit me while we were down there [in the empty site*
> *of the World Trade Center]: this was like Kenny's*
> *tomb. I realized that the rock had been pushed away*
> *and nobody was there. They had risen. That gave me a*
> *lot of comfort.*
> *—Danny Phelan*

Lieutenant Kenny Phelan, a firefighter from Engine 217, died on September 11. He served for eleven years in Engine 16-Ladder 7 in Manhattan until he was promoted to lieutenant in 1999. Eventually he was assigned to Engine 217, the firehouse where his dad, Danny, had spent nineteen of his twenty years as a firefighter. He loved being a firefighter, and he was proud that his brother, Lenny, his brother-in-law Eddie, and his dad, Danny, were all firefighters.

Kenny was a devoted husband to his wife, Patty, and a wonderful father to his four children, Kimberly, Erin, Danny, and Kenny. He was a supportive and much-loved brother to his four sisters, Marian, Jean, Mary, and Fran, and to his brother, Lenny. And to his parents, Danny and Helene, Kenny was the son we all yearn to have—a real treasure.

During the days I spent with Kenny's parents, we often sat around the dining-room table with cups of strong coffee and plenty of good food. Danny and Helene talked lovingly about their six children and twelve grandchildren. Often, we spent hours poring over old photograph albums. We chuckled as we looked at photos of Kenny growing up with his siblings. We smiled at pictures of the family of firefighters: Danny, Kenny, Lenny, and Eddie. We paused over the photos of Kenny with his youngest sister and godchild, Fran, who worked as an attorney on the eighty-fifth floor of the North Tower of the World Trade Center. And we wept as we looked at photos of Kenny with his wife, Patty, and their four wonderful children.

Over the weeks, I found myself embraced by this special family, and I appreciated their generous and caring ways to each other and to me. This is the story of one firefighter's family, who faced great challenges in their struggle to undertake an often painful and difficult healing process.

❖ ❖ ❖ ❖ ❖ ❖ ❖ ❖

Danny

When I first joined the fire department, in October 1957, Helene and I already had our first child. I wanted a more secure and stable job. Nobody from my family had been a firefighter before, so I had no expectations of what it would be like. The first day I went to work was the first time I went into a firehouse. When I walked in, it changed me. I became one of the firefighters.

Living with firefighters in close quarters is like living in a family, a community. We develop a tremendous bond with each other. We have to go into very difficult and dangerous conditions, where we bank on everyone doing their job. No one can put out a fire alone. Whatever we do well will make things easier for someone else, so we try our best not to let others down. Whenever a firehouse loses someone, it has lost a part of its family.

There are about ten thousand firefighters, who take care of the 8 to 10 million people who live and work in New York City. People are amazed that such a small group of people can handle so many fires. We have to be a well-trained team. Every person has an assignment, and all jobs are equally important. Everything is carefully planned and backed up. The ladder company goes in first, does the forcible entry if necessary, finds the fire, does the rescue work, and ventilates the building to allow the smoke and heat to escape. The engine company has the pumper and hoses and is responsible for extinguishing the fire. It takes every person at the scene to put a fire out.

There were so many fires, so many memories. The first time I found a dead child, it really hit me hard—he was only about six months old, the same age as my son Kenny. Another time we lost five children. While we fight a fire, the adrenaline is really flowing and there's a lot of excitement. But afterward when we sit back, we realize, "There were five little kids who died." I remember crying after that fire. I guess every firefighter has tears in their eyes at some time. We feel each loss as a personal loss.

At one fire, my company was inside the building and I was working on the street. I saw a firefighter at the top of a ladder with two little boys he had pulled out of the fire. I could see he wasn't able to get them both down, so I ran up to help. The boys were in really bad shape. When I got one of them down, I started mouth-to-mouth resuscitation. At first there was no response, nothing. I was afraid we would lose him. Then the most unbelievable thing happened. After I had taken a breath and was going to put my mouth back on his, suddenly his mouth came up to meet mine—almost like he was searching for the breath of life. My heart almost jumped out of my body. I knew right then that he was going to make it. His family and his grandmother were there, and they were all crying. I'll never forget that moment. But I know it wasn't me who saved him. I believe it was the Holy Spirit. I'm not a hero; I don't have lots of courage. Someone does it for you—makes you do something you couldn't normally do.

Helene

Our first son, Kenny, was born on a sunny day, on June 27, 1960, five years after Danny became a firefighter. He didn't start walking until he was almost sixteen months old. We tried all kinds of things to get him to walk. Then one day, he was sitting on the couch watching his sister eating a peanut-butter-and-jelly sandwich across the room from him. I guess he really wanted that sandwich, because he got off the couch, walked straight across the room, and took her sandwich.

Kenny was always a caring and serious boy. Sometimes I thought he was too serious. When President Kennedy died, we were constantly watching what was happening on television. Kenny was only three then, but often I saw him sitting quietly and looking sad. He was very sensitive to what we were feeling—even at that early age. He always loved sports. The Mets baseball team was new in New York when he was a little boy, so we got him a Mets uniform made of wool and he loved it. In fact, he didn't want to take it off. Even when it was hot, he slept in it, ate in it, and sweated in it.

As Kenny grew up, I always felt he watched out for me; he never wanted me to be slighted. He was very quiet and didn't try to be the center of attention, but he was always there if you needed him. He sometimes helped me take care of our younger children, or he would surprise me by washing the kitchen floor. Every spring he dug up the garden and helped me plant our vegetables. After he married and moved out, I stopped planting the garden.

Danny

Kenny was a very good boy—never any trouble. He was too young to play with the baseball teams I coached, but he came along with me as my batboy and he wore that Mets uniform. At one of the games, a player got sick, so Kenny had a chance to play with the older guys and he felt very proud. He was also a hard worker. When he was in grammar school, he had his first paper route. In the worst weather he was out early, delivering papers. Even after he broke his ankle, he didn't want to stop. So we drove him in the car, and he threw the papers out the window from the back seat.

When Jeanie, our third child, was going to have her first communion, we decided to paint the living room and dining room for her party. I patched up the walls one weekend. But then I injured my wrist and couldn't finish the job. Kenny, who was about nine, said he'd paint the rooms. And he did—all by himself—ceilings and walls, everything. I stood beside him and told him what to do. It was a huge job, but he just kept going without complaining.

As he grew up, I took Kenny with me to the firehouse occasionally, so he was familiar with the fire department, and the firefighters' kids became his friends. But he never said he wanted to be a firefighter. After studying accounting in college, Kenny served for eight years as a policeman before he joined the fire department. When he first became a firefighter, he served for eleven years in Engine 16 and Ladder 7 in Manhattan and he had my badge number, 176, until he was promoted to lieutenant.

Then he was assigned to a division to cover for other lieutenants who were on vacation. So he floated from one firehouse to the next. In the spring of 2001, Kenny was assigned to Engine 217, the same firehouse where I had been a firefighter for nineteen years.

Kenny was six when his brother Lenny was born. He included Lenny in everything he did, and Lenny looked up to him. They were very close and always together. They shared the same room until Kenny married Patty. Even after that, Lenny often went to their house on weekends and stayed overnight. Lenny also joined the fire department after serving three years as a policeman. Three years ago, Kenny, Lenny, their brother-in-law Eddie, and their friend Whitey (Danny White) studied together in our house in order to take the examination for lieutenant. They all did well and were promoted. Ironically, Kenny had worked enough years that he could have retired in July 2001—before 9/11 ever happened. But he wanted to take the examination for promotion to captain.

Helene

We saw Kenny the day before 9/11 when the four guys came over to study at our house for the captain's examination. When Kenny left, he stuck his head in the dining room where I was sitting at the table. "Mom, I'm going," he said. "Okay," I said. Again, "Mom, I'm going." Then he came over and gave me a kiss. I was taken aback a little, because he was always coming and going, but this time he told me twice he was going. I feel bad that I didn't give him a big hug; I just kissed him. That night Kenny and Patty came by to pick up their kids. That was the last time I saw him.

Danny

On September 10, as the guys were leaving, I asked them if they were working the next day. Lenny, Eddie, and Whitey had the day off. Although Kenny was supposed to have been off too, he had to substitute for the lieutenant at Engine 207. I remember Kenny saying to the guys: "From now on, we're going to study here two days a week until we take the captain's test in October."

The guys moaned a little, but they agreed. Those were his parting words to them. Then he came back to say goodbye to his mother.

On the morning of September 11, Kenny wanted to borrow one of our cars. He needed to go early to his firehouse to get his gear. So I drove the car to his house and picked him up. Then he drove me back home. We had about ten minutes together in the car. We talked about painting our house. Knowing Kenny, he would have come by after he finished work that evening to help me paint. As I got out of the car, he said, "I'll see you tonight." That was the last time I spoke with him.

I planned to start painting that morning. Helene was baby-sitting at Lenny's house for the day. It was about 8:15 a.m. I decided to read the paper for a while and then go to 9:00 a.m. Mass. I was sitting in the kitchen when I heard a news bulletin on the radio that a plane had hit the World Trade Center. Right away I thought, "It's such a clear day, so it must have been a small plane in trouble." I turned on the TV and saw that it wasn't a small plane.

My first thought was that our youngest daughter, Fran, who is eighty-fifth floor of the North Tower. That was close to where the plane had hit the building. I called her husband, Steve, and asked him if Fran had left for work. He told me she had been gone for quite a while. About then it hit me that Kenny would respond to that fire because he was across the river from Manhattan at Engine 207. Then I saw the South Tower get hit. At that point I was still worrying about Fran. Kenny had fought many high-rise fires in Manhattan. He knew what he was doing. I had a lot of confidence that he would be okay, but I was worried about Fran.

Later, when somebody came in the back door, I didn't even leave the TV to see who it was. I was relieved when it was Fran. She was crying because she knew the building had been hit near the floor where her offices were. Because she didn't feel well that morning, she started out a little late. She was on the express bus from Queens to Manhattan when it was stopped at the Midtown Tunnel and they were told to get off. She couldn't get any transportation back to Maspeth, where she lives across the street from us. It took her two hours to walk home. By the time she got to our house, both Towers were already down. She was very worried about the people in her company. We later learned that her law firm lost two women. A woman who had a birthday that day went in early with her friend to set up a small birthday celebration; both of them died. Others from the firm who were already in the building were able to get out. If the Towers had been hit later in the day, many more people in Fran's office would have died. Most of the attorneys didn't go in early, because they often worked late in the evening.

Lenny and Eddie, who had the day off, reported to their firehouses as soon as they could and picked up their gear. Eddie was sent to work at the site immediately, and Lenny was sent to another firehouse in Manhattan. He desperately wanted to be at the site, so he told the captain he had to look for his brother. He arrived late that afternoon.

When Eddie called from the site, he told me that they couldn't find Kenny or his company. People told him that when the roll call was taken to see who was missing, Kenny did not answer. But they were going to keep looking. Early in the evening, he called back again and said he thought we had a problem. When the second roll call was taken, Kenny and the men who had been with him missed it too. That's when it started to hit us.

Helene

Whenever I take care of Lenny's kids at their house, I usually don't turn on the television. And for some reason, the kids didn't turn it on that day either. Lenny called sometime that morning to ask if Fran was working. I didn't know. "Why are you asking?" I said. He told me a plane had hit her building, and he wanted to know what floor she worked on. I told him the eighty-fifth. He said it had hit above that floor, but he didn't tell me more.

Later I learned that Fran was okay, but even then I still didn't worry about Kenny. I knew he was working, but I didn't know he was with Engine 207 that day, nor did I know the extent of the problem. I had not yet turned on the television. About 11:30, John, the neighbor across the street, came by and told me that both Towers were down—down to the ground. He asked if Lenny was working, but I knew he was okay because he had the day off. When John turned on the TV, a man was being interviewed who said that as he and others were walking down the stairs, the firemen were going up. Then he said, "They couldn't have gotten out. I almost didn't get out myself before the building came down." That was when I realized that Kenny might have been there. I started to cry. I was so grateful when

John's wife came by and helped me with the children. All day it was "Have you heard from Kenny?"

It took me almost two hours to drive home. The traffic was horrendous because many of the roads were closed. I could hardly move, and I was so anxious to get home. Danny was on the phone when I got there, trying to find out if Kenny had been with Engine 207. The guy who answered the phone didn't know. So for a few minutes we had a tiny piece of hope that Kenny was somewhere else and was still okay. But he was there. Later we went to Patty and Kenny's house, where we continued to call the hospitals and the fire department. But all we learned was that Kenny was still missing. Still missing.

Danny

On the morning of September 12, I drove Lenny to the site. He planned to spend all day there helping with the rescue efforts. We got really close to the ruins, and when I looked down the street and saw what was there, I was afraid that no one could have survived. I guess I already knew then that Kenny wouldn't come back, but I still had some hope, and I didn't want to give up. I wouldn't ever do that.

Deep in my heart I knew that no matter how good a fireman Kenny was, when a building that size comes down, there's very little possibility of someone surviving. I had seen big buildings fall before, but nothing came anywhere close to the size of the Towers. More than thirty thousand people were rescued before they collapsed, but almost no one was rescued after the collapse. After a few days, I knew I had to face the truth and accept it— that it just wasn't going to be. But I don't think I ever gave up hope.

For several days we kept on making phone calls. Always the same thing: Kenny was still missing. We watched the TV almost nonstop for two days. Every now and then we would get our hopes up—like the time when they found some firemen who were rescued. But later we learned that they weren't from the original collapse of the buildings. They were rescue workers who had been trapped. We finally had to turn the TV off. We couldn't watch it any more.

The first week we were all together every day. Finally, on Sunday, we met and sat down as a family. Fran had to explain to the little kids what had happened. She used blocks to show them how the buildings had come down. We talked about how we were going to have to live. We couldn't continue as we were—with everyone together all the time, with so many people coming and going all day long, just waiting around. We had to get things under control to make things a little easier; we had to get ourselves organized. The kids had to go back to school. So we started to get back into our regular routines.

Helene

In the beginning, right after the Towers came down, I'd ask myself questions like, "What if Kenny doesn't come back?" But I knew he was strong. He was a fighter, and he had dealt with lots of pain. If he had one breath of life in him, I knew he would make it; he would crawl out somehow. Then I realized he could not be alive, or he would have come back. It was so devastating.

On Thursday the thirteenth, we were at Patty's house. I had been sleeping on the couch. I woke up really early—about five o'clock in the morning. I was sobbing with such sorrow. I wanted to go to the site and dig him out myself. Then all of a sudden, I felt a kind of calmness come over me. I could see water everywhere—like a river. And I knew then that Kenny was dead. But I felt peaceful, because I knew he wasn't suffering. Early the next morning while it was pre-dawn and still dark outside, I was crying again, when I saw an image of light and the Sacred Heart. Then I knew he was in heaven.

The next day I kind of lost it, and I told God, "I'll never be able to forgive you, God, if we don't find his remains. I don't think I can take that." But even then, something eventually came to me that said, "It doesn't matter; he's in heaven anyway." If I hadn't had faith, I would have been devastated. In fact, I don't think we could have gotten through this without our faith.

Danny

As time went on and we knew Kenny was not coming back, we thought it would help us if we could talk with the chauffeur of Engine 207 who had driven Kenny to the site that day. We wanted to hear what Kenny had said in his last moments. He was the only survivor of the firefighters that rode with Kenny on the truck. Even the records that reported where the companies had been on the site had been destroyed.

Earlier, we had talked with a firefighter from Ladder 110 who knew Kenny. He had seen Kenny near the escalator in the lobby of the North Tower and they said hello to each other. He also saw Kenny go to the command post to report in. When Kenny returned, he took the firemen who had come with him and walked away. Not too long after that, the South Tower came down. Kenny may have gone up the stairs in the North Tower, or he may have been sent to the South Tower. We will probably never know.

We knew that Kenny, as the lieutenant, would have sat in the front of the truck with the chauffeur and they would have talked. Right after the event, the chauffeur wasn't able to return to work. But in May when we called him, he was back on the job. He told us that an alarm came into Engine 207 that an airplane had hit the North Tower. Kenny must have just arrived at work. By the time the chauffeur got to the fire engine, Kenny was already sitting in it ready to go. At that point they didn't know that the second Tower had been hit. As they drove over the Manhattan Bridge, the chauffeur saw that it was on fire too. Kenny said, "Those buildings are so close together that the fire may have jumped across to the second building." When they got to Manhattan, the dispatcher told them to take the local streets. By that time, cars were already stuck all over the place. Because Kenny had worked there before, he knew the streets well. So most of their conversation was Kenny telling the chauffeur where to go.

When they arrived a few blocks from the Towers, around 9:30 a.m., they had to get out and walk. A policeman told them that the South Tower had been struck by another plane. Kenny had worked in high-rise fires before, and he'd been in the World Trade Center fire in 1993, so he told the other firemen to take a spare air tank. They each took a folded-up length of hose and a bag of tools and wrenches because they couldn't depend on the building having the right equipment. So they were carrying a lot of stuff. That was the last the chauffeur saw of them. He didn't know where they went. Later, after the Towers came down, he went looking for them.

Helene

There have been many things and many people who have helped us get through this difficult time. Certainly, my love of life and my enjoyment in living have helped me to heal. I don't really need or want big things. I love simple things like preparing a meal or having company come over for dinner. That gives me so much happiness.

Probably the biggest help for both of us has been our supportive family. Our grandchildren have helped heal our pain. Although we're hurting, the children need to go on with their lives, to go to school, to attend different functions. And now there's more that we need to do. We want to be at games and other events where Kenny would have been. The children bring a smile to our faces and help take us out of our grief. Somehow that lifts us.

It helps me to have the opportunity to care for all of our family—Kenny's wife and children, his brother and his sisters and their children, and my mother, his eighty-seven-year-old grandmother, who lives with us. She is suffering a lot, and somehow caring for her helps me go on.

We're thrilled that Kenny's youngest sister, Fran, had her first baby. When Fran was born, Kenny was nine years old and we named him to be one of her godparents. He was so delighted and enthusiastic. I often think how he must have been very concerned, thinking she was in the North Tower. I'm sure he would have tried to rescue her. Somehow Fran's baby was an affirmation that life goes on even in all the grief and sadness we feel. Although some things have been taken away from us, we think God has given us so much.

And there have been so many friends who have helped us. Our neighbors across the street, Virginia and Al, have been like pillars of strength for us. Every day they brought us a fresh yellow rose. And there have been others who we barely knew or didn't know at all. They showed us such concern and support, which touched us deeply. There were letters from people who had only met us once, and they wrote wonderful things. Their reaching out to us in some way has been very helpful.

Danny

The fire department has been especially useful to us in our healing process. They can't change what happened, but they are so caring. If we needed a ride somewhere this afternoon, somebody off-duty would probably take us without hesitation. For the closing ceremony at the site, they came to our house, picked up our entire family in vans, and took us to the firehouse, where they had breakfast for us and for the other families who lost someone. Then they drove us to the site so we were all together at the ceremony. All the off-duty firefighters from Kenny's Engine 217 were there; not one was missing.

Even though Kenny is no longer there, the fire department considers him to be part of their family. The companies where Kenny served—Engine 16, Ladder 7, Engine 207, and Engine 217—are always reaching out to Kenny's wife, Patty, their children, and our entire family. All of them have built beautiful memorials in their firehouses for Kenny and the other firefighters they lost on 9/11. They don't want future firefighters to ever forget them.

Helene

The fire department has also taken good care of Lenny. When Kenny was missing, Lenny wouldn't stay away from the site. He wanted to be down there all the time helping look for his brother. We were very concerned about him as well as about our son-in-law Eddie, who was searching on the site and who kept us informed about how bad Lenny was feeling. You could see the strain and stress on both of them. We were grateful that after a few weeks Lenny's former firehouse, Ladder 140, wouldn't allow him to go to the site by himself. They made sure someone was always there to watch over him and help keep him safe.

Early on, Danny had some really bad days too. Once when I was over at Patty's house, some of the firefighters from Engine 217 dropped by to see how she was doing. I suggested that maybe someone should go over to see Danny. They told me that somebody was already there. That kind of caring was reassuring. I'm sure it also helped the firefighters who did it for us.

Danny

People often talk about the possibility that someone they love might not be found at all and that there wouldn't be any "closure." But I don't think there ever is real closure. You can't put somebody out of your mind who was your child for forty-one years.

At Easter time, I started thinking about the fact that after the crucifixion, people came to the tomb where Jesus had been buried. But he wasn't there. He had risen. When our family went down into the empty World Trade Center site after most of the debris had been removed, there still had been no news about finding Kenny's body. It hit me while we were down there: this was like Kenny's tomb. I realized that the rock had been pushed away and nobody was there. They had risen. That gave me a lot of comfort.

Helene

I've learned a lot from this experience about reaching out to others who are hurting or who are in need. I know that I am grieving for the living as much as for the dead. When I see my children and my grandchildren, I know they are hurting. So I want to reach out and give something to them. I now believe I have something to give them—support, hope, and love. When I reach out to people, it makes me feel better and stronger.

When we went to the closing ceremony at the site, there was a beautiful young woman standing near us. She was all by herself, and she was crying quietly and looking so sad. At one point, I asked her who she was there for, and she said "my husband." He had worked for one of the companies at the top of the North Tower. Although I didn't know her, I felt such deep feelings of love for her that I found myself putting my arms around her. She said her husband's name was Andrew. I told her I would pray for her that night when we prayed for our son. Somehow that helped me too.

Having this chance to tell our story has also been healing and comforting to us. We have had the opportunity to say everything. Sometimes we are worried that it may be a burden for people to keep hearing about our sorrow and pain, that they might not want to hear about our grief. Now I know how important it is to listen carefully to people's stories—over and over. They may need to be heard.

Finally, I know that without our faith we would have been devastated. In fact, I don't think we could have gotten through this. We will never know why things happened the way they did; we'll never have the answers. But whenever we get really down, our faith helps us back up again.

❖ ❖ ❖ ❖ ❖ ❖ ❖ ❖

Within each of us, there lies a space that is as indestructible as a sacred scroll. It is this space that enables us to find the strength to rebuild our lives after tragedy. Not even death can have dominion over it.
—Naomi Levy

This inspiring story of a family's faith and love can teach us a great deal about coping with, and healing from, enormous personal losses and suffering. For most of us, our family is our most important community. When we are devastated by unexpected pain, deprivation, and grief, our biological family or our "family" of friends can be our greatest support system.

At times of horrific losses such as those that occurred on September 11, whether we are the ones who have been deeply wounded or the ones who are able to help others, we know it is a time to reach out to one another with great sensitivity and care. In the midst of such heaviness, we may need each others' presence and support just to help us move beyond the paralysis of despair and to get through the ordinary routines of life. At times we may need to step in and fill roles that others have played within the family. Certainly, during dark times we cannot forget to recognize and address our children's special concerns.

At the heart of this healing story is Danny and Helene's deep and inspiring faith. Even through their horrible grief, frustrations, disappointments, and sadness, they found comfort knowing that their son was with God. Research has shown that having faith in a higher power is an important factor in good mental and physical health and can help us come to terms with our losses.

Another key part of this story is how the roles of giver and receiver shift from time to time. Sometimes when we have been wounded and hurt, we are only capable of receiving others' support and sympathy. Yet at other times when we least expect it, we will find that we are strong enough, even in our anguish, to reach out to someone and give them something they might need. From that encounter, we may experience a sense of healing for ourselves. As Helene said, "I now believe I have something to give them—support, hope, and love. When I reach out to people, it makes me feel better and stronger." Being able to care for others and to receive care serves as a two-way street of healing that helps both the giver and the receiver to lift each other from their sorrows.

THE BAGPIPERS: LIFTING THEIR SPIRITS

As told by Charlie Fitzpatrick

*Because we played at so many [firefighters' funerals],
we thought we would get a little stronger and it would
be easier. But it never was. . . . I believe what really
saved us, what kept us going, was that we knew our
music was helping the families with their pain and
their grief.*

—Charlie Fitzpatrick

There simply are no words that can adequately express what music does for the human spirit. It has the power to change us by allowing us to discover parts of ourselves we did not know existed and to uncover feelings that have been buried deep inside our souls. It helps us to express our emotions of love and pain, and it puts us in touch with the divine.

Music is one of my oft-used healing tools. It can soothe me when I am stressed, energize me when I feel weak, comfort me when I feel sorrowful, and help me to recover when I am sick. It has the ability to express my yearning, my hopes, and my dreams, as well as my joys and sorrows.

Since September 11, whenever I've heard the haunting music of the bagpipes played at firefighters' funerals, I have cried. I've felt the pain and loss of so many people, but I've also known that my tears were cleansing me and helping me to heal.

One day I talked with Charlie Fitzpatrick, a member of the New York Fire Department's bagpipe band for thirty-seven years. I wanted to understand what it was like to be a part of this healing community and to play an instrument at firefighters' funerals that has the capacity to help people heal their grief and pain.

❖ ❖ ❖ ❖ ❖ ❖ ❖ ❖ ❖

It all started in 1966 when I saw my friend Jack Kelly playing the pipes in the St. Patrick's Day Parade. When I asked him how he had learned to play, he said, "Why don't you join us and learn to play?" I told him I had no musical talent, that I had never played an instrument in my life. I was surprised when he said, "Most of us don't have musical talent, and nobody played the pipes or the piano before they joined the band. McSwiggen, a nice Irish guy, will take you by the hand, give you a practice chanter—which is like a small flute—and a sheet of music and get you started." So I joined the band.

Every Monday we met with our instructor. At first it was hard for me, and sometimes I got discouraged—even a bit disgruntled—but at the end of each practice, when I listened to the seasoned guys playing such sweet and inspiring tunes, I knew I wanted to be a part of the pipers.

The Emerald Society Band was started about forty years ago so firefighters could play Irish tunes together and continue their heritage. When I joined the band, there were only sixteen members. There weren't many bands then, so we got by with a lot of mistakes and nobody knew it. It's different now. Today there are lots of good pipe bands, even in some high schools.

Over the years the band started to grow. Today we have seventy-five pipers, and drummers, and we play well. When we march down Fifth Avenue, we fill up a whole block. If someone wants to join, they have to be a member of the Emerald Society, the Irish-American members of the fire department. There may have been a couple of guys who sneaked into the band—like one Jewish firefighter who told us his great aunt had married an Irish guy. I don't think any of us really believed that. But he said if we let him in that he would guarantee good weather on St. Patrick's Day!

Before September 11, we played at a lot of Memorial and Labor Day parades. Sometimes we did little side jobs at weddings. We always like to play, so we take our pipes out at the drop of a hat. Since 9/11 we have mostly played dirges for firefighters' funerals. In fact, when we were asked to play at a wedding, we realized we had forgotten how to play wedding music. It took us a while to remember how to play street tunes, jigs, and reels because it had been such a long time since we had played them.

When we play at a firefighter's funeral, we walk in front of the hearse. About two blocks from the church, we start playing a slow march to "Dawning of the Day." When we get to the place where the fire companies are lined up outside the church, we put our pipes down and continue the rest of the way with only the drumbeat. As the coffin is removed from the fire truck, a solo piper plays "Amazing Grace." At the end of the funeral when the coffin is brought out of the church, we play "Going Home." Then we march out with the family and the firefighters behind us and end with "America, the Beautiful."

There were 343 firefighters who died in the tragedy. By the time we are completely finished, the band will have played at about 450 services. I have lost count of the number of funerals I've played at, but it's probably somewhere between eighty-five and ninety. Because there were so many services, we broke up the band into three groups: upstate New York, Long Island, and the five boroughs of New York City. We also played at memorial services for the firefighters whose remains were not found. Many of those families are brokenhearted because there was not a body or even a part of a body that they could bury. They, too, would like to have a grave or a place they can visit to say a prayer for their loved one. Where will they go? To the old World Trade Center site to remember that was the place their loved one died? It's very difficult for them.

If any body part was found and identified using DNA procedures, families also had a funeral even though they had already held a memorial service. So we played twice for some firefighters. There were a number of families who waited to have a service until they were certain that nothing would be found of their loved ones. Then they had a memorial service.

Some firehouses held lovely memorial services or dedicated plaques to hang on the firehouse walls honoring those who died. Usually only five or six band members played at each one of those events. We just wanted to have a presence.

Firefighters came from all over the country and from other countries to attend the funerals—Switzerland, Ireland, France, England, Germany. And since 9/11, the fire department has been invited to many places. It seems everyone has a soft spot for us because of what happened that day. However, the pipe band usually was not able to go, because we had to stay in New York for funerals. We were invited to a special event in Maryland but couldn't go because of a funeral. The people were so disappointed that we ended up sending six guys. One time we were on our way to an event in upstate New York when we got a phone call about another funeral. So we turned around and came back.

Playing for so many funerals has been very difficult. We usually did okay until we saw the families. Especially the little kids. That would just tear us apart. After most funerals, when we stepped to the side of the road and let the caisson—a fire truck with the coffin on top—and the family pass by, we almost always saw a car window roll down and someone wave at us or throw us a thank-you kiss. That has helped us and made it all worthwhile.

Perhaps the most draining and exhausting part was that after we finished one funeral we often had to get into our cars and drive to another to do it all over again. And then the next day, when we woke up, we did it again—and again. At one point we thought it might be better if we didn't go inside the churches. It was too painful hearing all the eulogies about the wonderful firefighters we had lost. But when the churches got too crowded, they started putting loudspeakers outside. So outside the church, we ended up hearing the eulogies anyway. Sometimes we walked three or four blocks away just to keep from hearing everything.

Durrell "Bronko" Pearsall, Rescue 4, one of our drummers, died when the Towers came down. Of course, we played at his funeral at St. Patrick's Cathedral. A couple of weeks after 9/11, the band went to the site in full uniform to the place where it was believed his company had been, where he might have died. After we played a few songs for him, we knelt down and said a prayer. As we marched out, a couple of the drummers threw their drumsticks into the pile of ashes and debris and yelled, "Keep practicing, Bronko." It wasn't too long after that that they found the remains of his body, close to the spot where we had played.

We had a wonderful funeral at St. Francis of Assisi for Father Mychal Judge, the fire department's chaplain, who was also our chaplain. He was killed by falling debris inside the lobby of the North Tower soon after giving last rites to a firefighter on the street outside. It seemed that everyone was at his funeral, including former Mayor Guiliani. Father Mychal wasn't a piper, but he was one of us, and he was always there for us. He was great to be with, and we all thought he was wonderful. We gave him a full uniform with kilts, the works. He was tickled pink. Every year he said a Mass at a special memorial service. In the middle of one service, he told us to stand up and hold out our hands. He was always up to something, so we never knew what he was going to do next. Then he started blessing our hands and our fingers. Later I asked him, "Father Mychal, now that you've blessed these fingers, are they going to play music like they're supposed to?" He laughed, "Charlie, you know the church believes in miracles, but let's not push it."

Because he was a Franciscan, Father Mychal usually wore his robes. At one service he surprised us when he came dressed in the piper's full uniform, complete with kilts. Later he came over to us and said, "I can't stay in this uniform too long. There's a group of nuns having a tea party over there, and I think they want to check me out." What a sense of humor! When someone sent the band a check for five hundred dollars that we didn't want to keep, we cashed it and gave the money to Father Mychal. "Don't worry; I'll get rid of that money for you!" he said. He took the money and handed it out in two-dollar bunches to poor people on the street.

Before St. Patrick's Day in 2000, Father Mychal wrote this letter to me:

> Dear Charlie,
>
> I could never tell you how much I feel about each one of you. As I stand in the door of the church waiting to greet the body of the fallen, there's an awesome silence that is broken only by the sound of your approach. It is the most moving of moments of the funeral. Chills move up and down my spine and tears come to my eyes. Nor am I alone, I'm sure. It is then that I want to move out and whisper into each of your ears how wonderful you are and how you touch each of us. I am sure you could never have realized when you first joined the band what a difference you would make.
>
> So recommit yourself to what you do, thank God for the very special gift that He has given you, and know that so many, so very many, love and appreciate you. You are wonderful.
> Father Mychal

Right after 9/11, many of the band members played at one or two funerals and then spent twelve or fifteen hours with their unit searching for bodies on the site. The next day they might play at more funerals and then head back to the site again. I remember one day, not long after the tragedy, we had to play at twenty-three services. In the breaks at the funerals when the coffin was inside the church, band members were lying on the lawn fast asleep. They were completely exhausted. When the fire department realized what was going on, they put active firefighters who played in the band into the ceremonial unit to do funerals only. After the site closed and the funerals slowed down, those guys went back to work again in their firehouses.

We're still in the middle of our pain. Before 9/11, I used to go to bed at ten at night and get up at six in the morning. I barely had to make the bed, because I fell into such a sound sleep—almost comatose. But since the tragedy, I toss and turn. I wake up three or four times a night thinking about all those young, bright firefighters who lived right here in my neighborhood who are gone now. Maybe when all of the funerals and memorial services are completely finished we will be able to move on. However, it will never be totally out of our minds. Now and then I've noticed there's a bit of nonsense beginning to surface again among the firefighters. Fooling around has always been our forte in the firehouses. After all, we have to be a little tough to be a firefighter. And we have to be emotionally strong to play the pipes at all those firefighters' funerals.

Often, people say to me that the bagpipe is special. It is both a happy instrument and a sad one, and its music can be used from weddings to funerals. People identify the sound of the bagpipes as sincere, as solemn, as emotional, and sometimes even earth-shaking. It's very hard not to get involved with them, not to let go, not to let the emotions start to break free. When we play the pipes, we can create a moment when an event is relived: we can make you laugh; we can make you cry; we can help you grieve.

Before a funeral, I've noticed that people wait for things to start. When they hear the drum major give the order and the pipes begin to play, they know it marks the true beginning of the event. As we start playing, we can see people's faces change. Even people not connected to an event who are just standing by the side of the road can be seen wiping their eyes. The sound of the pipes can touch them and break down their barriers.

It hasn't been easy playing at the funerals of our friends. Because we played at so many, we thought we would get a little stronger and it would be easier. But it never was. There were times when I could barely take it. When I looked at the other guys in the band, I saw that they too were fighting back tears. But I know those tears are helping the families and helping us to heal. I believe what really saved us, what kept us going, was that we knew our music was helping the families with their pain and their grief.

Perhaps Father Mychal was right. There really is healing in the music, in the bagpipes. It has the power to bring people together and to touch their souls.

❖ ❖ ❖ ❖ ❖ ❖ ❖ ❖

I am Music; I am eternal. In all ages I have inspired people with hope, kindled their love, given a voice to their joys, cheered them on to valorous deeds, and soothed them in times of despair. Through my influence, humanity has been uplifted, sweetened, and refined. For I speak to all, in a language that all can feel. I am Music.

—Anonymous

The story of the New York Fire Department's bagpipers holds a valuable lesson about the benefits of "sticking to it" when times are really tough. This community played the same music at more than four hundred funerals and memorial services for the missing firefighters, and they often had to repeat their performances.

The bagpipers understood that it would have been very easy to lose heart or to lose sight of their goal. There were times when it was difficult to keep going and to feel a sense of purpose. But they stuck with the same songs, the same routine over and over again. Although they were completely exhausted and distraught with the situation, they hung on to their belief that what they were doing was making a difference for the firefighters' families, people who needed them to do just what they did.

Paying attention to this superb example of the bagpipers' tenacity could be beneficial for those of us who feel that being around too much suffering or grief is discouraging or depressing. Often we would rather walk away or move on to something that would take our minds off the pain. At times we get tired of repetitive activities and would prefer not to have to stick with them.

But with the inspiration of the bagpipers, we too can try not to give up even when we are exhausted or disheartened with difficult situations. There may be communities who need us to keep going and to "play the same tune over and over." As Father Mychal Judge said to one of the bagpipers, "I am sure you could never have realized . . . what a difference you would make. . . . So recommit yourself to what you do." Yes, let's do that, and we just might make a difference!

THE HEALING TREES: REMEMBERING HEROES

As told by Kathleen Murphy

Planting the trees has helped me too. As a nurse, I'm very accustomed to helping people get better. And on 9/11 there were all those people that we couldn't do anything for. Now I feel that I have done something. I believe it will help other people too.

—Kathleen Murphy

When something terrible happens, most people have the natural desire to respond with kindness, to reach out and help someone. Ordinary people rush into dangerous situations without even thinking about what they are doing, about the possible harm or injury they might undergo. On 9/11, the firefighters, police, and other emergency workers rushed into the Twin Towers to rescue as many people as possible. Their desire to respond with compassion was so great that they gave little thought to their personal safety.

If we genuinely want to help, but we are unable to do so because of circumstances beyond our control, we may feel frustrated and upset. Many people who watched the disasters of 9/11 from afar and who were unable to reach out and help in some way reported that they experienced a sense of powerlessness and inadequacy, which resulted in their feeling sad, depressed, useless, and vulnerable.

Kathleen Murphy is an Irish nurse who was working in a New York City hospital on September 11. The staff hurriedly emptied out the hospital in preparation for the deluge of patients from the World Trade Center disaster they expected to receive that day. They were not prepared for what happened—no patients arrived. As the hours passed, Kathleen and her colleagues felt a sense of helplessness as they realized there was nothing they could do.

But Kathleen didn't stop there. Her efforts resulted in communities being organized in the United States and in Ireland that helped healing take place on both sides of the ocean.

❖ ❖ ❖ ❖ ❖ ❖ ❖ ❖ ❖

As a child, I dreamed of becoming a doctor, of making people feel better, of helping them to be healed. In the early sixties the economy in Ireland was very bleak, but in England there always seemed to be a demand for nurses, so I went there and trained and worked as a registered nurse. Later I applied for a U.S. visa and have been living in the States for almost thirty years.

On September 11, I was working in the outpatient unit of a Manhattan hospital in New York City. The unit is also used as a backup for the emergency room if there is a crisis. When the World Trade Center Towers collapsed, we immediately sent home the patients from the outpatient unit because they were not in critical need. Patients in the hospital who were well enough to go home were also discharged. We thought we would need the space for what we expected to be a huge influx of emergency patients from the disaster. We were anticipating a crisis.

We waited and waited. But as the day wore on, nobody came.

A group of out-of-town nurses who were attending a meeting at a hotel in the city left their meeting and went to hospitals around the city. They wanted to help, but there was nothing for them to do either.

People sat in lounge areas of the hospital watching TVs to see what was happening. Everyone had a very strange feeling. There was no traffic on the streets; the subways weren't running; people were wandering around in a daze not knowing what to do. We had volunteers lined up around the block. They left their apartments throughout the city and came to the hospital to donate blood. There were volunteers in a large auditorium waiting to help in any way. By evening, people were turned away because they weren't needed. Something awful was happening in the city, but there was nothing we could do. It was almost eerie.

At 6:00 p.m. we were told to go home. It was terrible knowing there were so many people lost in Lower Manhattan and we were waiting in a hospital with nothing to do. We were unable to do anything for the people who had been lost. We felt helpless. Eventually, I went home to Queens on a very empty subway. My sister called from our home in county Cork to see how I was doing. She had been trying all day to reach me at the hospital, but the phones were down. September 11 was my niece's fourteenth birthday. Her birthday will never, ever be the same.

Although I didn't lose anyone in the disaster, I felt a tremendous amount of the grief and suffering that was all around us. In the papers and on the news we heard about the families and their losses—sons and daughters and parents. We also heard about the emergency workers, the police, the firefighters who were missing. And from the firehouse near where I live in Queens, nineteen men died. That was a tremendous amount, a tragedy.

Long ago, my grandfather bought some land in Kinsale, county Cork, Ireland. The property has been in our family since the 1800s, and four generations of my family have lived there. I own a little part of that land. It's where I was born, so it's really home and very special to me. I wouldn't sell it for all the tea in China. Some time ago, I thought about planting a tree for each of my grandparents and their children on my part of the property. I love trees. They are a living symbol that continues on even after we're gone. They will be there for future generations to visit. After September 11, I decided to plant trees on my land for the firefighters who had been lost. At first I thought about just planting trees for the firefighters from the two firehouses located on either side of my home in Queens and for the two firehouses on either side of the hospital where I work. But one day when I was on Fifth Avenue and saw some of the firefighters' families, I knew I needed to plant one for each firefighter—not just the ones in the stations near me. That meant there would eventually be 343 trees.

A lot of the firefighters who died were young men with small children. Some of the children were not even born when their fathers were lost. Some children might not remember their fathers. I thought it would be nice for the children to be able to visit the trees that were planted for their fathers—especially those with Irish heritage. I think all of us search for our roots, no matter who we are or where we come from. The trees might be healing or helpful for the children, the families, and the co-workers of the firefighters.

We chose the evergreen oak and a selection of other evergreen trees appropriate to the area. We know we can call the fire department at any time; they are always present twenty-four hours a day. Evergreen trees are alive year round and would be symbolic of the ever-present firefighters. We wanted the trees to be planted on an area of the property where people could have easy access to them from the road; if people want to see the trees, they can just walk onto the property. We decided that the name of the firefighter and the company name would be placed on each tree and that trees representing firefighters from the same company would stand close together.

The community spirit around the tree planting has been wonderful. My brother, who lives on the property, selected and ordered the trees. Local people with machinery came to dig the holes for the trees. A retired Kinsale firefighter asked some pipers and drummers to play and made sure the fire trucks and fire department were at the ceremony.

On November 20, 2001, it was freezing cold, but the whole community made sure the first forty-six trees were planted. One of the neighbors, who had grown an oak tree from an acorn, delivered it to the site that morning. It was planted for Father Mychal Judge. There were prayers and music, and a priest blessed all the trees. The town fathers made speeches and asked that their condolences be conveyed to the families in New York. Then neighbors, friends, and family helped plant the trees. That night a special Mass for the firefighters was said in Kinsale.

The next group of eighty-six trees was planted on March 2, 2002. That, too, turned out to be a very special event. Three fire engines came from Kinsale, Carrigaline, and Charleville, and the firefighters wore their uniforms. We had a singer, bagpipes, and drums on the site. The grandfather of a firefighter who died at the World Trade Center came and planted the tree for his only grandson—the end of his family name. Also the aunt and uncle of another firefighter planted a tree for their nephew, who had been in Ireland the previous summer playing Irish music on the accordion. As they planted the tree and put his photo on it, they were crying. It was a sad but healing event for those families and a deeply moving time for all of us.

Families have contacted me and said how grateful they are for the trees, that they appreciate having a living memorial in Ireland for their missing loved ones. One family said their dad loved the outdoors and that he would have loved the trees. Recently, I learned that one of the firefighters had been in Kinsale on vacation with his wife the summer before 9/11, and now we have planted a tree for him.

Many firefighters' remains were never found. Perhaps the trees will be a living memorial to them. We all want to be remembered, and we want our loved ones to also be remembered. These evergreen trees will help the firefighters' names live on.

Trees are very special. In the past, people believed trees were powerful, and they talked to the trees' spirits. They are important in many ways: they help clean the pollution; they provide shade; they shelter birds. Someday, when I live near the trees that have been planted in memory of the firefighters, I will again hear birds singing the birdsongs I grew up with in Ireland. That will be healing for me.

Whenever I am home in Ireland, I spend time walking through the trees. I know each tree very well, and I like to check how each is doing. One day when I was looking at the trees, I found a memorial card stuck in one. Some family member or friend had obviously been there and had left the card. It was a real affirmation of the trees. I had been wondering if it was right to plant them, whether people would come to see the trees and whether it would mean something to them. Finding that card was very special, a kind of gift to me.

Planting the trees has helped me too. As a nurse, I'm very accustomed to helping people get better. And on 9/11 there were all those people that we couldn't do anything for. Now I feel that I have done something. I believe it will help other people too. When something is done for you, you are able to do something for someone else.

❖ ❖ ❖ ❖ ❖ ❖ ❖ ❖

Whoever it was that planted them
A hundred years ago,
Spread roots apart and tamped in earth
Would now be glad to know
Another man, tree-comforted,
Waits for their leaves to grow.
—*Paul Engle*

The feeling of being powerless or helpless is not something anyone enjoys. We prefer to take charge, to be in control, to be able to help in some way. When we are powerless, we feel weak and vulnerable. We may end up thinking that we are unable to do anything for ourselves or for others. It's understandable that we could become discouraged, despondent, and disheartened.

In this moving story of courage, we see how Kathleen's desire to do something made an enormous difference for several communities. Her enthusiasm and motivation to make her simple dream come true had the effect of empowering a community in county Cork, Ireland, who wanted to get involved with this healing project. And the community of firefighters' families in the United States will continue to feel the impact of her efforts for generations to come.

We can take heart from this story. Kathleen reminds us that "doing something for someone" can make us feel better. And we can have a positive effect on others—even if it seems small or inconsequential. After all, little deeds of goodness have a way of adding up to something significant.

THE DEPARTMENT OF SANITATION:
CLEARING SACRED GROUND

As told by Supervisor Frank Berran and Chief Michael Mucci, Deputy Director, Bureau of Waste Disposal

We believe we made a real contribution to the City of New York. We did what we were supposed to do, and we did it faster than was expected. Everything that fell down has been cleared out, and every street has been cleaned. . . . Our job was done well and done with respect for the people who died there.
—*Frank Berran*

Without the infrastructure of the sanitation department, the cleanup job would never have gotten done in ten months. Not only did we clean up the streets around Ground Zero and Wall Street, but during that period garbage was still collected for the entire city and there was no interruption in service.
—*Michael Mucci*

Almost from the day we are born, we yearn to have a sense of being appreciated for who we are and what we accomplish. When we are young, we dream of growing up to be influential and powerful, and we try hard to gain the respect of our families, friends, and communities. As adults, we tend to admire people who have made a name for themselves, whose titles carry a certain status that makes them seem important, even heroic, to us. We may unconsciously rank some people and groups as being superior to or better than others.

But occasionally we are completely surprised by the accomplishments of a community of people we barely noticed because they were not high on the totem pole of our approval. Without any real knowledge, we might have negative opinions about their worth.

When a tragedy like 9/11 occurs, the playing field can be completely leveled. People and groups have an opportunity to contribute, to excel, to be recognized and valued for what they are and do. Certainly, that was true for every group that worked within the twisted ruins of the World Trade Center. They became a part of the healing community.

Some of the least-honored but most critically important communities on the site were the ironworkers, the operating engineers, the construction workers, and the sanitation workers. They worked tirelessly at their dangerous jobs with valor and dignity—and without a single complaint. Through their efforts, they helped to accomplish a miracle: millions of tons of debris were searched and removed from the site without any serious casualties and way ahead of the projected schedule. They more than earned our highest respect and appreciation for a job well done.

I chose to interview one of those "unsung heroes": the Department of Sanitation of the City of New York, a group that is so vital to the essence of the life of the city but that rarely gets our appreciation or thanks. This "community" was responsible for moving and removing every inch of the rubble from the World Trade Center site to the Fresh Kills Landfill in Staten Island. There it was carefully searched again and finally buried in a sacred site at Fresh Kills where it will never be built on.

I met Frank Berran, a supervisor for the sanitation department, during a coffee break at St. Paul's Chapel near the site. Frank and many of his colleagues meticulously and determinedly cleared away every piece of the debris at the site until it was closed in May 2002. Later I met Chief Michael Mucci, who supervised the work at the Fresh Kills Landfill, the final resting place for the remains of the World Trade Center. These men told me an amazing story of healing that started at Ground Zero and ended at the sacred burial site at the Fresh Kills Landfill.

❖ ❖ ❖ ❖ ❖ ❖ ❖ ❖ ❖

Frank Berran

The day the Towers went down, I was working in a sanitation department garage in the Bronx checking out trucks when someone said, "Hey, a plane just crashed into the World Trade Center." I could actually see the Towers and the smoke from the garage where I was working. Then I saw another plane crash into the second Tower and a huge ball of fire shooting up into the sky. To this day, I think about that sight maybe ten times a day.

I started working at the site on the second day after the Towers came down. As a group of us approached the site for the first time, there was a lot of anticipation. We had no idea what we were going to see or find. A couple of blocks before we got there, we saw the smoke rising in the air. The spotlights were already on. It felt like we were going to a movie set. It looked so unreal—like something had destroyed everything. All of us just sat in the van staring at the debris in total silence. Then we saw some guys slowly walking off the site. They were completely covered with dust and dirt. It was in their eyes and noses—everywhere.

At the site I thought of my friends who had been in the Towers and who were missing. Then I thought about my kids and how much I loved them. I wasn't worried about my own safety, what was in the air, the dangers to my own health. I just knew there was something very important that we had to do. The highest part of the pile of debris must have been about ten stories high. It was full of rubble and twisted steel. I saw the cops and firefighters with their buckets crawling around on the pile. They looked like little ants. Right then I realized that we had a very big job ahead of us.

The first few weeks we talked constantly about the experience of being there. After a while, well, it wasn't like we accepted it, but it became "our job." We had to do something to help; we had to do our work. The area around the site reminded me of what it looks like after a very bad snowstorm. Ashes and debris were hanging on fences, on top of lampposts, everywhere we looked. But with snow, the sun helps melt it away. There, we had to clean everything ourselves. We started with buckets, shovels, and barrels, and we just worked our way through. I encouraged everyone to wear masks all the time. We didn't know what we were dealing with, and we probably won't know for a long time. We hauled tons and tons of debris off the site twenty-four hours a day. We had about forty dump trucks on each shift. After they were loaded up, the debris was either driven directly to the Fresh Kills Landfill on Staten Island or dumped on barges that were taken there.

At first we worked twelve-hour shifts, seven days a week. We never had any problems or complaints from any of the workers, and almost nobody called in sick. They just kept pushing themselves and working hard all the time. Everyone who worked at the site for the sanitation department volunteered to work there. I had the choice of saying no, but I knew I really wanted to be there to offer my help.

We used all kinds of equipment to try to suppress the dust. When trucks were loaded up and taken off the site, they were driven through an area where they were hosed down. The FBI got on top of the trucks with flashlights to do another check. If they saw anything that resembled body parts, we dumped the load and checked another time. All of us saw all kinds of body parts and things that were really difficult to see. I don't think any of us will ever forget that.

Everybody felt driven in the beginning. Working seven days a week, twelve hours a day, we soon lost track of time. As the months went by, everyone became exhausted. I saw firemen, cops, and construction workers in their overalls lying on the steps of neighboring buildings or on the pews in St. Paul's Chapel. We started giving people days off, so they weren't working every day. Everybody on the site really put their hearts into whatever they were doing—no matter who they were—and they all did their jobs well. I remember watching in awe and respect the way the ironworkers hung suspended high in the air doing the very dangerous work of cutting down the twisted beams.

For several months, when I went home at the end of my shift I'd lie in bed and think about what I had seen that day. I talked with my wife, Tracy, about what had happened. She was always very understanding and supportive of the fact that I had volunteered to be there. And I talked with my kids. That helped me get through those difficult days.

When "the cross" was found on the site, the sanitation department got involved with helping set up the outdoor worship services. "The cross" was made of several twisted beams of steel approximately fifteen feet high that appeared in the debris after the Towers fell. When Father Brian Jordan came to the site and offered to lead services, there was so much debris around the area that there was no place to hold them, so we went to work and cleared a space.

At the first service, there were only about six to eight people who showed up. Soon the police, the firefighters, the construction workers, and the ironworkers started coming too. Even when it was extremely cold and rainy, the services went on. At times there were so many people that we thought we would have to move it to another location. Eventually family members of the missing began to come too. Sometimes they made informal speeches thanking the workers for what they had done. They said they were grateful because they saw how hard people were working as they searched for remains and cleared away the debris. Sometimes they said something like: "My [missing] daughter thanks you too." It was heartbreaking, but we really appreciated their acknowledgment and their gratitude.

Whenever any bodies were found on the site—of firefighters or cops or civilians, all work stopped. The firefighters and cops lined up and saluted as the bodies were carried off the site. The first few days, as sanitation workers, we just stepped to the side and stood quietly. But after two or three days, we also lined up and saluted with the others. We, too, were showing our respect and honoring the people who had lost their lives as well as those who had given their lives on 9/11.

While we were working on the site, nobody had time to think about what we were seeing and feeling. We were caught up in the job; we were on a mission. We were pushing to get it done. And we ended up being way ahead of schedule. But after the job was finished, it started hitting a lot of people what we had been doing, what we had seen. The sanitation department has an Employee Assistance Unit, and a representative spoke to us several times, inviting people to come for counseling. There were many people who needed help, and they took him up on his offer.

Although my family didn't lose any close family members in the tragedy, a number of us still decided to volunteer at the site. My cousin Charlie, a fire battalion chief; my brother-in-law Mike, another firefighter; my sister Pat, a podiatrist; and my cousin

Johnny, a retired Port Authority cop, all worked at the site. It was our way of helping others, and maybe a way of healing ourselves too.

Whenever I worked on the site, I thought about my kids and their safety. My two daughters, Aileen and Bridget, who are eighteen and twenty, don't live with me anymore. Before 9/11, they rarely called me. But when those Towers went down, they were both in touch with me right away. "Dad, where are you? Are you okay?" My four sisters live all over the place. After this happened, I wanted to call them more and talk with them. In a way, this tragedy really brought us closer together. Suddenly people were thinking more about what they have, what they might not have. I tried to put things in perspective for my family as much as possible.

Like other sanitation workers, I took many members of my family to the site, because I felt it was important for them to see what had happened. When I took my daughters to a service at the site, I saw Aileen looking around and her eyes were getting a little moist. She's a lot like me; she keeps stuff inside herself. I could see it was bothering her, so I hugged her. I remember thinking, "Here's my daughter looking at the largest cemetery in the world with no tombstones." Later I said to her, "Just be kind. Don't have any enemies. Don't be mad at anybody. Always look at the other side." I didn't want her to be angry about anything. Because we just don't know. Bridget knew several people who had died there, but she's more open and could talk about her feelings.

When I took my six-year-old son, Brian, to the site, he looked around and asked, "Dad, where were those two big buildings?" Then he asked, "Where does Uncle Mike work?" Later he looked around and asked me, "Do you think a plane could hit that building over there?" So it was definitely on his mind. One night I took him to a Mets baseball game at Shea Stadium near LaGuardia Airport. There were a lot of planes flying over the stadium. He was really into the game when suddenly he turned to me and said, "I wonder, Dad, if that plane is going to hit a building." I got a little lump in my throat as I realized how sad it is that these days kids have to think about these kinds of things. It's probably on their minds more than we know. It's frightening what this has done to our children. I believe we have to try to be as honest with the kids as we can be, without scaring them.

Now I begin to understand more about how people felt in Oklahoma City. I don't think New Yorkers understood a lot about that tragedy until the Towers came down on September 11. Then it really hit them about how bad it had been in Oklahoma. And we're beginning to understand what other countries in the world experience with terrorism. It's a whole new way of living for us.

On the site, whoever you met—a cop, a steelworker, a firefighter, a state trooper, a sanitation worker—you nodded and asked, "How you doing?" It felt like a supportive community of people working together. Anything anyone asked for, we were more than willing to do. Everybody talked with each other and was friendly and helpful to each other. Whenever we parted, we shook hands or hugged each other and said, "Be safe."

On the last day of work at the site, we had a barbecue. Everyone was there from all the different departments— firefighters, cops, sanitation workers, the ironworkers, everyone. About 7:00 that night it started hitting me that we were going to have to leave. The job was done, and we had a good sense of accomplishment, of satisfaction. There had been no arguments. Sometimes when we clean up during major snowstorms, after about four days of it we have guys screaming at each other. Although we were working long hours on the site, nobody got on each other's back. We had a real sense of camaraderie, of community.

The other day I ran into some of the guys I had worked with, and we hugged one another. It was great to see each other again. We talked about how we were doing since leaving the site. Almost everyone said the same thing: "I really miss being there." One guy said, "I miss the feeling of family we had." It's a big adjustment to come off of that. The sanitation department doesn't get as much of a "family feeling" like the fire department and the police department. Their dangerous work helps to build a sense of camaraderie or community. But we had that at the World Trade Center site—we had the feeling of a real community. We will have to try our best to hang on to that feeling. We'll try to remember the special times we had as colleagues, although it will likely never be quite the same as it was there.

So as horrible and horrendous as this situation was, it showed the better side of the city. It brought the good out in everybody. Maybe people who didn't even know they had good inside them were able to see that. In many ways, it brought the city a little bit closer. We believe we made a real contribution to the City of New York. We did what we were supposed to do, and we did it faster than was expected. Everything that fell down has been cleared out, and every street has been cleaned. And we continued to service the area. Our job was done well and done with respect for the people who died there.

Michael Mucci

On September 11, I was the director of the Fresh Kills Landfill in Staten Island. We were getting ready for the landfill's final closure. At one time, all of New York City's garbage was taken there—about thirteen to fourteen thousand tons a day, until the city started a program of exporting its garbage to other sites. We were cleaning up the area and getting ready for trucks to bring in dirt. We were building roads that made it possible to drive to different areas on the site. That certainly made dealing with the tragedy easier.

On the morning of 9/11, someone told me a plane had just hit the World Trade Center. We went to the top of the landfill to see from there what was going on. It was a beautiful, clear day, and we could easily see across the harbor to Manhattan that the Trade Center was on fire. As soon as the first tower collapsed, I knew that Sanitation would be involved. Nobody had to tell us to get ready. We knew what we had to do.

As the day progressed, we started getting phone calls. The FBI wanted to take a look at our facilities and barges. Fresh Kills was to be reopened to receive the debris from the World Trade Center. The first truck filled with rubble from Ground Zero came into Fresh Kills at 2:20 a.m. on September 12. Everything escalated from there. Before long, we were taking in ten thousand tons of debris a day in trucks and barges twenty-four hours a day, seven days a week. We had gone from being closed to a full-scale operation in a couple of hours.

When the trucks and barges came in with the debris, everything was separated and sent to the appropriate area: search areas, a stockpile area, a place for steel, a place for smashed and burned vehicles such as the fire trucks and police cars. In the beginning it was really eerie, because the police cars' radios were still talking. Alarms were going off. Some of the newer cars had automatic lights, which went on when it got dark. Finally the FBI cut the cables so that didn't happen.

Searching was done by hand when we first started. Eventually it evolved into a very efficient way of searching. After the steel was separated, it was shaken to be sure nothing was in it. The rubble was sifted and separated into different sizes—down to about a quarter of an inch. Then it was searched on conveyor belts by the FBI and police. Once it was cleared, we removed it and buried it. Approximately fourteen hundred body parts were found at Fresh Kills that had not been found at the Trade Center site, and there were thousands of rings, watches, and credit cards.

We never got used to what we saw and did, but we just did what we had to do, although it was not pretty or easy. The sanitation department's counseling department provided counselors if we needed them, and a priest was on-site almost every day.

Within a few weeks, Fresh Kills became a small city. The cooperation between the different bureaus and unions was amazing, and everything went smoothly. Each morning all the people representing every one of the agencies, from the police department to the FBI to the Army Corps of Engineers, sat around a table to work out anything that had to do with the operation of the site. At the height of the operations, there was a tremendous amount of equipment and about fifteen hundred people working on the site at the same time. So it's amazing there were no major injuries—only one broken arm.

Probably no other city in the world could have handled this kind of operation. No other city moved its garbage by barges. The infrastructure, equipment, and personnel were ready to be used. Usually when there is a disaster, the Army Corps of Engineers comes in and takes over, but they didn't have to do that at Fresh Kills. When we met with them after the completion of the operation, they were astonished at what we had done. They said it was the most efficient, smooth-running operation they had ever seen. It just shows that whenever people get their heads together and want to do something, they can do it. The Army Corps is developing a plan for the nation based on what we did.

Certainly, there was a sense of sadness as we worked at Fresh Kills, but there was also an attitude of "we have to do whatever we can." Something positive came out of all of this pain. We saw what people are really made of. Everybody was helpful. People from stores and restaurants drove into Fresh Kills with food, cookies, and soda. Nobody called them and said we needed sandwiches; they were just there. People donated flowers, Christmas trees, everything. They'd say, "We thought you might need this." One guy drove up with a tractor-trailer full of showers and toilets. Someone brought seven thousand buckets. Everything just poured in. Retired sanitation workers called: "I can answer the phone. I'll do anything. Just let me help you in any way." Somehow the tragedy brought out the best in us. The hearts of people were really big.

During the most difficult times, what kept the workers going was the outpouring of thanks we received from people throughout the country. Schools from all over the United States sent us cards and banners. One school sent us three hundred pairs of work gloves with small notes tucked inside. We really appreciated the support.

Now the Fresh Kills Landfill is officially closed. There are no more efforts around the 9/11 work. Some of the steel from the World Trade Center site was kept for memorials. Some crushed vehicles were given to museums or kept to be used for memorials. About 1,275 million tons of debris and material have been buried in a forty-acre section on the western slope of Fresh Kills. It's been covered by a foot of dirt and seeded for erosion control. Eventually, there will be some type of memorial out there. We call that place the "Sacred Ground."

Without the infrastructure of the sanitation department, the cleanup job would never have gotten done in ten months. Not only did we clean up the streets around Ground Zero and Wall Street, but during that period garbage was still collected for the entire city and there was no interruption in service. The sanitation department went on with its work in the rest of the city as though nothing had happened. Everybody worked and pulled together from all over the country and from all walks of life. We saw that there was no difference between us. Hopefully this will never ever happen again, but we know what we can do if we have to. We don't have to do anything spectacular. We just need to work well together and do our job.

❖ ❖ ❖ ❖ ❖ ❖ ❖ ❖

And what is it to work with love? . . . It is to charge
all things you fashion with a breath of your own spirit,
and to know that all the blessed dead are standing
about you and watching.
                                        —Kahlil Gibran

There are so many things we can glean from reading this story. It's astonishing how a devastating and traumatic event can have the effect of pulling us together and bringing out our best. Although the working conditions at Ground Zero and at Fresh Kills were dreadful and people worked long and grueling hours, they didn't complain, there were no fights, and people were kind and gentle with each other. They treated each other as equal members of an enormous team.

One of the most inspiring parts of this story is how such a huge job was completed ahead of schedule using buckets, shovels, and barrels. Likely that happened because people pulled together and became a community. Many workers on the site told me that even when they were absolutely drained of all energy, another person inspired and encouraged them to muster up the strength and courage to do a little bit more.

When terrible events happen, or if we face a monumental job, it's easy to become disheartened. We can also feel discouraged if we are always working "behind the scenes" and never have an opportunity to see the results of our efforts. At such times, we would do well to remember these brave, unsung heroes. It's possible that we will find the courage to emulate their example and to approach the most difficult of tasks with kindness, compassion, and respect for one another. Working as a genuine community, we may be surprised how easily we can achieve our goals.

St. Paul's Chapel:
Creating a Haven

As told by the Reverend Lyndon Harris

It seems clear to me that St. Paul's Chapel was spared, not because we were holier than anybody who died across the street from us, but because we had a job to do. . . .
                        —the Reverend Lyndon Harris

A few days after September 11, I went to the site of the World Trade Center to pay my respects to the people who died in the destruction of the Twin Towers. I felt overwhelmed with sadness as I looked at the rubble of those once tall, sleek buildings. The smells of smoke, ashes, jet fuel, and chemicals oozing from "the pile" penetrated my lungs like a dagger. I watched hundreds of people crawling over the debris, searching for survivors. I knew they were holding onto a tiny shred of hope that someone might still be found alive. It felt like my heart was being torn apart.

As I stood near that sacred spot where so many souls had departed this earth, I silently prayed for healing for those who were suffering, and for peace in the world. At St. Paul's Chapel, the oldest church building in New York City, I stared at the undamaged, stately steeple that was silhouetted against the spotlights on the site. The chapel was so close to the burning rubble that I marveled how it could still be standing after the earthshaking collapse of the huge towers just a short distance behind it.

Not long after that, I started working as a volunteer at St. Paul's Chapel. On the fence outside the chapel were thousands of letters, cards, photos, flowers, and supportive messages to the families of the victims, the rescue workers and the City of New York. Inside there were more letters and cards plus huge banners about hope, love, forgiveness, and courage that had been sent by people from all over the world. They hung on every inch of wall space and every pew with their special messages: "Peace," "We love you, New York," "Never give up hope," "Remember to forgive." Thousands of volunteers from New York, the United States, and the world came to the chapel for the privilege of helping hand out food, coffee, bandages, socks, gloves, and of providing care for the exhausted workers who did twelve-to-eighteen-hour shifts on the site. Weary firefighters, police, sanitation, and construction workers entered that space for sustenance, rejuvenation, rest, support, and encouragement. Seven days a week, around the clock, we volunteers kept the vigil candles lit, listened to people talk, served food and drinks, gave out hugs, and made sure the workers were comfortable.

One night an exhausted policeman told me he was afraid to fall asleep—that he might not wake up on time for his shift. I encouraged him to rest and promised to wake him at 3 a.m. I shall never forget how he thanked me, dropped his tense shoulders, and slowly took off his bulletproof vest in the safety of that holy place. When he finally allowed himself to lie down on one of the pews to sleep, I covered him with a beautiful quilt donated by a family from Ireland.

For me, working at St. Paul's Chapel was the closest thing I had ever experienced to being in what I think of as God's blessed space, open and welcoming to all. Whenever I worked a twelve-hour shift, I always walked away from it feeling that I had received more hope, energy, love, and healing than I had given. There was a sense of community, of family among all of us: the volunteers in the chapel, the families of the missing, the souls who had departed, the workers on the site, the City of New York, and people from around the world who were there in spirit. St. Paul's Chapel was a most restoring place, full of boundless love and compassion. It was truly a healing community.

The Reverend Lyndon Harris, the priest and pastor at St. Paul's during the nine months it operated as a house of hospitality, was often present when I was there. I asked him to tell the story of how this haven for healing had been created.

❖ ❖ ❖ ❖ ❖ ❖ ❖ ❖ ❖

In March 2001, I went to St. Paul's Chapel to create a laboratory for alternative worship and urban evangelism for the Episcopal Church. Prior to my arrival, there had not been a priest on staff at the chapel for nearly twenty-five years. There was an 8:00 a.m. Eucharist and a shelter for homeless men. During my first months, we put together a jazz ensemble and experimented with multimedia presentations on the big screen. We were planning to reconvene on September 17.

On September 11, I was in my office at Trinity Church waiting to attend a videotaping of a speech by Rowan Williams, who has since been installed as the Archbishop of Canterbury. While I waited, I furiously sent out e-mails about the start-up of services at St. Paul's. Then someone told me something had happened at the World Trade Center. Outside I saw paper coming down everywhere. I began running toward the World Trade Center to see if I could be of any help. I got as far as Liberty Street, a street just south of the South Tower, when the second plane hit that Tower. At that point I knew it was not an accident. So I ducked into the closest building, the American Stock Exchange, to avoid falling debris. I stayed there for a few minutes before I went back to the Trinity building.

When the South Tower collapsed, an ominous black cloud descended upon us in horrific fashion. It filled the building with smoke, and we could barely breathe. Our eyes burned, and we couldn't see. We put wet paper towels over our mouths to filter out the smoke. The first thing we did was evacuate the children in the preschool in our building. Most of us picked up and carried a child. I was carrying a little girl. She was very calm, not crying. We went out the back of the building and made a run for it. We tried to get away from the Towers by heading for the Staten Island Ferry Terminal at the end of Manhattan. About halfway there, the North Tower collapsed, totally consuming us. The dark smoke, paper, and debris were like a huge formidable wall chasing us down.

I guess if I had been in my right mind, I would have been afraid. But I wasn't thinking about that. I was just trying to figure out what we had to do next, what kinds of strategies we needed to develop, where we should go.

After what seemed like an endless walk through the smoke and darkness, we made it to the ferry terminal and were evacuated by bus to Thirty-fourth Street. Then I walked home to my apartment in Greenwich Village. My thirteen-year-old daughter, who was in school, had called home to see if I was okay, and my wife told her "of course he is." But at that time, she had no idea where I was or what was happening to me. Although everyone in my family was badly shaken, we were fine.

On the morning of September 12, I got up early and with some trepidation started walking down Broadway. I expected to see that St. Paul's Chapel had been demolished. I couldn't believe it when I walked near City Hall and saw the spire in the distance. I felt my breath taken away when I realized that it was still standing. I couldn't believe the chapel could possibly have survived when the Towers had collapsed just behind it.

Walking into the building for the first time after the attack was an amazing experience. I was all alone, and it was almost scary. But it was a tremendously powerful and emotional moment for me. There was a lot of energy in the building that I could feel as soon as I stepped inside. It just felt like Holy Spirit energy. As I walked inside the building, I saw that the place was covered in ashes and debris, but the building was intact—not even one window had been broken. I'm sure the old sycamore trees that stand behind the church next to the Towers helped protect the chapel. Also there was one window on the balcony upstairs that was accidentally left halfway open. One of the guys who slept in the homeless shelter the night before must have forgotten to close it. That probably also helped with decompression and prevented the windows from breaking.

It seems clear to me that St. Paul's Chapel was spared, not because we were holier than anybody who died across the street from us, but because we had a job to do—and that was what we had to try to do.

Several days later, people from the Seaman's Institute and General Theological Seminary, along with some of my friends, set up a hot dog, hamburger, and drink stand on Broadway in front of the chapel. We weren't sure if the building was safe to use until it was checked out by a structural engineer, so we started barbecuing on Broadway, eventually doing about two thousand meals a day on the street.

A week later, after the engineers found that the structure of the chapel was sound, we opened the doors and started offering different things inside. From that day on, St. Paul's stayed open twenty-four hours a day, seven days a week, until the rescue work on the site was officially ended and the chapel was closed for cleaning and renovation on June 2, 2002.

One thing led to another, and the services at the chapel just started to grow. We served a half million meals around the clock during the nine months. The rescue workers began sleeping and resting on the pews. Different people came to us with special gifts, and we included whatever we thought would be helpful. There was an abundance of offers by professional volunteers. We had grief counselors, massage therapists, podiatrists, and chiropractors.

The podiatrists were deeply appreciated by the emergency workers, especially in the first four months, because they were working on a site that was still on fire and their boots were melting off their feet. Often I joked with them, "You work on the soles, and I'll work on the souls." Actually, we were mainly concerned about the care of the body and physical relief. Certainly, it's all connected. You can't have your soul feeling good if your soles don't feel okay—or your back. The chiropractors and massage therapists were extremely popular too. Anyone working on the site was welcome to use any of these services. We never discriminated against anyone.

The Music Givers Union came to work with us, providing free concerts at the chapel three times a day for seven months. They did everything from jazz piano to string quartets. Many people commented on how soothing it was to come into St. Paul's and have the anxiety and the weariness of working on the site washed away by the music.

Every day we had a Eucharist at noon for those who wished to participate. If people didn't want to join in, that was fine. But we felt it was important to do that—as a witness to ourselves and to others. Everything we did in that sacred place was connected to what we had been called by God to do and had vowed to do—to seek and serve Christ in every person.

Although I was priest and pastor at St. Paul's, the hat I wore the most was that of manager. We ended up running a large financial operation. It was a huge undertaking to supervise. Fortunately, I have a background in management, so I was able to call forth some of those skills. Trying to manage a staff and a full-blown operation as well as trying to be a priest and pastor proved to be a real juggling act.

At St. Paul's, we tried to create a haven for people, an oasis of hospitality, a place where they didn't have to do anything, a place where they could come to be inspired and uplifted and healed— perhaps literally and figuratively. We never proselytized, and whenever people came in to try to do that, we kicked them out. We wanted the space to be respected so people could come in to unwind, to hear a good concert, to have a good meal and a cup of coffee. We always tried to do what was right, and we tried to do our best. We wanted to make a difference.

Every day I saw God present in the people on the site. Any person who worked sixteen hours a day in that hellish pit looking for body parts has a heart that is filled with love that comes from God. That person has a courage that is inspired by God and a commitment that goes beyond selfish achievements. I believe that was the Spirit of God at work. I felt that on the site and at St. Paul's.

We experienced some amazing examples of God's love over the months. Late in September, an elderly African-American woman in the South Bronx heard that a man working on the pile had hurt his leg. She must have been in her eighties. She got on the subway and traveled all the way to Lower Manhattan. She talked her way through the police lines—which at that point in time was no small feat, came into St. Paul's Chapel, and gave us her only cane. Then she hobbled off. For me, that's the story of the whole experience, that kind of selfless love, that giving that went beyond the comfort level. It was completely transforming.

I will always remember Father Lapsley, a priest from South Africa who came to St. Paul's. He was one of the first white priests who stood against apartheid. Someone sent him a mail bomb to thank him for that. It blew off both of his hands. He celebrated the Eucharist with his prosthetic devices and hooks for hands. I assisted him at the liturgy that day. When he elevated the host and broke it with those hooks, I felt a shudder go down my spine. His sermon was all about forgiveness and healing and love. If that guy can talk about forgiveness and healing, then I think we would do well to listen.

For me, it was truly a privilege to do anything for the people who worked so hard in the hell of Ground Zero. I was their pastor, and I saw them as my congregation. I tried to pass through the site as often as possible to check in with people and to be a presence—to be a visible sign of God's love even in that place. It was an extraordinary experience to be present and to do something for those wonderful people; it was an honor to be there for them and to be in charge of St. Paul's Chapel during this point in history.

In many ways, the crisis of 9/11 was an opportunity for us to try out a new way of being the church—to minister to body, mind, soul, and spirit. What happened at St. Paul's was that God gave us a glimpse of what might be possible: a glimpse of the church of the future, a glimpse of love which was genuine, a glimpse of integrity, a glimpse of a healing community. For those of us who experienced that, it changed us forever.

❖ ❖ ❖ ❖ ❖ ❖ ❖ ❖

Hospitality is the virtue which allows us to break through the narrowness of our own fears and to open our houses to the stranger, with the intuition that salvation comes to us in the form of a tired traveler.
—Henri J.M. Nouwen

In its critical location next to the ruins of the World Trade Center, St. Paul's Chapel had a unique opportunity to carry out a very special role in history. It also had a chance to demonstrate the genuine meaning of being a "healing church" to a community with enormous needs. Sometimes when a terrible tragedy occurs, a community can discover what its true identity is, what its real purpose is, and what it was created to do or to become.

On the last day of services at St. Paul's Chapel, the emergency workers stood up and paid tribute to what the chapel had meant to them. A construction worker, who had lost two brothers in the Towers, stood up with tears streaming down his face and confessed that he had lost his faith in God. But in the healing space of St. Paul's he had seen God in the eyes of the volunteer workers—at all hours of the day or night—and he now could go on with life.

All too often we try very hard to figure out what our mission or purpose in life should be or what role we should play in a tragic event.

Sometimes it can be revealed to us if we merely are receptive to it. All kinds of doors and windows to incredible possibilities may be unlocked for us if we can relax and let it happen. And if we have big, wide-open hearts—big enough for people to walk right in—we too will create blessed spaces like those at St. Paul's Chapel.

Our Children and "Ordinary People":
Touching Angels

As told by our children and Mike Bellone, Bob Barrett, Battalion Chief Jim Riches, and Principal Maureen Burgio of St. Patrick's School

> *Whenever possible, we focus on the positive [in our presentations]. We want these kids to feel better, to grow up strong and brave.*
> —Mike Bellone

> *There's so much that is bottled up inside of [kids]. One kid said, "I was so happy to talk with someone who was there, who really knew what had happened." Some of the kids are desperate to be heard.*
> —Bob Barrett

> *Dear Mike and Bob: . . . I learned from you that everybody can be a hero, not only the big and the strong, but also the small and the weak.*
> —Fifth-Grade Student

It has often been said that our children are our hope for the future. Indeed, the future of the world is in the hands of our children. How they develop, how they mature into adults and leaders of tomorrow depends on how we care for them, how we love and nurture them, how we help them cope with difficulties and trauma.

The horrible events of September 11 caused severe harm to enormous numbers of children. The vivid images of the World Trade Center Towers collapsing with thousands of people trapped inside has been etched forever on children's minds—whether witnessed firsthand or from repeated television viewing. Many children are irritable, violent, suffer from nightmares, have eating problems, and have difficulty concentrating on their schoolwork. Unfortunately, a large percentage of these children have not been given appropriate support, nor have they had an opportunity to express their fears and anxieties.

The literature is filled with information about how children's personalities can be damaged if they have experienced or witnessed trauma, abuse, or violence—especially if they are unable to express their feelings or if they are not supported in a healing process.

While working as a volunteer at St. Paul's Chapel near the site of the ruins of the Twin Towers, I met Mike Bellone, an emergency medical technician who became a fire safety director on the site, and Firefighter Bob Barrett from Ladder 20. They were concerned about the thousands of children who had been deeply wounded by the tragedy of 9/11 and decided to do something to help them heal. During the day, Mike and Bob traveled to schools and day camps, providing kids with an opportunity to meet and talk with two "ordinary people" who worked at the site of the tragedy. At night they returned to the unbearably sad work of digging for the remains of victims. Often I traveled with these courageous men in order both to lift my spirits and to learn what children were feeling—before and after they met Mike and Bob.

What these "ordinary people" did was extraordinary. It was nothing short of miraculous.

❖ ❖ ❖ ❖ ❖ ❖ ❖ ❖

Fourth-Grade Student

Once I visited the Twin Towers. I saw lots of people working at the bottom selling pizza and ice cream. Then I went to the top and looked down. Everything seemed so tiny—the people and the cars. When the Towers fell down, I thought about the people at the top, who must have been really scared. And I thought about the people at the bottom, who looked so tiny. I wonder if they were all killed. It made me so sad. I couldn't stop thinking about that.

Sixth-Grade Student

On 9/11, my dad lost three of his friends who worked in the Trade Center. That made him so upset that he wasn't able to go to work for a while. My best friend lost her aunt and her cousin. Another friend lost her dad, and she had to go to counseling for a long time. Since 9/11, I'm afraid we might have a fire in my apartment building. Maybe we would be trapped. It's very scary.

Eighth-Grade Student

I think 9/11 was the worst day ever. Now there are lots of kids who don't have moms or dads anymore. It could have been my mom, because she works in a tall building. For a long time I didn't want her to go to work, and I was nervous whenever she left our apartment. A friend asked me, "What if people are really scared? If they tell someone, will they have to go to a psychiatrist?" I don't know what the answer is.

Bob Barrett

God works in mysterious ways, because my group wasn't working on September 11. When a plane hit the World Trade Center, I called my firehouse, Ladder 20, and learned they were there. Right then I knew I had to go too, so I went to the nearest firehouse and headed in with them. Both Towers were already down when we got there, about 11:00. I was in my sneakers and shorts. I had no gloves, no mask, no boots, nothing. We started frantically digging with our hands in the burning ruins. It felt like the end of the world. Later I learned that all the guys from my company were gone—fifteen from my firehouse—including my best friend, Dave. We had worked as partners for twenty-four years. On 9/11 our partnership was broken.

Mike Bellone

On the morning of September 11 I was at home watching television. I'm a Red Cross–certified Emergency Medical Technician, and I respond to any kind of emergency. On the television screen it said that anyone with medical experience should report to the Trade Center, so I hitched a ride into Manhattan. By the time we got there, it was completely dark, like nighttime. When I looked up to use the World Trade Center Towers as a guide, they weren't there. I felt totally disoriented, like a blind person whose furniture had just been rearranged.

At the site I tried to help in any way I could. Nobody was forced to stay, but it was difficult not to be there. It's like when you can't see where someone is, you begin to worry about them. So I worked every day. One day Battalion Chief Jim Riches from the fire department said he wanted me to be a part of their unit. He encouraged me to enroll in the John Jay School of Fire Science and I became a fire safety director on the site.

Chief Jim Riches

Mike was always on the site right from the beginning, working every single day, rain or shine, cold or hot, until the last beam was taken away. He didn't have to be there; he didn't get paid. Whenever we needed something down in the hole and we saw him coming, we'd say, "Thank God Mike's here." He was like an angel coming to bring us what we needed. As we worked together, I asked him to become a part of our team. In my mind, Mike goes way beyond the image of the Good Samaritan. He showed me what friendship is about and what caring really is. After losing my own son Jimmy on 9/11, I can say that something good did come from this tragedy, because I met Mike.

Mike Bellone

There were many days when I worked twelve to eighteen hours. Then I'd head over to St. Paul's for a couple of hours of sleep, and I'd read a few of the children's letters and poems from around the country that covered the walls and pews. They somehow gave me the strength and courage to keep going.

One night in March when Bob and I had been sleeping in St. Paul's, I woke up and read one of the letters taped on the back of the pew in front of me: "Dear Fireman, When I grow up, I want to be a fireman just like you—up until the part where you die. Your friend." I said to Bob, "Look at this letter, how precious it is. But kids shouldn't be writing about death, or about buildings falling down, or about how sad they are that we lost our friends. They should be doing their homework, playing softball with friends, hanging out with their buddies. We have a serious problem. We're in a country that has everything, and kids are talking about death and destruction. We can't sit here and let this happen. We have to do something." I also talked with Chief Riches about this idea.

Chief Jim Riches

Near the site we were given hot meals and coffee at the Red Cross, the Salvation Army, and St. Paul's. In all of those places pictures and letters from kids were taped up all over, and they were rotated every week. It was uplifting to have children's messages of encouragement when we were digging in that horrible hole. When we came up and saw the letters and pictures the kids had made for us, it gave us hope.

But as we started thinking about their pictures, we realized that most of them were filled with buildings on fire, planes crashing, people looking disturbed. We couldn't help but wonder what was going on inside these young kids' heads. Most of the pictures were about devastation, destruction, and distress, so there had to be a lot of pain on their minds. Some kids were only four or five years old. How was this going to affect them when they got older or when they became adults? Would they always be filled with anger and hatred?

Mike was already thinking ahead. He started talking about going out to speak to kids in schools. I told him I thought it was a great idea. The kids had seen people dying, crying, screaming, and suffering on television, and it had to affect them in a harmful way. It was important to have someone soothe them, calm them, answer their questions, and tell them it was only a few bad people that had done this terrible thing. Not everyone was bad.

Mike Bellone

I spoke to my friend Justina Romano, who is a first-grade teacher in Public School 226, an elementary school in Brooklyn. "My friend Bob and I would like to stop by the school to see how the kids are doing. Would that be okay?" She was delighted. So we talked with her class. Then she organized another event for the whole school. While we were there, a television crew filmed us. After that aired, we had lots of requests to do the same thing at other schools in New York. So we went to schools during the day and returned to the site to work the night shift.

When we go to schools, we usually start by asking the kids questions, and if they guess the right answer, we give them fire department patches. That's how we get their attention. We ask, "Does anybody know how tall the Twin Towers were? How many acres are there at the site? Do you know what happened on December 7, 1941?"

Then we give the kids a chance to ask us questions. They ask some amazing questions, like "How did you feel the day the Towers fell down?" That's something many kids are concerned about. They may be afraid to ask their parents or teachers, who might not want to talk about it or are unable to deal with their questions. We always try to answer them as honestly as possible. We tell them the truth: "We were scared out of our minds." We can see the kids start to relax when they learn that two big men who worked at the site were also afraid. It makes them realize that they weren't the only ones who were frightened nor were they crazy to feel that way. It validates their feelings.

Or they ask, "What would you do if it happened again? Is it safe to go into a tall building? How many people died? How many got out of the buildings? Were there a lot of people who helped?" Again, we tell them the truth, but always gently and with a positive slant.

When we ask them, "What is a hero?" they usually answer, "A policeman, a firefighter." But the answer we say is that they are the real heroes, because they supported us with their letters and prayers. Then we break the word "hero" down and let them guess what each letter stands for:

H—health: to be a hero, you have to be healthy, eat good food, don't use drugs, don't smoke, and be sure to exercise.

E—education: go to school, do your homework, read, listen to your teachers.

R—respect: respect yourself, your parents, and your teachers. If you give respect to others and you respect yourself, you'll gain respect.

O—our future: if you do these three things, our future will be in good hands with you.

We've received thousands of drawings, posters, banners, postcards, and letters from kids of all ages around the country thanking us for our visits. If they ask questions, we try to respond to them whenever possible.

Bob Barrett

Some of the letters were barely legible, but we knew the enormous effort that went into writing them. They have deeply touched our hearts. Here are several that brought tears to our eyes:

Dear firemen, Please rebuild the World Trade Center, but this time hide it. Don't tell anyone where it is.
Your friend

Thank you for telling us that we helped you get to your goal. Before, I thought that kids could not help—until you guys came and said so.
Your pal

I thought your presentation was very good because we learned that we are the heroes not the losers. Thank you for showing us what the word hero really means.
Your hero

I know the sadness you're going through. My grandfather just died. But as you said, when you see a closed door, look for an open door. That's all I will say!

Your friend

Sometimes the depth of the kids' questions surprises us. We realize they've been thinking about this for a long time. Almost everywhere we go, someone asks, "Did you lose any of your friends?" I explain, "I lost my best friend, but now I have Mike as a friend. Sometimes when something is taken away, God gives us something else, if we are open to that. So when one door shuts, we need to look for an open one." We try to help kids see that it's not what you've lost but what you still have left that counts.

Kids in the seventh, eighth, and ninth grades don't talk much, because they're at that awkward age where they don't want to sound silly. They have other things on their minds and lots of peer pressure going on, but usually after we finish, a lot of these "cool" kids come over with tears in their eyes and give us a hug.

Sometimes parents want to shield their kids from what happened, but that's impossible, because the 9/11 event was just too big. The kids want to make a contact with someone who was on the site. They want to ask questions and get some answers.

Mike Bellone

Often someone asks, "How could God have allowed this to happen?" We answer, "But God didn't cause the tragedy in the Trade Center. And look what God has given us: our families, our friends, our life, this beautiful earth." We remind the kids that God helped us save between thirty and thirty-five thousand people from the Towers, that there were fewer than three thousand people who died, and that God replaces our losses. We talk about how we felt God's presence on the site, how God helped us during the rescue operation, that no one was seriously injured on the site—there was only one broken leg. It's astonishing to watch the kids' faces light up. They feel better, because we've given them "an answer"—not that it was the best or only answer, but it's some kind of an explanation. Whenever possible, we focus on the positive. We want these kids to feel better, to grow up strong and brave.

Since we first started, we have been invited to hundreds of schools, day camps, play groups, and children's hospitals in New York and many states around the United States and to other countries, including Japan, Taiwan, Korea, and England. We've spoken at several colleges and universities, including the Massachusetts Institute of Technology (MIT) and Harvard. Two professors at MIT told us before our talk that their students were only interested in hearing information regarding the technical aspects and conditions of the Trade Center's collapse, not the emotional impact. They were concerned that what we might say wouldn't be effective with their students. But after we finished our presentation, I don't believe there was a dry eye in the group—men or women. And every student gave us a hug before we left. Later the professors told us that in their twenty years at MIT, they had never seen such an emotional response.

Bob Barrett

Many people won't talk about what happened, and that makes it worse for kids. Children need to ask questions, to talk about their feelings. There's so much that is bottled up inside of them. One kid said, "I was so happy to talk with someone who was there, who really knew what happened." Some of the kids are desperate to be heard. We try to give kids a chance to ask questions, to hear some answers, to be validated.

The tragedy of 9/11 has been difficult for kids because they felt they weren't able to do anything or to help anyone. Being so far away, they saw things happening on TV, but they couldn't participate. We tell them, "Each one of us has been touched by 9/11. Your letters, prayers, and fundraising efforts helped support us while we were on the site. So you're a part of our team." The kids have always been involved emotionally—even from a distance. But now we've given them the status of "You were there with us."

Our work with children may have helped heal some of their wounds, but it has also personally helped heal some of mine. I've been trying to figure out why I'm still here. I'm alive because my group didn't work on September 11. But why? I believe I'm here to give something back to someone, maybe to the kids who wrote all those wonderful letters that supported us, that gave us chills as we sat in St. Paul's Chapel.

Recently I had a dream that I was talking to a priest. He asked me, "If you had one wish, what would you want?" And I said, "I'd like to be a good guy." Suddenly the priest was transformed into Jesus, and he said, "I can't make you a good guy by saying you're a good guy. In order to be a good guy, you have to leave a trail of good deeds. You have to earn it."

Maybe the dream is about our purpose here on earth, why we are still here. Life is so short, every moment so precious. And we have to leave a trail of good deeds for the kids. Perhaps then it will be possible for them to grow up to be strong and loving people. Mike and I really want to make a contribution, to spend our time doing good things and giving ourselves to others.

Fifth-Grade Student

Dear Mike and Bob: I feel touched by how you told us that we and our letters were a source of energy for you. I learned from you that everybody can be a hero, not only the big and the strong, but also the small and the weak.

Fifth-Grade Student

The program with Mike and Bob was great. I didn't know some of my friends were so scared and they felt the same way I did. We never talked about that. The best part was when Mike told us about the big cross being found in the ruins at the site. I thought that was pretty amazing.

Seventh-Grade Student

I used to think I would sound stupid if I asked questions about 9/11. Bob and Mike said we could ask any questions and say what we wanted. Now I know it's okay to be scared when something terrible happens and that we should talk about it. That way we can start to feel better. That felt really good.

Ninth-Grade Student

I used to have bad dreams about the people who jumped out of the Towers. But Mike and Bob said they didn't jump, that it may have been their bodies reacting and falling out. That made me feel a lot better. Mike and Bob told us that God was with them at the site. So maybe God and some angels were in the Towers helping take care of people when they were trapped. Mike said God doesn't stop bad things from happening. But God is there to help us when we are hurt.

Chief Jim Riches

Mike and Bob have chosen to take care of our children, to reach out and spread a healing message to them. They will always work to encourage kids to be involved, to tell them that they helped us after 9/11, that they are our future, that they can make the world a better place.

Principal Maureen Burgio

On 9/11, St. Patrick's School was part of the disaster at the World Trade Center. Our children saw it happening out the windows of our building. When I heard children screaming upstairs that morning, I ran to the third floor. The children had witnessed the plane hitting the first Tower. It had a terrible impact on them.

I believe in the healing process and want to give our students a positive approach to life's problems. We offered them different forms of therapy; however, many of the children were unable to express their feelings verbally. We tried to help them work through their fears and anxieties through music and art. I also bring programs to the school that are constructive, so the children can see there are good things in the world. I invited Mike and Bob to talk with the students at an assembly. It was one more step in the children's healing process. We needed to come together to think about 9/11 in a beneficial way.

During the hour and a half of their presentation, the students missed History, Social Studies, and English classes. But whatever they might have learned in those classes could never compare to what they learned from these two gentlemen. There aren't words to describe how helpful and healing this was for everyone. They helped us see positive things within the disaster—even at the site of the ruins. They left us a special part of the World Trade Center, a cross that was cut from one of the fallen steel beams.

I believe God gives us people like Mike and Bob who can help us to understand things better, to make our load a little easier, to give us courage, strength, and hope to endure.

❖ ❖ ❖ ❖ ❖ ❖ ❖ ❖

Jesus said, "Let the little children come to me, and do not stop them; for it is to such as these that the Kingdom of God belongs."
                                                    —Luke 18:16

From the first time I met Mike and Bob, who call themselves "ordinary people," I felt I too had been touched by angels. When Mike sat in that pew reading a child's letter and came up with the idea of helping children, he set into motion a remarkable community effort—something we all have the potential to do. Since then, he, Bob, and others have spoken to thousands and thousands of children, lifted their spirits, given them hope, and helped heal some of their wounds. Now this community of angels has dreamed another dream and are forming a children's organization to reach out to children affected by other traumatic events.

There's a lot to learn from this inspiring story. Sometimes when we have a tiny seed of an idea like Mike and Bob had, it can grow into something very important, something bigger than we ever dreamed it could be. All of our communities and each one of us have the potential to help many people, to make a huge difference in life. If we allow things to happen and if we are open, our little dreams can snowball and grow into exciting healing possibilities.

When Chief Jim Riches described Mike, he said, "He was like an angel coming to bring us what we needed. . . . Mike goes way beyond the image of the Good Samaritan." Taking a look at the story of the Good Samaritan might be a worthwhile effort for every community. After all, the Samaritan wasn't a priest or a powerful ruler with important credentials. He wasn't anyone special. He was just an "ordinary person" who felt deeply moved by the suffering he saw and who opened his heart to reach out to someone who desperately needed help.

Perhaps this story will inspire our "ordinary communities" to reach out to children, to encourage them, to help them grow to be strong and healthy, to let them know that they are our heroes and that they can make the world a better place.

CONTEMPORARY ROMAN CATHOLICS (CRC):
RUNNING WITH GOD

As told by Monsignor Tom Leonard; and Dave Cervini and Liam O'Brien, CRC Members, Holy Trinity Church

> *The church needs to be there to help [people] along, not to solve their problems—we have our own problems. We must try to give them a good experience of what church can be: a community, . . . a feeling of belonging, a sense of their gifts and their power.*
> *—Monsignor Tom Leonard*

> *If the CRC had never come about, I probably would be spiritually dead or in rehab today. It saved my life. Now, in my own way, I can give something back, and I feel great about that.*
> *—Dave Cervini*

Part of the group's success was having a supportive
pastor who let the group find itself. [Monsignor
Leonard] allowed the group to grow organically
without a tremendous amount of oversight, and
certainly no form of interference.
                                        —Liam O'Brien

These days many of us feel a kind of emptiness, a dark isolation filled with anxiety and uncertainty. The world seems to be filled with too much pain and confusion, and our lives feel fractured, uncertain, fast paced, even purposeless at times. Often we try to drown our fears and our feelings of hopelessness in anything we think will give us comfort: material goods, empty social gatherings, alcohol, drugs, sex, meaningless relationships.

Although we yearn for a supportive community, and for connections to others that will fulfill us, we might be unwilling to move away from the security we know. We may be too afraid to risk taking a step into the world of the unknown. Even prisoners released from years of confinement sometimes gravitate back toward the familiar, their life in jail. We are reminded of the man who was lying beside the pool of Bethesda for thirty-eight years, unable to get off his mat whenever the healing waters were stirred (Jn 5:2). Perhaps, like him, we might feel uncertain if Jesus asked us the poignant question, "Do you want to be healed?"

Today, one of our greatest hungers is the desire to have some kind of spiritual life, to be in a community where we feel integrated, safe, and spiritually nurtured. In the last decade, hundreds of books about spirituality have made the bestseller lists. Unfortunately, many of our religious institutions have not known how to address these needs; they continue to offer the easy, well-known routines of worship services. Many churches are almost empty except for a handful of elderly people sitting in the pews. Others have become what I call "fast-food churches"—quick fixes that leave people hungry for something deeper and more meaningful. Almost before they've heard the final blessing or sung the last hymn, people are racing out the door to return to their lives of isolation and emptiness.

One day I heard about Holy Trinity Church in New York City. I could hardly believe that hundreds, maybe thousands, of young adults in their twenties to forties were flocking to the church to worship, to socialize with each other, and to serve: "running with God." I knew I had to learn what was happening at this unusual community in New York City, a city where young people rarely rush to church. So I interviewed Monsignor Tom Leonard, the pastor, and two members of the Contemporary Roman Catholics from Holy Trinity, Dave Cervini and Liam O'Brien, and learned about this extraordinary healing community.

❖ ❖ ❖ ❖ ❖ ❖ ❖ ❖ ❖

Monsignor Tom Leonard

A parish can be a very healing community, especially if it provides a supportive place for those who have been away from the church and who want to come back to build a relationship with God or to build a relationship with others. At different times in our lives, we may feel uncomfortable with God. We might even leave the church, particularly when we are young. When we go to college or are out from under parental authority, many of us drift away from God. Because of our fear of being punished, we may feel we cannot rebel against our parents or society too much, but we can easily rebel against God.

However, at some point in our lives, we may begin to ask questions such as, "Why was I born? Why am I alive? What am I here to do?" Then we will likely start to realize that we need to find some kind of anchor for ourselves. We might even consider whether or not we want to be a "religious" person.

About eight or nine years ago, two young people in the parish came up with an idea that they thought would appeal to young people. When they presented it to me and asked if they could organize it, I said, "Sure, do it." It's not that I have great expertise in the area of working with young people; it's just that I allowed them to use the facilities and trusted that they had the talent to do it. I truly believe the church should try to empower talented people to do things themselves.

The original plan was quite simple: to make an announcement at the Sunday evening Mass that everyone was invited after the service to go to a neighborhood restaurant or bar where they could get a sandwich and a drink and have a good conversation. Eventually this concept developed into what is now a very active group known as the Contemporary Roman Catholics (CRC).

We're not just spiritual people; we're physical too. We would rather that young people go together to a restaurant or bar with others who have just come out of a worship service than to play the singles bar scene, not knowing who is there and what they are getting into. At least they are with others who have been to church and they are only committing themselves to conversation and shared food. There's a line from A. E. Housman that we often quote: "Malt does more than Milton can/To justify God's ways to man."

Over the years the number of young people attending has increased significantly. We now have nearly fifteen hundred people on our e-mail list. People hear others talk about what's happening, so they come from all over—even outside the city. Here they meet people, they feel comfortable, they are accepted, the preaching is good, the liturgy and the music are excellent, and there are many other young people. Most importantly, they find people on a similar journey who are looking for something—not necessarily a husband or wife—but a real sense of meaning in life.

When we finish Mass at 6:30 p.m., nobody goes straight home—they stand out in the front talking to one another, as in the old days. Forty-five minutes later they might still be out there. I believe that's the way church should be. As clergy, we too are out in front of the church talking to people. We get a lot of work done out there.

At the core of the success of the CRC is the people's involvement and their feeling of being empowered to do things on their own. But the other part is the mystery of faith: their relationship with God and how God pursues them. I believe the rudiments and foundations of faith that these young people received thirty years ago are coming to being now, partly because they feel a sense of emptiness. Also, time is passing rather quickly for the young people. And when they go through an event like 9/11, they suddenly realize that life can be gone, that there has to be more than this. They get a feeling of "I don't have much time to make my mark, and I want to count for something." Suddenly, it's not enough to make a name in business or to be successful on the job. It's then that the deeper questions of life touch them and they want to ensure that they are contributing something, that at the end of their life something good will be said about them.

As priests, our challenge is to be the question mark to someone's conscience and to the conscience of the community. We need to walk with them and understand that we are all on this journey. Sometimes we may be a few steps ahead of them in age, but not necessarily in holiness or intelligence. As clergy, we need to recognize that there are very intelligent and sensitive people out there. We must try to help them weave together those pieces of their life that they have not been able to pull together. We are here to welcome them into the church for baptisms and invite them into eternity at death. And in between we have to figure out how we can touch their lives so they can have their own distinct relationship with God.

The people in this parish are great people; they know what is going on in the world. The church needs to be there to help them along, not to solve their problems—we have our own problems. We must try to give them a good experience of what church can be: a community, good music, good preaching, good liturgy, a feeling of belonging, a sense of their gifts and their power. Then when they move to another place, they know that church doesn't have to be "boring." They can liven it up, they can do something about it themselves.

Dave Cervini

About seven years ago, I moved to New York City and started working for a radio station. I hadn't been to church for about ten years and didn't feel any connection to it, but I knew I had a sense of spirituality.

In the city, my friends from high school were married and my friends from college had moved away. I didn't want to hang out with the people from my radio station; they tended to be into sex, drugs, and rock-and-roll. I had already been through that. So I was feeling rather empty. One day when I was sitting in my apartment feeling sorry for myself, I went through half a bottle of vodka. I knew I had to get involved in something more meaningful.

So I took out the phone book and looked up all the Catholic churches within walking distance of my apartment. At the first church I visited, I didn't feel anything. But twenty minutes after I walked in the door of Holy Trinity, I knew it was where I wanted to be. Although the church was getting a new organ at the time and it was totally disheveled with boxes and pipes everywhere, I felt welcomed and embraced.

One Sunday I saw an announcement in the bulletin for a Wall Street Catholic Singles Dance. I said to myself, "You really need to get out and meet people, and this is what you have to do." But in my mind I was picturing that the group was a bunch of really nerdy people. I didn't know what to expect. There was also an announcement that the 5:30 Sunday Mass was for young, like-minded people who would go after the Mass to the Raccoon Lodge, a biker bar around the corner from the church. I thought, "Wow, a biker bar; this has to be pretty cool." So I wound up, still a bit guarded, going to the Raccoon Lodge about a half an hour before the group arrived. I was too cool to be a part of the crowd. About fifteen people walked into the bar. After my second Martini, I plucked up enough courage to introduce myself. I learned that two guys had come up with the idea of getting together after Mass because there were lots of people in their twenties and thirties who attended it.

Not long after that, we started exchanging ideas about going to movies, to plays, on trips, and things like that. We never meant for it to be "a group." It just started out with a few people from the church gathering together outside after Mass. Soon the group went from fifteen, to twenty-five, to thirty-five, to forty people. About five of us from the original group formed an informal committee. In about two months we had developed a deep friendship. Soon we started doing fundraising events for the church. One night, while sitting together at Joe's Fishshack, I said, "It is really cool to hang out with your church group. We should call ourselves the Cool Roman Catholics—the CRC."

When we had a Christmas party and fifty people showed up, we realized there was a sense of community that was building. We sent out mailings about different events. After six months, over a hundred people were coming to different activities. Soon there were camping trips, volunteer opportunities, and fundraisers for the homeless shelter in the church. Then some spiritual things and community service projects began to develop. We had become a real community. But the 5:30 Mass on Sunday remained the main focus of the group.

Today we have more than a thousand people on our e-mail list. There are about seven hundred people that actively participate in our events. In the archdiocese there are fifty-two young adult groups that cater to people in their twenties, thirties, and forties. When the archdiocese saw what was happening here at Holy Trinity, they invited me onto the pastoral council for young adults, to help them develop similar things around the city.

Because our people are very involved, we have grown into a dynamic, active group. We don't schedule an event or a fundraiser and assign somebody to do it. Every activity is run by someone who has a passion for it. For example, one guy who is very spiritual loves to organize retreats and spiritual discussions. A chef puts together cooking classes. Another person does wine-tasting events. On any given month, we may have twenty events scheduled.

Certainly, this isn't a typical church group. When we first started, we made up flyers with a picture of cakes with a line drawn through them, meaning "no bake sales, no bingo." We were just a bunch of people who were working crazy hours and who lived in the big city. Many of us had been away from the church for a while; others were attending church but were searching for some kind of spirituality, some deeper meaning. After a while we figured that the name Cool Roman Catholics was a bit too much, so we changed our name to Contemporary Roman Catholics. But I still think we are "cool," no matter what. When I first joined the group, I confess I thought it might be a way to meet somebody, the love of my life. That hasn't happened, but I have the best friends ever and it's absolutely wonderful for me.

On September 11, things really changed for all of us in the CRC. That morning, I was at work at the radio station. Our offices are high enough that we could see the World Trade Center. Somebody told me that a plane had hit one of the Towers. When the second plane hit, we knew the world had changed for us forever.

Midtown Manhattan was almost completely evacuated. But a radio station is a crucial source of information. So I spent the day talking back and forth on the phone with the Red Cross and getting information on the air. About 5:30 I felt really drained; I didn't know exactly how I could help. You couldn't donate blood, because the lines were so long and there were volunteers all over the place. Because I needed to do something, I walked to the Red Cross Center. There were thousands of people in the streets. It was total chaos. It dawned on me that I could tie in the radio station. Using my ID card, I finally reached the communications director and told her that I worked for a radio station and that I could make announcements. "What can I tell people on the radio to do?" I asked. She said, "We need food for the volunteers."

So I did a report on the radio about the need for food. Then I got on the phone with CRC people, and suddenly the group just came together. We went to local shops, restaurants, and businesses in our neighborhood and got food from them. Then we made sandwiches, wrapped and labeled them, and delivered them to the Red Cross volunteer center. Within three and a half hours, ten people made more than a thousand sandwiches. The communications director was so appreciative. Then she asked us to do breakfast the next morning. We quickly sent out e-mails asking if people wanted to volunteer to do breakfast. You wouldn't believe the number of people who came. Suddenly people with skills in organizing things just did what they had to do. We used the radio station to get resources and to legitimize our efforts. We invited people to come to the church. We used the radio station's vans to pick up donations around the neighborhood. We sent two hundred loaded trucks of supplies to the Red Cross. It was phenomenal.

After a while the Red Cross stopped taking donations at their site because they couldn't handle them. So they sent people with donations to our church, where we categorized, boxed, and delivered them to the right places. After September 13, we had the only trucks that were getting through to their center bringing batteries, goggles, gloves, food, nonperishables, clothing, and other things. When they couldn't take more donations, they put us in contact with other centers around the city that needed supplies. Eventually we started bringing things directly to Ground Zero at the Trade Center.

In a few days, we were operating at full capacity. Many people came to help who heard on the radio what we were doing. We registered people and told them what they could do.

The Murphy Center, a huge room underneath the church, was stacked from floor to ceiling with boxes categorized and ready to send out as needed. We also delivered hot meals to the fire and police stations on the Upper West Side. We kept up the food donations for about a month by enlisting restaurants in the neighborhood to provide food for volunteers. We collected

$225,000 in donations. It was an amazing business process that came together. Several television pieces were done on our work.

During the first days, we learned that three people from our group had been killed on 9/11. Many of our parents, relatives, and friends also died. When somebody came into the room who had been directly touched by the tragedy, the huge bustling center that had been alive with conversation and energy just stopped as we comforted that person. It was very moving. All of this activity took place for about a month. After that, we did a few fundraisers, mostly for the firefighters and their families. We bought savings bonds for families at the firehouse on Seventh-ninth Street. We learned which kids were fatherless or motherless and got them bonds.

During the early days, I didn't think about the destruction of the World Trade Center. I didn't even think about all the people who had died. In a way, I avoided having to think about it by getting busy. My own involvement with this really helped me to deal with the tragedy of that day. It was a blessing that I didn't know anybody personally who was killed, because I would have been so involved in grieving that I may not have been able to help organize things.

About five months after 9/11, things started to settle back to our normal routines. But at every gathering someone always brings it up and talks about what happened that day, what happened here, how our people were affected by it. Without a doubt, 9/11 brought people in our group closer than we had ever been. The membership probably doubled because of the tremendous effort that we made. The sense of community was heightened to an incredible level. And the healing, well, it all goes back to the idea that we are there for each other. It's like having a friend you can count on, and "the friend" is this community.

Somehow this tragic event made me feel better about who I am. I was having some trouble with that before 9/11. From time to time, we all have doubts about our abilities. Sometimes something like this helps us see what we can do well, that this is where we belong. I know that I "belong" doing this kind of work. It made me more energized and wanting to help people. I felt like I was doing the work for God.

Not long ago, I left my job. I want to make a difference; I don't want to go through my life working until 9:30 every night and then go home and not have time for relationships or time to enjoy the gifts that God gave me, the gift of this world, the gift of helping other people. I sat on a mountaintop and spent some time thinking for a while. I was with myself, my thoughts, and God. Now I know that everything that has happened in my life has been divinely given to me. I was so involved in doing things that I didn't have time to listen to what God was telling me.

If the CRC had never come about, I probably would be spiritually dead or in rehab today. It saved my life. Now, in my own way, I can give something back, and I feel great about that.

Liam O'Brien

My mother was born in county Clare and my father was from Tipperary, so I spent a good amount of my childhood visiting my maternal grandparents in Ireland, my second home. Therefore, I became involved with Holy Trinity in a very "Irish way": I didn't go "shopping" for a church; I found the nearest Catholic Church in my neighborhood, Holy Trinity, and that is where I went to Mass on Sundays. It was simply my good fortune that Holy Trinity blossomed into such a lively community.

Holy Trinity always had a vibrant liturgy, but at the end of Mass people went their different ways. There wasn't a sense of a unified community. So many communities, not just church communities, are very fractured and disintegrated these days. We are pulled away from our families, our traditional organizations, even our cultures. We work, we socialize, we go to church, but there doesn't seem to be a continuous connection in our lives. Even though we are very successful, we are also very prodigal. We go into the world on our own, and we abandon the things that nurtured us—perhaps, in retrospect, the greatest things in our lives.

At Holy Trinity Church, we wanted to recenter our lives around our church community, to reintegrate our lives by placing the church and our faith back at the center of our world. The approach we've used is getting people for whom faith is an important element of their lives, to start meeting each other. Not just bumping into each other during the liturgy, but after the liturgy, meeting each other socially as a community. This helps everyone who participates realize that they are not alone in the pursuit of a more fulfilling faith.

Part of the group's success was having a supportive pastor who let the group find itself. He allowed the group to grow organically without a tremendous amount of oversight, and certainly no form of interference. He trusted his parishioners and supported their ideas. When we first started meeting after church in a local bar to eat, drink, throw some darts, and talk, people said, "This is nice, but what else should we be doing? How are we going to build on this?" So we started public service projects, spiritual groups prayer groups, and book-reading groups—anything where there was a strong interest. If someone wanted to volunteer to paint classrooms in public schools, start a Rosary group, visit an old-age home, volunteer with children, do food and clothing drives, organize blood drives, whatever, they could advertise it through the group to see if there was an interest in their idea.

We've done some very special things. We have participated in programs for the old-age homes that are nearby. The homes asked for volunteers to pray with the elderly. We were invited to come to some of their dances—especially anyone who knew how to do the dances that older people remembered, like swing and ballroom dancing. We threw a Christmas party for an AIDS hospice for young children and infants, and CRC members help staff the parish homeless shelter.

There have never been any events that appeared to be unchristian. The people are very committed to the group and so happy to have found it that they are careful only to do things that nurture it. What's remarkable about this group is how it attracts a lot of people who never thought of themselves as church people. When I invite people to the group, I tell them we are a collection of people who have recognized that all of our many pursuits have left us still feeling disconnected, still dissatisfied, still alone in the world—even though we may have good families and friends. The group reorients anyone who participates to start focusing on other people rather than on themselves. When we stop being self-motivated and self-centered and start focusing on genuine relationships with other people and God, it has a remarkable effect. It ends up nurturing us.

Perhaps the story of the Tower of Babel in the Old Testament is relevant for our group. When people couldn't communicate with each other at Babel, they just dispersed and the community disintegrated. I think the CRC is trying to reverse that, trying to undo the damage of Babel by collecting people together in a community and getting them to speak the same language and communicate together spiritually and socially.

❖ ❖ ❖ ❖ ❖ ❖ ❖ ❖

Heartful practice is about keeping the heart open to the world around us—to people, places, ourselves, and the divine. . . . It's about seeing the connections, the interlocking webs of energy among people.
—*Belleruth Naparstek*

The success of the Contemporary Roman Catholics of Holy Trinity Church is very exciting and impressive, especially during these times. This exceptional story has some powerful lessons for almost any community.

At the heart of the accomplishments of the CRC are what I call the "basic rules" for a thriving grass-roots community: everyone is welcome, every persons' gifts are appreciated and utilized, members are invited to design and create policies and activities for the group, the hierarchy or "leaders" do not superimpose the structures or guidelines, members are empowered to do what they have a passion for, and participants are trusted to do their best for the community.

What I especially appreciate about this story is how the CRC community recognized that people who come to church are more than just spiritual entities. Indeed, we are physical, emotional, social, and spiritual beings, and we need to address all of those parts to be whole. Somewhere in the core of all of our souls, we likely have a desire to worship, to socialize with one another, and to serve those who are in need. Therefore, we might want to add another "basic rule" for communities—that of nurturing all parts of ourselves so that we can become the people we were created to be.

THE CAREGIVERS:
CARING FOR OUR SOULS

As told by the Reverend Cari Jackson

*In our work as "ministers," we work with other
people's spirits, other people's hearts and minds. I
don't believe any one of us has the right to engage in
such sacred work if we don't also do self-care.*
—the Reverend Cari Jackson

Within every human being, we have a "natural instinct" to care for people in whatever way we can. We reach out to our friends if they are in trouble, or we try to cheer people who are feeling depressed. We take pleasure in doing something useful for someone in need. We try to be good caregivers.

For several years I worked as a volunteer in the pastor's office at the Union Theological Seminary doing spiritual direction and leading workshops. Early in September 2001, the Reverend Cari Jackson, the seminary's interim pastor, asked me to lead a workshop on "Keeping Compassion in Caregiving Ministries." I had just written up the flyer that was to be distributed later that month:

> Caregiving and leadership can be oppressively demanding,
> exhausting, even potentially wounding. Often we "put out"
> more than we get back, and we may feel guilty if we are
> upset about it. In times of stress and loss, we can suffer deep
> fatigue, depression, and burnout. We need to take seriously
> caring for ourselves if we work in caregiving ministries.
> While "feeding the sheep," we need to be "fed" too.

But then September 11 changed everything. Eventually I led that workshop, which was postponed until late October. I added a subtitle: "And Avoiding Burnout in Difficult Times."

I doubt that there is anyone who has dedicated more energy and thoughtfulness to the ministry of caregiving than Cari Jackson. She understands that the "community of caregivers" requires nurturing and support in order for them to care for their flocks' physical, emotional, and spiritual needs—in order for them to be a healing community.

❖ ❖ ❖ ❖ ❖ ❖ ❖ ❖ ❖

At the Union Theological Seminary, there has always been a long-standing history of advocacy, compassion, and care for the community. As an academic institution, it is easy for people to become absorbed in their scholarly work, but the seminary has also been very committed to serving God and God's creation. So when 9/11 loomed so large in people's lives, it was understood that students could not just study. Indeed, what did study matter if we were not also serving at a time when the need was so great?

The school year had begun the previous week and everybody was trying to get settled in. But immediately after 9/11, students started asking, "Why am I here? Why has God brought me to this place at this time? What is it that God wants me to do?" People were walking around in a daze. Many were glued to the TV and were being traumatized again and again. The cycle had to be broken; being locked in to the television had to end. They needed to do what God was calling them to do—to serve.

It's my strong belief that when we are physically and emotionally exhausted, we can reach into the Spirit to re-energize. This brings clarity, strength, focus, and renewal to our lives. When we feel frozen, we can meet God in our service, and

God will give us what we need to serve the people, whatever situation we might encounter.

So a group of twenty to thirty students, faculty, and staff began going as close to the World Trade Center site as we could. We didn't know what we were going to do or where we were going. We tried to listen to the Spirit about what was needed and to meet people where they were. We just walked through the streets singing and praying, inviting people to join us in the circle of prayer. In that time of crisis, it was easy to walk up to strangers and ask, "Are you waiting to hear about a loved one?" Or we asked, "May I pray with you? I'm with a group of people from Union Theological Seminary, and we're here to remind people that even now God's comfort is here." Some people desperately needed to talk, and some needed to be held.

We prayed with workers who were searching for bodies. We prayed with people who were waiting for news of their loved ones. We prayed with others who didn't want to go home, who needed to be there. Sometimes people held our hands very tightly. Perhaps it felt like an anchor for them. Often we had huge circles of strangers and people from Union, all interspersed. Just doing that was a powerful and healing experience. If people weren't able to go home, we tried to find housing for them. We made a list of people at Union willing to open their homes. Whatever people needed—food, shelter, money, prayer, a hug—is what we tried to give them.

Several people told us that they didn't know if they really believed in God, but they thought it was nice to have God there through us. Person after person expressed their gratitude that we had taken the time to be there. We hadn't expected that. We weren't doing anything. It was just a ministry of presence. Many people said our presence gave them a sense of hope. I believe that was what people got: hope for the recovery of loved ones they hadn't heard from, hope that they could continue to do what was needed in removing a body, hope that another attack would not happen, hope that they would be able to return to their homes soon, hope that this nation and this world would learn something we needed to know to prevent these kinds of tragedies from happening again.

I believe God meets each of us where we are, and that we are called to meet people where they are. We should never go to people with our own little packages: "We want to pray with you, and we have housing"—especially when people are not ready to pray or are not in need of housing. If people want to curse, that's what they need to do. We can't "fix things" either, because if we try to make things look neat and tidy, we'll miss out on a rich encounter with God. God comes in the rough places of our hearts, our emotions, our minds, and our lives, and that is when healing and transformation can happen.

Each time, before and after we went to the site, we did something that was vital to doing effective ministry near Ground Zero. We took time for the ministers to talk about how they felt. We discussed feelings, and we prayed. In the days and weeks after we stopped going to the site, we checked in with each other to see how everyone was doing and to support one another. Perhaps what was most healing for the students was that they had a real sense of why they were in seminary. Some of the professors, no matter what the content of their courses, took time in their classes to try to bring understanding about how 9/11 related to their courses and their experiences so the students could see the linkage between study and service. It was a critical aspect of the formation of their ministry. The students who were emotionally and spiritually ready to do the work around 9/11 are going to be much more powerful and effective as ministers than they would have been had they not had that experience.

In the days immediately following September 11, I started getting telephone calls from clergy who were exhausted and depleted. For the most part, they sounded like they were in control. Likely they felt they needed to be that way in order to be effective in working with strangers and people in their congregations. But many of them were in shock and filled with rage. I could hear that in our conversations when occasionally something slipped out indicating their level of fear, anxiety, and confusion. Many people were wrestling with the question "Where is God in all of this?" Meanwhile they were trying to provide stability, safety, and security for others because they didn't want to cause more trauma.

It was obvious that clergy needed a safe space where they could rest and restore, but most of them couldn't take a whole weekend off. So a half-day retreat was planned with a discussion of practical self-care strategies, one-on-one counseling, and massage therapy to help caregivers take care of themselves. In that healing setting, people's pain, anger, and confusion came out—along with their fatigue. They admitted they were asking the same questions as the people they were serving. Person after person said they had not felt it was acceptable for them to be exhausted, depressed, or to have such a depth of sadness. But they needed to express all of that.

I used to ask people, "Are you taking care of yourself?" They usually said yes, and I'd wonder, "Are they lying, or are they not even aware of their need?" So I changed my question to "What are you doing to take care of yourself today?" That way they had to think about it. Sometimes people answered, "I think I'm burning out." Then we could strategize what might be helpful to them.

In New York City, schools handled the issues of 9/11 very differently. Some said, "We are not trained in trauma, and we are not going to talk to students about this." Students in those schools didn't have a place to deal with their fear and confusion. Other schools provided a space for students to talk about 9/11. Some educators said that when they called the school board, they would get a different answer about whether or not it was okay to engage in dialogue with students about the disaster.

In one school district where teachers and counselors were not supposed to touch the subject or talk with students, a teacher reported that the tension among both students and teachers was high because of the undiscussed and unmanaged stress and anxiety. She really wrestled with this problem before deciding to work one-on-one with students to see how they were doing. Even though the school didn't hold an assembly or conversations in classes, she tried to reach as many students as possible. Yet there were no real supports available to teachers.

This example cites another reason we need to work with caregivers—including educators—because if they are confused and conflicted, you can imagine what happens in their work with students. At a caregivers renewal retreat for educators, we tried to help people get centered and have more clarity. We did some bodywork, including exercise, yoga, and massage, to help them open up their concerns and blockages.

I have always felt that an important and major part of my ministry is ministering to "ministers." As I was growing up, I experienced religious and spiritual abuse by three pastors. So when I was nineteen and God called me to ordained ministry, I said no for sixteen years. I had seen how ministers got off the mark of their ministry and ended up abusing people. I didn't want to injure people or their spirit. When I finally said yes, I told God that I would only enter a ministry if I could do it without engaging in any kind of abuses to people. In order to do that, I knew I would have to do a lot of intentional, reflective self-care. That was the root of my passion for caregiving.

Early on I thought self-care was only a spiritual process and that if ministers had problems it was because they weren't praying enough or not having enough quiet time with God. I now understand that many ministers have emotional pains from their childhood that they have never dealt with that show up in their ministry. They may have never reflected on an issue, or they might dismiss it as just something that happened long ago. Many people have wounds that never get healed or have needs they try to satisfy in the context of their ministry.

Looking at my own life, I see places that are still in the process of being healed and other places that haven't even begun to heal. I have to be very intentional about how those issues impact my life and learn how to deal with them in healthy ways. Otherwise, they will show up in my ministry.

Pastors and counselors are especially in need of support groups and collegial space where they can talk in a safe place. Because they are always listening to everyone else, they need places where they can talk without being interrupted, where things can be said in total confidentiality, and where they can choose to receive advice or prayer.

In the winter after 9/11, we held a Bible study at the seminary specifically for ministers on the spiritual power of lament—that too was another way of caregiving for the caregiver. Within Christianity we often want to rush to victory, to resurrection, to power, to healing. We don't stay long enough in the grieving, the sorrow, the pain, and the lament. In Lamentations, we read words like "Where are you? How long, O God? Have you forgotten me?" The ministers said, "This is my story, these are my questions. It's okay for me to say this to God." They had been afraid that if they asked such questions, God would zap them. The Bible study freed them to wrestle with their questions and doubts, knowing God still loves them.

During the eight weeks we met, the study became a support group and a healing circle as well. Group members began sharing very personally some of their own lamentations that were at the core of their hearts. We also did some bodywork, because places of lament were stuck in our bodies. It ended up being a holistic approach to lamentation, a wonderful dance between head and heart. It was transforming. I believe that is part of what a caregiving space can provide.

Caregivers renewal has many different elements: pastoral counseling, retreats, support groups, Bible study, information seminars on dealing with trauma and grief. By offering a smorgasbord of services, we are providing healing support to many people, because they can find something that will meet their particular needs wherever they are.

The purpose of caregivers renewal is to ensure that professionals such as clergy, counselors, physicians, nurses, social workers, and educators are consistently able to provide high-quality care to those whom they seek to serve. All of these professions come into contact with large numbers of people, so the expanse of the injury they could do is great. Having experienced abuse, I know that unhealthy people can have an enormous impact. In their woundedness they relate to parishioners, clients, patients, students, family members, co-workers, and neighbors.

When I consider what just one unhealthy person can do, I think of the powerful metaphor of a stalled car on a roadway. One stalled car can jam up traffic for miles. We have to be concerned about the stalled car—or one car with faulty brakes—and its impact on all those other cars.

Self-care for caregivers is not something we do as ancillary to ministry. When it is treated as ancillary or secondary, it is easily squeezed out of our time. I believe it is integral to ministry and that ministers must engage in self-care in order to minister effectively—whatever their ministry. Working as a pastor, physician, counselor, teacher, or social worker are all forms of ministry.

In our work as "ministers" we work with other people's spirits, other people's hearts and minds. I don't believe any one of us has the right to engage in such sacred work if we don't also do self-care. We all must engage in healthy self-care for the good of others and ourselves.

❖ ❖ ❖ ❖ ❖ ❖ ❖ ❖

Our seminary taught, and taught well, how to counsel others, how to listen to others . . . but no one taught us how to listen to ourselves, to our own inner needs and wounds.
                                                        —*Flora Slosson Wuellner*

This chapter is filled with many useful messages about caregiving that are spelled out loudly and clearly for all caregivers—pastors, physicians, therapists, counselors, teachers, social workers, family members, friends, every one of us. Certainly, during times of crisis, we need to go beyond the theoretical, the academic, and textbook learning, as Union Theological Seminary did after the events of 9/11. To be effective in our work as caregivers, we have to be grounded in reality and in the practical. Cari encourages us to have the wisdom to accept and serve communities right where they are—not where we think they should be or want them to be.

Many of us are members of communities that help others. Therefore, it would be beneficial to pay close attention to the advice this chapter spells out. We need to allow ourselves to recognize and deal with our real feelings, especially the ones we try to hide from the people with whom we work: anger, depression, sorrow, grief, pain. It is absolutely essential to take care of ourselves, to take respites and retreats. And we need safe places where we can go to lick our own wounds and gear ourselves up to return to the frontline to serve those in need. If we "listen" carefully, the words "healer, heal thyself " are right behind what is being said.

Without safety measures, burnout could be just a breath away. There is much work to do, and we don't want to crash and burn and thereby stall everyone else on the highway of life. Perhaps it's time to consider finding a safe space, to take some time out and have a serious tune-up in order to restore our souls.

THE REPUBLIC OF IRELAND

INTRODUCTION

*Many of the sacred facades have been pulled down in
the domains of religion, politics and finance. The
unmasking has revealed corruption in all of these
domains. . . . The positive side of this is that it relieves
us of overdependence on false crutches; it invites us to
depend more on our own courage.*
—John O'Donohue

In the last two decades, Ireland has undergone some
astonishing changes and transformations. Mainly driven by
investments in global technology, a huge economic boom has
taken place that has had an enormous impact on the economy, on
Irish institutions, and on peoples' lifestyles.

Positive results of this boom can be seen throughout the
country: fewer people live below the poverty line,
unemployment rates have lowered, and levels of emigration
have been reduced. In recent years, extreme poverty has no
longer been the powerful force driving Irish people to look
legally or illegally for jobs in other countries. The present
generation is the best educated, most employed, and most well
fed ever in the history of Ireland.

Yet many people have voiced their concerns that the Celtic
Tiger of rapid economic growth and spiraling costs has had a
negative impact on the country, that it could contribute to rising
numbers of emigrants who are unable to afford to remain in the
country. Certainly, whenever major changes come to any country
or community, people often experience some apprehension about
the possible loss of their identities or of familiar roles.

In Ireland today, a number of problems have accompanied the
rapid growth and abrupt changes that have occurred within the
society. Consumerism has become a substitute for many of the
more traditional family and cultural pastimes. People are
overwhelmed with the fast pace of life, intense stress, and the
aggressive behavior of people on the street and on the job. They
no longer feel they have much control over their lives or their
families' lives. Crime and violence are on the rise, making

concern and anxiety almost constant companions for those who are defenseless.

Without a doubt, the Ireland of several decades ago has disappeared. On the positive side, the quality of education and health care has improved. Women today are able to get an excellent education and better jobs. They can go to work after marriage and can choose when to have their children. But on the negative side, the high cost of living has forced both parents to find work; this, combined with the expenses of child-care, means that many children come home to empty houses. Parents are absorbed in long, stressful working hours and can find little time to spend with their children. In the past, the family played a pivotal role in ensuring the health and stability of Irish society. But now the backbone of the family has been weakened. Many of today's youth are turning to alcohol, drugs, and meaningless activities. Without the embrace of the protective family or community, the elderly and the young are more vulnerable and less protected. Fewer people have a meaningful community to belong to where they can find solace and support.

In his book, *Working Towards Balance: Our Society in the New Millennium*, Father Harry Bohan wrote:

> Technology has transformed the nature of Irish society and its effect is multiplied by the fact that the economy—and therefore the society—is driven by investment from global technology companies. . . . We are now very much part of the global society. However, when a society decides to fly on one wing, the fallout can be serious, particularly in the area of relationships.

Perhaps one of the most tragic effects is that people think they have lost a spiritual dimension in their lives. Many feel a sense of isolation, loneliness, competition, and detachment. The breakdown of community life, of family roles, and of institutions such as the church has had a damaging effect on Irish society.

But in these encouraging chapters we have the opportunity to hear what some communities in Ireland are doing in response to the problems that are occurring now, as well as to those from the past. They are creatively and courageously dealing with the issues and difficulties of isolation, discrimination, urbanization, addictions, and abuse. They are working with compassion and diligence to find a sense of balance, to provide a better quality of life for families, neighborhoods, institutions, groups of people, and the community in general.

Let us "listen" to them and learn from them as they tell us their stories. Perhaps we will come to understand how we too can be more courageous in approaching the problems, the issues, the pain, and the suffering that is found in all of our communities.

The Church:

Facing the Truth

As told by Bishop Willie Walsh

A bishop has to be available to any victim who wants to talk with him. It must be a priority of ours. . . . And we have to be honest, open, and accountable. We cannot be defensive.
—Bishop Willie Walsh

In recent times, it seemed like barely a week went by without our hearing another heartrending and incriminating accusation of child sexual abuse by the clergy of the Catholic Church, both in Ireland and in the United States. The media has been filled with tragic stories of abuse victims, and with numerous complaints directed at the leadership of the church for its failure to deal adequately with the allegations.

Unfortunately, this has taken an enormous toll on the victims and their families, as well as on innocent priests. All have experienced a sense of isolation, pain, sorrow, and anger. Unquestionably, it has had a very negative and harmful impact on the church's credibility, undermining many of its commendable contributions to society. Victims and their families, clergy, and the entire church community are in great need of healing because of this terrible betrayal.

As I walked through the simple but lovely Cathedral of Ennis in county Clare, I was surprised to see a poster in the nave of the church with these words:

> With God all things are possible. The church has always had its limitations and sinfulness, but child sexual abuse by priests and religious is one of the saddest manifestations of this reality. Such exploitation of the vulnerability of children is a betrayal of trust of the gravest kind. . . . Many lay people in the church have been shocked and appalled at what they see as a cover-up and lack of candor on the part of our church leaders. It is a fact that many victims did not experience the church as compassionate, understanding, and ready to listen to allegations of misconduct with an open, nondefensive posture.
>
> Our bishop and others have stated and restated that the healing and well-being of victims remain the priority. We, as the parish community, need to understand this profound concern for victims, this profound sadness for the tragedy they have experienced. . . . The beginning of healing is facing the truth. Victims must be encouraged to come forward and speak the unspeakable. The diocese has set up procedures to ensure that appropriate opportunities are afforded every person who has a complaint to make. In addition to the healing of victims we all share a responsibility for the protection of children. We need to exercise vigilance and support measures to ensure that we rout the evil of abuse from our families, our church, and our society. The collusion of silence that has for so long committed the innocent to misery must be broken. . . .
>
> Our church needs a new kind of listening. . . . We need a listening where the church itself can be informed and even on occasion transformed. Can the church be healed? With God all things are possible.

After reading this very candid and courageous message, I felt a sense of hope when I learned that the bishop referred to as "our bishop" in the statement was Bishop Willie Walsh, the humble and gentle man I was about to interview.

❖ ❖ ❖ ❖ ❖ ❖ ❖ ❖

My own background is typical of many Irish priests; I was born in the 1940s and brought up in a country farming community in north Tipperary. I was the youngest of six children, four boys and two girls. Both of my parents were quite religious. My mother was a traditional Irish mother. My father, I believe, was a man of great integrity with a very strong faith, but not in any ostentatious way.

So I was reared in a house where there was a lot of value set on religion and on priesthood. Although there was no pressure from my parents, I knew they would be pleased if I became a priest. Eventually I came around to the idea of being a priest and was ordained in 1959. It was a time of great hope in the church. Fortunately, I had the opportunity to study in Rome for seven years, which proved to be very important in my own formation. The Italians have a wonderful approach to life and a great humanity about them. I think of them as a warm and strong family of people. Whenever I visit Italy, I feel very much at home. In Ireland at the time, the church was rather severe and fairly strict. There was more of the fear of God rather than the love of God in our images. The Italians had a more trusting belief in a forgiving and loving God.

After my studies, I spent twenty-five years teaching in post-primary schools. I found teaching very enjoyable and rewarding. The contact with young people really challenged me— particularly in the sixties and early seventies, the years of what we call "the angry young men." Those angry young men were a most stimulating group of people; they were out to change the world and to change it very quickly. As a young priest, I too was in a hurry to change the world, so I identified with the things they said and the challenges they presented.

But the students who opted out or showed signs of disillusionment also made a deep impression on me. I tried to help those young people. Any time I made an effort to get to know a student disillusioned with life, I found that he always had a serious problem in his background. That taught me never to judge, never to condemn. We have no idea about the difficulties people experience in their lives. To this day, whenever I sit down with struggling people, I find there is a depth of goodness that may not appear on the surface. Indeed, often the opposite appears. If I were to list the most important influences in my life, I would put at the top of the list my involvement, in the late sixties, with the Catholic Marriage Advisory Council, which is now known as Accord.

Over the years I attended a number of training courses with all kinds of people, mostly, of course, married people. We worked together, very much as equals, in marriage preparation courses and marriage counseling. These people had a significant effect on my life. They offered me support, friendship, and intimacy, which perhaps many priests don't have. Having close intimate relationships was a special privilege. In working with marriage counseling, I had the opportunity to be in contact with many broken people. All of these things helped shape my approach to life.

In 1994, I was invited to become bishop of the Killaloe Diocese. Although priests had talked over the years about my being a possible candidate, nonetheless it was a bit of a shock to my system. I was appointed coadjutor bishop to succeed Bishop Michael Harty. I expected to have a rather comfortable entry into the job, but within six weeks of my appointment, the bishop, who was in full health, died unexpectedly. Suddenly I found myself thrown fully into the job before I was actually ordained a bishop. I was fortunate that I was still in the familiar surroundings of Ennis. In each of the three major changes in my life I have moved only half of a mile.

When I first became bishop, I was rather nervous about taking on the job. I thought it would be a lonely life and I might be very isolated. I haven't found that at all. I still have the same friends and do the same things for recreation that I did as a priest. Apart from the inevitable occasional loneliness of the life of a celibate priest, I don't feel cut off from people or isolated. I have a strong sense of support, of community, and of friendship with both priests and laypeople. This really keeps me going. Overall, working as bishop has been a happy and fulfilling experience.

There has, however, been one aspect of the work that I would describe as a nightmare—the whole issue of child sexual abuse. That has been a great source of sorrow to me. Over the years I have met people who were abused by priests. Each time I am struck by the enormous pain caused and the destructive nature of the abuse. I have spoken also to priests who have abused; they too carry immense pain and shame in their own lives. It's not only the abuser and the victim who suffer, it's the victim's family and the abuser's family too. The pain surrounding this whole issue is enormous. It has done a great deal of damage to the church in Ireland.

I believe the victims must always come first, but this problem has also seriously damaged the morale of priests who have not been abusive and has to some degree undermined our confidence as bishops. The picture that is often painted is one of uncaring bishops who are only concerned about the good name of the church. That's not a fair or complete picture. We have been deeply saddened by the pain this has caused the victims, and we want to do anything in our power to try to bring about reconciliation. I realize that when we talk about the possibility of reconciliation and forgiveness, that too can be hurtful to victims who are perhaps not ready for that.

In 1999, in preparation for the end of the millennium, I thought it was an appropriate occasion to try to express our sadness about what had happened and to hold out a healing hand to victims— not just to victims of sexual abuse, but to anybody who had been hurt by priests or laity or anyone connected to the church. To do that, we decided to do a walk through most parishes in the three counties across the diocese. We called it "A Pilgrimage of Reconciliation."

First we wrote to every household in the diocese explaining that we wanted to acknowledge that serious hurt had been done over the years, that people had suffered because of sexual and emotional abuse as well as other forms of abuse. We wanted to acknowledge all of this and to ask for forgiveness. That was the purpose of the pilgrimage of reconciliation. This is what we wrote:

> Dear Friend,
>
> I write to you about a pilgrimage which we are planning to make in the coming weeks across the Diocese of Killaloe from Loop Head in West Clare to Kinnity in South Offaly. I am hoping through this pilgrimage to promote Reconciliation, Healing, and Forgiveness as we prepare to enter the new millennium. These themes are central to our celebration of Jubilee 2000 and indeed are at the core of the mission and message of Christ. In the Bible a jubilee year was a special time for forgiving debts, and being reconciled with each other and with God.

Over recent years we have become painfully aware that wrongs have been done and hurts caused by some members of our church. As we approach the end of the millennium I want to acknowledge the wrongs done and the hurts caused and to ask pardon for them. I do so on my own behalf as bishop and I believe in doing so I am also speaking for priests, religious, and laity in our church.

In acknowledging the hurts caused I ask pardon from you if any injustice has been done to you, or if you have been treated with disrespect. I have especially in mind anyone who has been abused physically, emotionally, sexually, or spiritually by anyone who claims to belong to our church. I have in mind people who, for whatever reason, have felt excluded or unwelcome. I recognize that your hurt may be such that you find it impossible to forgive at this time.

If this acknowledgment and asking for forgiveness has some meaning for you I now in turn issue a gentle invitation. Wherever human beings interact with each other there will be hurts caused. Which one of us can say, "I have done no wrong; I have caused no hurt to anyone"? Can I invite each one of us to pause a while and consider if there is a need to acknowledge some hurt caused and to ask for pardon—hurt caused to husband or wife, parent or child, colleague or friend. To ask pardon for hurt caused and in turn to try to forgive . . . asking for forgiveness, offering forgiveness, being reconciled to each other . . . is there a better way to end the old and to begin the new?

We are all pilgrims on our journey of life. This particular pilgrimage will give concrete expression to our desire to make amends and to be reconciled with each other and with God. Maybe in meeting one another, or in walking a few miles of the road together, we can grow toward understanding, and eventually, forgiveness and reconciliation. If you wish to go a little further I invite you to join us at any of the various gatherings which are going to take place in churches across the diocese between now and Christmas. There will be opportunities to join in prayer for reconciliation and to be reconciled to God through the Sacrament of Penance. If it has been a "long time" you will be all the more welcome.

Thank you for reading this message. May the God of Gentleness be with you as we cross that mysterious boundary from the old into the new millennium and begin our celebration of the Great Jubilee 2000.

With kind good wishes,
Willie Walsh[2]

From November 26 until December 19, we walked across the diocese in rainy, windy, and cold weather. We began each day with liturgy in the local church on the theme of reconciliation. The service opened with these words:

Jesus told a story about two people who went into the temple to pray. Only one of them returned home at rights with God. That was the one who humbly acknowledged he was a sinner. On this pilgrimage of reconciliation each one of us is invited to acknowledge our own story and undertake our own pilgrimage: a journey of authentic conversion.

Afterward we set out walking. In the middle of the day we usually stopped in a church hall for tea and sandwiches and relaxed for an hour or so. Then we began our walk again, usually arriving at another parish church around sundown. We ended each day in a church with a liturgy of reconciliation. Large numbers of people turned out for that service. One of the verses of our pilgrimage prayer was "May all of us who bear the name Christian be true disciples of the Lord Jesus. May we be signs of healing, bringers of forgiveness, and sources of reconciliation."

I never walked with fewer than forty or fifty people. Usually on weekends we would have a group of a few hundred because the youth and children joined us too. The last day we had something like a thousand people who walked with us on the final part of the journey to my own hometown of Roscrea, where there were another one and a half thousand people waiting for us.

It was quite an extraordinary experience to simply walk the roads with parishioners and priests from all the parishes throughout the diocese. I was often asked, "Why are you doing this at this time of the year? Why don't you do it in the middle of the summer?" I think there was something special, perhaps even healing, about walking through the wind and rain. As we walked, I heard some astonishing stories. People came to me with significant hurts that had been carried through their family for more than seventy years. These had been passed on from generation to generation. There were serious injustices done by the church and by priests over the years. When there was an injustice done, we tried to undo the wrong as far as possible. I remember one family who had suffered a significant injustice in the 1920s. They continued to be friendly with priests in the parish, but never told any priest about the problem. It was a constant source of pain and anger for them. I had a number of meetings with the family and listened to their story. We talked together a great deal. Eventually they seemed to feel a sense of forgiveness and healing.

Perhaps of all the experiences I've had as bishop, that pilgrimage was the most moving for me. It seemed to strike a chord with people, because it was a public acknowledgment by the church—not just by the priests but by everybody. There was a wonderful equality about it all—just walking and talking on the road in the rain and wind. I believe the whole pilgrimage did effect some sort of healing.

On a wider scale, I'm involved in a subcommittee on abuse for the Irish Bishop's Conference, which is trying to bring about healing and reconciliation. Certainly there's no magical formula for that. A lot of work has to be done on an individual level. A bishop has to be available to any victim who wants to talk with him. It must be a priority of ours that a victim is welcome to do so. And we have to be honest, open, and accountable. We cannot be defensive.

At times it can be quite difficult to say what you want to say. There's an intimidating atmosphere if you speak about reconciliation and forgiveness. You can be misunderstood, as if in some way you are trying to "get away" with things. And people can easily think you are trying to avoid paying compensation. We have to face the reality of rebuilding damaged lives; we have to be prepared to do that. And if that rebuilding requires large finances, so be it.

But we need to understand that there can be no complete healing without at least the beginnings of reconciliation and forgiveness. At the moment, that's also a difficult message to put out there, because it too can be interpreted as not wanting to accept the consequences. But we have to do it—in as gentle a way as possible. And we must make it clear that we will cooperate in every way with civil authorities, that any cover-up or any lack of cooperation with civil authorities is totally out of the question and not in keeping with our Christian obligations.

Another tremendously sad factor is that sexual abuse of minors is fairly widespread across Irish society. A recent scientific report, the Sexual Abuse and Violence in Ireland Report, indicated that this problem is not just found in the priesthood and church. Many people have been abused by people from all sectors of society, but again, we have to be careful in saying this, because it can be interpreted as excusing what priests have done. There is no excuse for priests or religious abusing children. None whatever. I believe that journalists have done a good job of drawing attention to the issue of priests and sexual abuse. Sometimes their criticism has been a bit unfair, but by and large they did us a service by exposing this serious evil. Now I want to invite journalists to paint the fuller picture and to search for what we can do to diminish the suffering and pain of all abuse victims.

As a church we have to ask some tough questions. It's not good enough to simply say, "Sexual abuse is happening across society." We, after all, preach the evil of sexual abuse. Priests and religious are supposed to have a special calling with high ideals. So what has happened? There are questions arising from the issue of sexual abuse which I don't like asking—the answers may be uncomfortable, but they must be asked.

- Has celibacy been a contributing factor in the area of abuse?

- Has our training as priests and religious in some way stunted our growth as sexual beings?

- Does priesthood attract more than its share of people with psychosexual difficulties?

- Have we as bishops in some way been more concerned about power and control than about service—above all service to the message of Christ?

- Have we as church been too concerned with laws and ortho-doxy and too little concerned with human development and human relationships? Have we neglected the supreme law—the law of love?

- Has the virtual absence of any female input into either Sacramental Ministry or decision-making areas of the church been a serious distorting influence?

We need to seriously examine how we have trained and cared for those who are, as it were, the foot soldiers or perhaps foot servants of the local church. The priests in the frontline have suffered greatly in recent times. Many feel that they are paying the price for the abuses of privilege by others in the past.

In many ways the abusers and their families are also victims and are in need of healing. Many of the abusers have been abused themselves as children. I find it heartbreaking to face a colleague and to have to ask him to leave his ministry. We're just beginning to help priests who have been guilty of abusing. There are now several groups around the country who work with them. We must do more.

Certainly, the prime factor in healing of abuse cases should be a pastoral response rather than a legal one. When abuse or marriage issues get into complicated legal battles, it changes the situation. That's not to say that victims aren't entitled to go a legal route. But once they go that route, the "healing process" becomes more complex.

It's very important to acknowledge the reality of our own lives; I'm grateful that in today's church we can recognize and admit that we are a sinful, frail people. All of us are pilgrim people together on a journey, and we are far, far from perfect. Each one of us shares in the sinfulness and the goodness of humanity. This is an important theological theme for our church in this century. We need to recognize the sins of the church over the centuries and the hurts it has caused. Certainly, that touches on an area of church life like ecumenism.

In north Tipperary, where I grew up in a farming community, many of our neighbors were Church of Ireland people. We had a helping and cooperative relationship among us when it came to farming, but there was a boundary when it came to practicing religion. When I was about nine, there was a serious crisis in my home. A Protestant neighbor had died, and my mother didn't want my father to go to the funeral because it was against the church rules at the time. My father insisted on going because the neighbor was a decent man whom he respected. A number of years later I learned that my father had been involved with other Catholic neighbors in a land dispute, and they had boycotted that Protestant man. But he had forgiven them and had held out the hand of friendship. I believe that was the reason my dad insisted on going to his funeral even though he knew that doing so was considered a sin in the eyes of the church. Reflecting on that in later years, I felt the Catholic Church's attitude toward non-Catholic churches was to some degree unchristian. Especially the idea that you couldn't even go to another person's funeral and join with the congregation in prayer.

Another issue that has caused enormous hurt to many people is interchurch marriages. A Protestant boy or girl literally had to leave their own community and family if they wanted to marry a Catholic girl or boy. There was a decree that the marriage had to take place in the Catholic Church, and the Catholic party had to make a solemn promise to bring up any children as Catholics. There was no consideration of the convictions of the Church of Ireland person, nor was the couple allowed to decide what was best for their children. That appears to me to have been quite arrogant on our part. At an ecumenical event I gave a talk and expressed regret for the pain we had caused. As a result, I received a number of letters from people who had been hurt in precisely this way over the years. There also was a bit of controversy about my expression of regret—some people believed I was being disloyal to church teaching.

Thankfully, there has been considerable improvement in the relationships between churches in recent times. Two years ago Bishop Edward Darling of the Church of Ireland and I set up a committee and produced a small booklet on interchurch marriages, trying to address some of the difficulties. In the Foreword we wrote: "We acknowledge, with regret, that much hurt has been caused in the past to couples themselves and to their respective families by lack of cooperation between our churches. It is hoped that the sort of cooperation envisaged in this document will lessen the possibility of hurt in the future. We are happy that the emphasis in the document is on our shared vision of the sacredness of Christian marriage while at the same time recognizing the differences which separate us."

I believe that in the past the Catholic Church has been arrogant in its approach to interchurch marriages. And there continue to be problems. Catholics still have to make a promise to do all they can to bring up their children as Catholics. In our booklet we wrote that the Church of Ireland person could feel an equal obligation to bring up the children in his or her faith. Ultimately, it is the decision for the couple to make. We tried to recognize the sacredness of both faiths. Some people may have felt that I was not totally in keeping with the teaching of the Catholic Church, but I believe any sort of exchange between Christians should be based on a deep respect for the other. Any lack of respect would be unchristian.

I'm also uncomfortable with our position regarding sharing in the Eucharist. When I go to a Church of Ireland ceremony, I am saddened that I can't share in their Eucharist. They see sharing the Eucharist as sharing food or nourishment for the journey towards unity. Catholics regard sharing of the Eucharist as a sign of total unity. We all subscribe to the belief that Christ is present in the Eucharist. Sometimes I wonder if the Lord wants us to fight over the nature of his presence. I don't believe it would be disrespectful to share together in the Eucharist, but because I take my role as bishop and my loyalty to church teachings as a serious obligation, I continue to follow the rules of our church. However, I believe there is room for further development regarding the sharing of the Eucharist.

Today most Catholics believe that the issue of justice is a most important one for any Christian. Whether it's the question of the distribution of wealth, health care, care of the aged, or other justice issues, the church has a strong obligation to stand for and speak out on issues of justice. Recently I've become involved with the issue of accommodation for the Travelers. It's a problem that has been with us for a long time. An enormous gap has developed over the years between the Traveling Community and the settled community.

About half a century ago, the Travelers moved from place to place as tinsmiths. Local people accepted them in that role and helped them by giving them food. The Travelers just parked along the side of the road and then moved on. In the last thirty years the tinsmith business has ended and traditional halting places where the Travelers stopped and parked their vehicles have disappeared with the changing of roads and the increase in traffic. We now have Travelers on the side of the road who are constantly being moved on with nowhere to go. The proposed solution is a Traveler accommodation with either houses or halting sites, but it has not solved the problem. Whenever a local authority attempts to get a halting site, the settled community immediately tries to stop it. So there are still Travelers with no place to go.

In various discussions I have learned that there is an enormous gap in understanding between the Travelers and the settled people. Most settled people think, "I have nothing against Travelers, provided they behave in the manner in which I think they should behave." In other words, provided they behave as settled people. The reality is that they are not settled people. Behaving like settled people is quite meaningless to them; they don't understand that.

The Travelers, the settled community, and local authorities have all had some fault in this situation. Each group has simply seen it from their own point of view. The biggest difficulty at the moment is that there is almost no communication between the groups. Travelers do not talk to settled people, and settled people do not talk to Travelers. I need to talk more with them, because every time I do, I get a better insight into how they feel. By and large, Travelers feel alienated. They feel badly treated, that they are being pushed from one place to another. They feel settled people do not respect them and regard them as a nuisance. I know if I'm treated in that way I'm not going to respect the other person. Often we hold up our hands in horror at the prejudices we see in Zimbabwe or in South Africa. We think, "Isn't it dreadful the way they treat the black people!" But somehow we fail to see that there is a strong parallel between how we treat Travelers and how black people were treated in South Africa.

Ultimately, I think we need to be concerned for what happens to the Travelers' children. They seem so natural and unspoiled. If we don't solve this problem, we are doing a serious injustice in allowing children to be raised in dreadful conditions. I hope that settled people and Travelers will talk to one another, to try to get a better understanding of each other. Perhaps all of us can learn something from each other.

In Ireland today there are many other issues facing church and society. One of them concerns education. Up to now the church has been very much in control of primary education and a large part of postprimary education. We need to reexamine our position in that regard. Increasing numbers of people are looking for different choices of schools. One of the questions facing the church in Ireland is, Do we want to continue to have Catholic schools that only cater effectively to practicing Catholics, or do we want schools that welcome everybody of every faith and of no faith? Perhaps specific Catholic teaching could be done in a place either inside or outside the school. Certainly, I don't have immediate solutions to these issues. But we need to examine carefully the idea of control and power. Having too much control and power can be a dangerous role for the church—or for anyone.

Finally, a deep concern of mine is what our modern Ireland is offering to young people today. I don't want for a moment to turn back the clock to the closed and oppressive Ireland of the forties or fifties. There are wonderful things about our society today— an openness, and perhaps a greater honesty than ever before. But we need to challenge the commercial messages that claim material possessions or alcohol or drugs make you happy. I worry a great deal about the atmosphere that has developed in our towns and cities—the Friday and Saturday night disco scenes with lots of drinking and easily available drugs. A significant exploitation of young people has been going on, which will have negative consequences. Again, there are no simple solutions, but somehow this too has to be challenged because it's damaging our young people. The increasing number of suicides among the young is very disturbing.

I have a sense at this time that most people are struggling with many things in their lives. Although I regard myself as a very fortunate person, I too find myself struggling—struggling with life, struggling with faith, struggling with priesthood. I believe the church could help us to heal by identifying and acknowledging that we are all struggling and frail pilgrims.

❖ ❖ ❖ ❖ ❖ ❖ ❖ ❖

Throughout the gospel it is evident that Christ was
overwhelmingly aware of human weaknesses. Yet, he
looked beyond mere human limitations and saw the
potential of every individual. Aware of this potential,
Jesus worked to transform the person.
— *Loughlan Sofield, Rosine Hammett, and Carroll Juliano*

What a blessing to have had the opportunity to be in the presence of Bishop Willie Walsh, a very humble and courageous representative of the church community. The actions and efforts that Bishop Walsh and his colleagues have undertaken to encourage forgiveness and reconciliation in the church could serve as a role model to many communities.

One of the important lessons we can take away from this powerful story is the reminder that each one of us is a human being with our unique defects and blemishes. We do and will make endless mistakes and blunders, we can and will easily slip up or fall, and we have shadow sides that we might not want to admit to others—or to ourselves. Indeed, if the truth be known, even when we are feeling strong and powerful, we are still fragile and weak.

Once we are able to acknowledge and accept our flaws and errors as individuals and as communities, we are more likely able to forgive ourselves and others. We can begin to appreciate that everyone has both good and bad qualities. Then we will discover that we need not condemn or judge others who are less than perfect—who are really just like us.

As Bishop Walsh reminds us, we are all pilgrims struggling on the journey of life. We can speak the truth, even the unspeakable. We may be surprised to learn that within each one of us there is a sacredness that can be found in facing the truth.

CUAN MHUIRE ADDICTION CENTER:
FINDING A WAY FROM HELL

*As told by Sister Consilio and recovering
alcoholics and drug addicts*

*I don't know of anyone who hasn't been helped in some
way. Thousands have made it. It would be almost
impossible for any person who lived in Cuan Mhuire
for any length of time not to go out a better person.
They will have discovered more of their own
inner goodness.*

—*Sister Consilio*

*Someday I hope . . . I can give back some of the things
I have learned here. . . . Certainly, it helps me to help
others. I want to live the life that Cuan Mhuire has
given me—a belief in myself and a life I didn't
have before.*

—*a recovering alcoholic*

*Here at Cuan Mhuire, I wake up in the morning and
scream that it's great to be alive. I'm not reaching
under my bed and taking out a needle. Just for today I*

am clean, and just for today every one of us is clean.
That's all I care about today.
                    —a recovering drug addict

No matter where we live or what culture or class we may come from, almost all of us have been affected in some way by the tragedies and problems associated with addictions. We know people whose lives have been damaged or completely destroyed because of alcohol or drug addiction. Some of us may even be caught up in the dangerous web of our own or other's addictions.

Sadly, most addicts feel unloved and unlovable, and they often suffer from a sense of unworthiness. Sometimes they feel deeply ashamed about their troubled lives. Although they desperately want to change their predicament, they rarely know how to go about doing so.

On my last trip to Ireland, I was surprised to learn that addictions are rapidly increasing and becoming a serious problem within the country. Many young people start abusing alcohol at an early age. In the last six years drug use has gone up by more than 40 percent. There may be as many as one hundred thousand youngsters between fifteen and sixteen years of age who are multidrug users. Many start using as early as thirteen or fourteen. Sadly, in the fast pace of today's Irish society, there is little time to hear children's longings or to acknowledge and accept their need to be seen, heard, and unconditionally loved. Many children no longer feel there is a "safe harbor" for them. As a result, they feel lost and are turning to alcohol and drugs.

Fortunately, there are some "safe harbors" in Ireland, and I was privileged to visit one. Cuan Mhuire, "Harbor of Mary," is a beautiful place filled with compassion to help the wounded heal from their addictions, as well as their low self-images. It is lovingly guided by an extraordinary woman, Sister Consilio, and her dedicated colleagues.

❖ ❖ ❖ ❖ ❖ ❖ ❖ ❖

A recovering alcoholic

About seven years ago, I was gambling and drinking to numb the pain of everything in my life. Once I took my first drink, my life went totally out of control. Sometimes I disappeared for weeks on end. I thought by going away the pain would go away.

I remember someone saying, "If I could just go away and leave my head behind me, I'd be okay."

Although I tried to fight my drinking problem, I didn't have the right program. I didn't know how to express my feelings, and anyway I didn't want anyone to know how I really felt. So I bottled up my emotions and became very depressed. Whenever I tried to give up drinking, my depression got worse. I didn't know that I was beating up and persecuting myself. When a psychiatrist gave me antidepressants, I was still drinking. So I sank deeper into the black hole of depression and drank even more. Eventually that brought me to the brink of suicide.

In February 2002, I arrived at Cuan Mhuire. I was so lucky to have found this place, because I was on the verge of giving up completely. One of the first things I learned was the importance of "self-forgiveness." Until I came here, I had never heard those words. That started me on the right track. I had been blaming everyone but myself for my problems. I wanted to change everyone but myself, and I wanted answers immediately. I was living too much in the past and planning too much for the future. Cuan Mhuire taught me to live life in the moment, that I only have today, and that answers don't come quickly or easily.

Our daily program—meditation in the early morning, meetings, counseling sessions, one-on-one sessions, and lots of work—puts routine and discipline back into our lives. When I first came here, I wasn't able to sleep and my mind was racing like crazy. They say it takes two years for the brain to get back to normal. Eventually I learned to relax.

Now every morning I want to get up to live. When I was drinking, I only wanted to get up for one thing: the poison I had the night before. It was a slow form of suicide, and I know where it would have brought me if I had kept at it. I always had a belief in God, but I blamed him when things didn't go right for me. Now I'm inspired to do things I hadn't done before I came to Cuan Mhuire, like writing. In my early days, I wrote: "Each a unique and individual story . . . all having suffered similar days and nights and often years of mental and physical turmoil, living in a haze that never seemed to clear until they discovered Cuan Mhuire—a heaven away from the hell of addiction."

Since being at Cuan Mhuire, I have experienced ups and downs. But I'm learning to let go. Daily I remind myself where I came from and of what drinking will do to me if I ever return. I caused my family so much pain and hurt by not being there for them. I know people who have had relapses and are dead now because of an overdose or an accident. It reminds me what alcohol can do, how alcoholism is a disease that will be with me the rest of my life. Now life for me is my sobriety. I cannot say "never," because tomorrow is another day and I can't live for tomorrow, nor for yesterday. I have to live now, in this moment.

Over time I have become physically and mentally healthier; even my spiritual well-being is better. I just came back from a ten-day break at my home. People said they saw a big change in me. Someone asked, "Why don't you drink anymore?" My answer: "If I drank, I wouldn't have what I have now. Peace of mind."

After I finished the program, I decided to stay and work full-time for Cuan Mhuire. Someday I hope to train to be a counselor so I can give back some of the things I have learned here. Maybe I can help someone get what I have. Certainly, it helps me to help others. I want to live the life that Cuan Mhuire has given me—a belief in myself and a life I didn't have before.

A recovering drug addict

I'm an addict. My drug of choice was heroin. Some of my problems stem from my childhood, but I never realized it. As a child, my life was in the hands of a man who basically betrayed that trust. From the age of about five until thirteen, I was sexually and physically abused. At the time, I didn't understand what was happening to me. Even though he's dead, he still has a certain amount of control over me. I hope to deal with that here at Cuan Mhuire.

I grew up for eight years without a father and never had the courage to ask my mother where he went. I thought it was because of me that my mother and my biological father split up. Today I know his name and where he lives. Over the years I have had so much hatred and anger inside me, which all went against myself. Some people told me that I was stupid and no good, that I'd never go anywhere with my life. After a while I too believed that lie. I started bouncing checks and robbing cars to get money for drugs.

At the center I'm learning that what happened twenty-four years ago when my father left has nothing to do with me. In this group I share everything about my fourteen years of abuse because I know they won't judge me; they understand how I feel. And I want to get well. At first it was hard for me to trust anyone, because the trust I gave as a child was abused.

Most of us drug addicts and alcoholics have only negative feelings about ourselves. We don't realize that we can have good feelings too. Plenty of times I've thought about going out that gate, but there are always these lads who help me see the goodness that is in me, that I couldn't see myself. The other day when someone asked me where I lived, I said, "Cuan Mhuire is my home." I've been in other treatment centers where hurtful labels were used; even if I told someone here that I'd done something terrible, they wouldn't label me.

Without drugs, I'm starting to have feelings. I'm very emotional, and I cry over things. Drugs take away feelings. Now I'm beginning to love myself. None of us loved ourselves; we only cared what other people thought about us. I tell myself that I don't care what other people think. That's their stuff, their problem. If someone likes me or wants to talk to me, that's brilliant. I'm helping them, but I'm also helping myself. We all have our good and our bad days. Thank God, I now have more good days than bad. I've been here for about three weeks. When I first came in, I wasn't looking very healthy; I was really thin. I've put on two stone [twenty-eight pounds] since I came into the detox.

When I'm in active addiction, a lot of people are hurt emotionally: my mother, my father, my little sister, my ex-girlfriend, and my son. Even though he's very young, he's hurt because I'm not there for him. I was just a shell of a person while I was using drugs. But I'm not empty anymore. Now I'm maybe three-quarters full. I have my emotions, my feelings, this "family" around me, and a support group. It's super. I wake up at half six [6:30] in the morning and feel brilliant. When you are sick on drugs, you don't even "wake up" at all. These days, I don't have to worry where I'll get my next drugs. I don't have to worry about going out and robbing people. I've started praying that my self-hatred will be taken away. In the morning I pray for strength to get me through the day and to make the right choices. At night I thank God for a day of being clean and sober.

Here at Cuan Mhuire, I wake up in the morning and scream that it's great to be alive. I'm not reaching under my bed and taking out a needle. Just for today I am clean, and just for today every one of us is clean. That's all I care about today. I have other problems that I will deal with as they come along. But for today, I am clean.

Sister Consilio

About forty years ago while working in the hospital down the road, I came into contact with lots of people drinking wine on the road. I got to know them well. I learned that most of them were well-educated and had come from good backgrounds. I wondered how people of such high caliber could reach such a state. I always thought how much their mothers would worry about them if they knew they were on the road. I wondered what my mother would think if my brother were in that situation.

Over time, I began to realize that these were my brothers, and I said to myself, "Someday, somewhere, somehow, I will have a place that these lads can call home." I thought if they could go to work in the morning, it would restore their dignity. If they came home at night to a fire and a meal and someone to love them, their troubles would be over and everything would be resolved. I was foolish enough to think that I was going to be the one to love them. I forgot about all those people who had loved them long before I showed up. Later I realized that the person whom they most needed to love them was themselves. They needed to learn what was best inside themselves. And they needed to find out that the main causes of their addiction and its symptoms were a poor self-image and low self-esteem.

It's been thirty-seven years since I got involved in this work. As a nun, it was an impossible dream to take care of the men on the road. One Sunday I heard about an Alcoholics Anonymous (AA) meeting in a nearby town. Immediately I thought of those lads and got permission to go to the meeting with the matron from the hospital where I worked.

At the meeting, a man sitting next to me loaned me his pen to jot down some points. About a week later, he called into the convent to see me. He kept coming for the next five or six weeks. I thought he was coming because he was interested in AA, but he told me having somebody listen to him was helping him to stay sober. Soon he told other people, and they started coming to the convent at all hours, drunk and sober. I developed a lot of problems in the convent as a result of that—especially because they often came at about 9:00 at night when we were supposed to be having silence.

At first I apologized to the other nuns because it was so late, but after a while I stopped apologizing, because I knew I'd be doing the same thing the next night. One day I noticed a doorway near the entrance of the convent that hadn't been opened in years. Inside was a small music room. I asked the Reverend Mother if I could use that room and when people called we could talk there, rather than in the convent parlor. She agreed. It wasn't long before it became too small.

Eventually, I was able to get an old dairy from the convent in Athy. By that time several of the lads were sober. One was a plasterer and another a builder. So we converted the old dairy into what we called the first Cuan Mhuire. Then a doctor, who also had a problem with alcohol, came to help work with the men who were in dire straits. Until then, they had to go to the hospital if they were sick or needed detoxing. That was very expensive, and often by the time they finished the treatment they were back drinking again. I thought it would be marvelous if we had a place where people could come in and recover. There'd be the sheer joy of seeing them recover, and they wouldn't be handed a costly bill as they left.

In the early stages, I tried to help people dry out in their homes, but that was very complicated because it was nearly impossible to supervise them. I would be out half the night with them, and then I went back to the convent in the morning to do my work. Meanwhile I was terrified that they might take a drink while I was out getting medication for them.

In 1965 I got permission to keep a woman—a friend of the nuns who had a serious drinking problem—overnight in the old dairy we had converted. From then on, I kept anyone who needed to stay in the dairy. Because our doctor was very interested in the Irish language and in boats and harbors, we decided to call the dairy "An Cuan"—"the harbor." And because I couldn't survive without Our Lady, it became "Cuan Mhuire"—"Our Lady's Harbor," or "the Harbor of Mary."

When people started coming, we had no expectations that they were going to get well. We thought we would give them and their families a break and a caring place. Likely people started getting well because they were being offered love, friendship, and fellowship. Certainly, there were plenty of pubs in the area where they could easily have gone to get a drink. And my work at Cuan Mhuire was just part-time, because I had major responsibilities in the kitchen at the convent and in the school. So these lads had to look after each other. I believe that was the real key: when they took responsibility for each other, they started getting well. And that's how they recovered.

When people started to recover, they felt grateful and they felt part of the Cuan Mhuire community. It was very much a family for them. So when they left, they brought back other people who needed help—in the middle of the night or anytime. It wasn't long before we had thirty people staying with us. As the Convent of Mercy gradually became vacant, we got more space there. It was quite primitive and very poor; we had little or nothing. We had a mug on the mantelpiece, and if anyone had a couple of shillings, they put them into the mug to buy a meal. There was no social welfare.

It was through the pure grace of God that we survived. Very little money changed hands. Some of my friends helped us. And, of course, I was cooking in the kitchen in the convent. At first the other nuns thought I had a very big appetite. But some, those who knew what I was doing, added a portion of their dinners to "my dinner." So "my dinner" went around a long way. Eventually people who had been helped at Cuan Mhuire started doing fundraising events to keep us going. To this day they are still involved.

Most people who come to Cuan Mhuire feel they are no good, or not good enough. They don't believe they measure up to the expectations they have for themselves, or that they think their parents or others have for them. Almost everything goes back to childhood. A very simple thing can affect a child's life and future.

Yesterday evening I was called to the drug unit because one of our boys was suicidal. He told me about voices he heard telling him to finish it all. So I sat with him, listened to him, and asked him about his childhood. He told me that as a small lad other children said bad things about his big ears. It was the only thing he could remember that had ruined his childhood. I said, "Your ears are perfect, no bigger than anyone's ears." He told me they had been very large when he was a child, the same size as now. He was so desperate last night; he was full of fear and shaking with terror. We said some prayers together, repeating very gently, "I am good, I was always good, and God made me good." And then we said, "I am really safe. I am very safe." We repeated that until he fell asleep. When he woke up this morning, he seemed much better.

All of us at Cuan Mhuire believe that one young person is more valuable than every material thing in this world. No matter who the person is or how ill they are, every one is beyond a price tag. It is a huge privilege to be able to welcome them into our house. It's why we are here: to be truly present and open to them, to help them feel safe, loved, and secure.

People who come to us because of drug addictions probably started using when they were thirteen or fourteen years old. Even though they are in their twenties now, they haven't really lived a day since they started using. They're in a kind of cloud and haze. Two lads came out of their haze this weekend. When I asked them how it felt, they both said it was like being born, like getting out into a life they never knew. One said, "I can't believe how nice the flowers smell. I never really smelled a flower before." The other said he was terrified. These young people don't really know their parents, their homes, their lives. It's like they were living at a slower rate because the drugs blotted out everything for them. So our program has to help these people with their formation. It has to encourage them to grow from age thirteen on, even though in reality they are twenty-four or twenty-five years old. In a fourteen-week course, we try to bring people up to the age they really are.

Our program is about self-discipline—not army discipline or enforced discipline. Every person has to become responsible for themselves, be attentive to what they do, and discipline themselves. Those are our conditions. The program is very structured. We know things need to be constant in formation. So every day it's exactly the same, and we don't move or deviate from it half an inch. We provide everyone with time frames and plenty of work opportunities so that they know what they are doing from the moment they wake up in the morning until they go to sleep at night. Everything is detailed, from prayer time to teatime to cigarette breaks to work times. Repetition is the key to wisdom. It is about being positive and healthy.

Addicts have lived so much in their heads that we often joke with them that they've become head cases. We teach them how to be attentive so they can live at a deeper soul level. Attentiveness brings them right out of the racing-head stuff. They also need to learn to live in the present, the only reality there is. If they are to grow beyond their condition, they can only do that from their inner being. Not from their head or my head or anyone else's head. Young people take to the spiritual dimension at Cuan Mhuire like ducks to water. They might not have said a prayer in years or might not remember ever having said one, but they are hungry for the spiritual life. They are so fearful, so alone, that they are delighted to know that God is there for them. It's amazing how they can experience peace, joy, and contentment from it.

In our house in Northern Ireland, we have a cross section of all denominations. All our meditations are nondenominational. When people realize that they are made in the image and likeness of God, it doesn't matter what denomination they belong to. We have a Muslim chap in the drug unit. I gave him the option of not coming into the religious classes, but he decided he wanted to come. He doesn't participate in taking holy communion. Whatever he believes is fine with us; whatever we believe is fine with him.

If drug users try to use drugs while they are here, they are not allowed to stay. People spend two weeks in detox, and then they stay another fourteen weeks beyond that. Nobody asks them to leave, and some stay longer. Drugs are much more difficult to deal with than alcohol. With drug addiction, nothing matters one inch—parents, family, girlfriends, children—except the longing for the drug of their choice. Most of our people turn out very well. One lad who didn't make it the first time is here now, but he seems to be doing quite well because he is much more mature. After they leave, they come in for a urine sample every week for two years. On one Saturday of the month, they can come to talk or be in a group. A lot come to AA meetings.

In the drug unit, they come in thin as whips and they are not able to eat. They look like they're not going to live. But within a number of weeks, everyone has put on a stone or more. They are smiling and cheerful. Their parents say they don't know them when they come to visit. I believe it is because they experience unconditional love and they practice caring and giving. They learn not to expect anything in return. They practice their prayers, and they begin to believe in God's power within themselves. This creates enormous healing. If it weren't for all that healing going on, I would have burned out years ago.

Here at Cuan Mhuire we try to call forth what is best in each person. We see that young people have a hunger and thirst for something meaningful, something deeper than the pleasures put before them in society. Some are beginning to understand that "pleasure" can be a very shallow thing and that real joy and peace are everlasting gifts that they have already within themselves. Then they can experience and share them with other people.

There's a story of a banquet, which is about both hell and heaven. At the banquet everyone has huge forks. They are so big that if someone picks up one of these forks, their arms are not long enough to get the fork to their mouths. The people that make it hell struggle to get them into their mouths, which is impossible. But the people who make it to heaven are the people who feed each other.

We live as a family at Cuan Mhuire. The people who make the best recovery are the ones who respect and watch out for others, who live and care for everything as if they were in their own home. I don't know of anyone who hasn't been helped in some way. Thousands have made it. It would be almost impossible for any person who lived in Cuan Mhuire for any length of time not to go out a better person. They will have discovered more of their own inner goodness.

A recovering alcoholic

Cuan Mhuire is my home. I've been here just over two years. When I came in, I felt worthless. My marriage and my children were gone because of my drinking. The drink came before anything else in my life. Nothing else mattered. Cuan Mhuire took me in when nobody else wanted me.

There was a lot of abuse in my home as I was growing up. I had a difficult childhood and a very, very strict father. At nineteen, I married for the wrong reason: to get away. Then I had children. While they were small it was the happiest time of my life. When they started school, I took to the drink straightaway. After five years I had a serious drinking problem.

When I drank, I thought nobody wanted me. When I arrived at Cuan Mhuire for the six-week program, I felt useless, no good at all. But I liked what I saw happening. Every day, people were recovering and feeling good about themselves. It was like they were being given a new life. I started to believe that I wasn't a bad person; I was a good person. That gave me some self-respect. As a good person, I could help others. I loved going to women in the unit and just sitting and listening to them, just being there, having a cup of tea with them. And I learned how important it is not to live in the past or the future as we alcoholics seem to do.

After I finished my six weeks, I decided to stay for another few weeks. Eventually Sister Consilio asked me if I would like to work here. I said, "Yes." I do cooking and cleaning in Galilee House, where the trained counselors are. During the last two years my two grown sons have started visiting me, but I don't plan to go back home, because my life is here now. If I'm able to stay away from the drink for three years, I want to train to be a counselor.

In this house in Athy, we have 140 people, and there are three other houses—in Limerick, Galway, and Newry. There's also a halfway house in Dublin, where people can stay while they look for a flat or a job. Many people come to Cuan Mhuire for the six-week program, and then they try to make it work outside. Some people are lucky and get it the first time. Others return, because it doesn't always work the first time. It's tough out there. Usually on the second round they make it.

I know I would not have this wonderful life I have today without this community. I also understand that just one drink would take away everything I have now. I never want that to happen, because that life is a hell. So I will stay away from the drink—one day at a time.

A recovering drug addict

I came to Cuan Mhuire because I knew I had a serious problem that I couldn't deal with on my own. It took me twelve years to realize that. When I first came in and went through detox, I had it in my head that I was only going to stay for a few days and then I was going out again, but once I got in the unit I decided to give it a shot.

Over the last two or three weeks, I've been getting different feelings. When we are on heroin, we suppress them. We cut ourselves off from society by robbing or abusing people. We don't know how to love people—especially ourselves. I can share anything with this group, no matter what I feel. In my heart I know that I will be listened to and heard.

As a child, I wasn't heard. Things were lacking in my life, so I went looking for something. I found drugs and took to them like a duck to water. When I first started using, I just thought I was a junkie. But we aren't junkies; we're addicts.

Cuan Mhuire is a lifeline for me. Without it, I would be dead or in prison. As soon as I joined the group, I felt how positive they were and saw how much they wanted to get better. We don't get "better," but we can keep the addiction away on a daily basis. We try not to think of the future. If we can wake up in the morning and stay clean, don't pick up drugs, and get back to our beds in the evening without using drugs, that's a great day.

I have so much respect for Sister Consilio and all the staff here. They make us feel as though we are welcome, as though we are a part of this special community. Everyone tries to help us. They worry about us and pray for us. I never believed in religion, but since I came to Cuan Mhuire I started praying. Now I pray in the morning and in the evening, and I go to Mass and do the Rosary every night. At the start of each group, we pray for each other's families and for our intentions. I find that very calming, knowing that people around me are praying for my family, for my sister's recovery, and for me.

This is a great place to be. This course is only four months long, but if I need to be here longer, I don't have to go back outside that gate. In most of the programs around Dublin, you have to leave after six weeks. You are turned out into the same place you left. If I go back there, I'd hang around with the same people, with the same drugs. At Cuan Mhuire I can stay in the big house for months. I can do other courses and find out more about myself. When I'm ready, I can go out for a weekend to see how I adjust back in society. If I leave and relapse, it means that I am still missing something, but I can come back and do the program again and again. Hopefully, I will only have to do it once. That's not to say I'm certain that I won't go back out there and use again. But I'm trying to live for today—just one day at a time.

❖ ❖ ❖ ❖ ❖ ❖ ❖ ❖

There are those who give little of the much which they have—and they give it for recognition and their hidden desire makes their gifts unwholesome. And there are those who have little and give it all. These are the believers in life and the bounty of life, and their coffer is never empty.

—Kahlil Gibran

The addicts who have been fortunate enough to spend time in the safe harbor of Cuan Mhuire don't leave this special place without some very useful tools to help them continue their journey of recovery. Sister Consilio and those who work with her in these extraordinary havens value each person so much that they give endless time and energy to helping them heal from their addictions of low self-esteem, of feeling unlovable and unworthy. They try to ensure that each person learns the essential lessons of self-discipline and of self-worth.

Like the people at Cuan Mhuire, all of us would benefit by learning about our own addictions of negativity, pessimism, self-hatred. Perhaps we would be helped if we spent a few days in a safe harbor learning how to be connected to some of the more positive things in life, such as confidence in our own abilities and a belief that we have unique gifts to offer.

As I listened to the stories of these recovering addicts, I couldn't help but think about how easy it would be for any of us to seek comfort in alcohol or drugs. When life gets difficult, what do we reach for to drown our sorrows, to soothe our souls? If we have the disease of alcoholism or drug addiction, it doesn't take much to slip deeper into this bottomless pit—this hell of addiction.

This chapter also teaches us about the value of "tough love," the kind of love that demands that we shape up and get well because we are so valuable. People who really care about us want the best for us and won't allow us to abuse ourselves through our negative addictions. They may be the most important people in our lives.

MOUNTJOY PRISON'S DÓCHAS CENTER:

CREATING NEW LIVES

As told by John Lonergan, Governor of Mountjoy Prison; Kathleen McMahon, Deputy Governor of Mountjoy's Dóchas Center; and women in Mountjoy's Dóchas Center

> *Our philosophy is based on promoting the good in people, giving them an opportunity to do something positive. . . . In the process, we help them develop their humanity. If we only emphasize the bad in people, we will get more badness out of them.*
> —John Lonergan, Governor of Mountjoy Prison

> *I've never been in any other prison, but I hear stories about the old place. If I had ended up in a prison that was anything like that, I probably . . . wouldn't have survived. So I'm grateful that there is a place like this.*
> —a woman in the Dóchas Center for transporting drugs

Prison. The word alone can bring to mind frightening and ugly images of solitary confinement, jangling keys, endless locks and gates, bars, overcrowded cells, handcuffs, gang rape, severe punishment, absolute fear.

A former prisoner once told me that, when he first entered prison, he felt he became just a number, no longer a human being. For him, every day behind bars was about misery, loneliness, and fear.

In numerous interviews with other prisoners I've been told that in order to survive inside, you have to learn to beat the system, to pay people off, to cheat, to steal. You have to learn to become a "successful convict." It has been said that when innocent people or petty offenders are put into prison, they will likely become hardened criminals by the time they are released.

In Dublin, I visited the famous Mountjoy Prison, where more than five hundred thousand people have been confined over a period of 150 years. Interestingly, the story of Mountjoy had its beginnings in the American colonies. Until the outbreak of the American War of Independence, thirteen thousand Irish criminals, who were not wanted at home, were punished for their crimes by being transported to the American colonies for periods of up to fourteen years to work on labor intensive plantations. After the war ended, the newly independent American citizens were no longer willing to receive foreign criminals. On March 27, 1850, the first prisoners arrived at Mountjoy. Over the years, Mountjoy has held all kinds of criminals, from murderers to political prisoners to drug addicts. It has gone through many crises, changes, difficulties, and alterations.

In 1984, John Lonergan became Mountjoy's Governor. According to Tim Carey, author of *Mountjoy: The Story of a Prison*,

> He has been the single most important influence on the prison. After years of suspicion he introduced an open and humanitarian attitude towards prisoners and staff. . . . Governor Lonergan's influence in the prison has been immense. But he is perhaps best known for his efforts to influence the outside world. While recognizing that his responsibility is to manage prisoners, he also believes that society should take its share of the responsibility.[3]

One day I visited with Governor Lonergan and spent hours locked behind the heavy metal door of the Dóchas Center of the Mountjoy Women's Prison. I admit when I first heard the bang of that door as it locked behind me that I had a moment of bone-chilling anxiety: "What am I doing here? Maybe this wasn't such a good idea." But once inside I was allowed to wander freely and mingle and talk with the women. I wasn't always certain who was a staff member or who was a "prisoner," as almost every person I met wore civilian clothes and there was a sense of community and fellowship among everyone.

During my time inside Mountjoy, I heard some amazing stories and learned some very special lessons about healing.

❖ ❖ ❖ ❖ ❖ ❖ ❖ ❖

A woman in the Dóchas Center for transporting drugs

I've been in here for three months because of importation of drugs. I never took drugs, believe it or not. The father of my children set me up and got me to do the job for him. We had a really bad relationship, so probably if I hadn't done the job, he would have murdered me. Or I might have been in here myself for murdering him.

Everything happened so fast. I knew when I was caught that I was facing a long sentence. But I kept hoping that I would get out quickly so I could be with my children. It's very hard for me because my children are small and I miss them so much. My mam is looking after them, but she finds it difficult. They are very young, so she has her hands full.

Being in here has helped me a lot. I'm starting to change my life around. I've had time to think things over, and I realize now that I was in bad company. Another positive thing is that since I've been here, I've been going to school full-time and have done every one of the courses. I've done all the computer courses, as well as courses in speedwriting and business organization. I passed all the classes and will go on to college soon. I'm delighted, because I get to go out on day release.

The staff has encouraged me to do things, and they have been very helpful to me. They understand that I want to have a better life. I also work in the kitchen and spend a lot of time cleaning my room at night. That's the way I am—I try to do things to forget about the past. Now I'm starting to overcome some of my fears, and I'm learning stuff about myself. I've never been in any other prison, but I hear stories about the old place. If I had ended up in a prison that was anything like that, I probably would have done something stupid and I wouldn't have survived. So I'm grateful that there is a place like this.

Although the last couple of years have been really difficult, I believe everything is going to work better from now on. In the past, I wasn't in the right frame of mind. Even praying in here has helped. I strongly believe I'm in here to get myself sorted out. I think this place is helping me grow up quicker than I expected. Now I'm a lot more mature. I am still young enough, so I'll have an opportunity to get on with my life. When I get out, I need to further my education so I can get a good job and support my children. Hopefully, I will get there. No, I *will* get there.

A woman in the Dóchas Center for shoplifting

I've been here for five months for shoplifting. I don't have a drug addiction. I was in the old prison once before, and I was in a prison in England as well. When I lived in the old prison, it was very rough. There were cells everywhere, and it wasn't a very healthy place. Sometimes there were ten people in a room with you. That was bad, because people on drugs were put together in the same place with people who were not on drugs. The prison was overcrowded and noisy. I never could think in there, and I always felt afraid.

When this prison opened, we had some space, we had our own shower, and we could put curtains on the windows. It was like having our own bedroom. I never had that before. We eat breakfast in the communal kitchen in our own house. It's nice in here, and there are good officers. I get on great with them. If I need anything, they help me with it. Sometimes we even get days to go shopping in town.

I get out of here in another ten months. I'm a little bit nervous, but I think I'll be okay. Right now I'm taking a twelve-week course called "Options." It's about the way I should speak to people, about making eye contact, about having community skills. It's about things I should do when I get out. I also work in the kitchen, where I'm learning a lot. That makes me feel good. Before I leave here, I want to do the course on child minding. Maybe I will be able to get a job doing that when I get out. I want to make my life better than it was.

John Lonergan, Governor of Mountjoy Prison

I was appointed Governor of Mountjoy Prison in June 1984. Mountjoy is Ireland's largest prison, accommodating up to six hundred men and one hundred women. The men's prison was built in 1850 and the women's prison in 1858. The women's prison originally accommodated up to five hundred women and children; however, during the early 1900s the number of women in custody dropped dramatically, and by the 1950s the daily average number of women in custody in Mountjoy was as low as twenty. In 1956 most of the women's prison was redesignated as St. Patrick's Detention Center, a detention center for boys aged between sixteen and twenty-one years. As a result the women's prison was confined to one basement floor. It was a small, dark, depressing place with a most austere regime.

After I left Mountjoy in 1988 to serve as Governor of Portlaoise Prison, the B Wing of St. Patrick's was refurbished for the women. On my return to Mountjoy in May 1992, I was shocked to find that the refurbished wing was totally unsuitable for use as a women's prison. It was worse than Alcatraz—wire, cages, steel bars—everything about it was over the top. I decided, "This has to be stopped, women cannot go back there." As luck would have it, Maire Geoghegan-Quinn was appointed the first woman Minister for Justice around this time. and she took a keen interest in the whole issue. Soon after her appointment she approved the building of a new facility specifically designed for women, with women having direct and major input at all stages of its design and construction. The new facility needed its very own identity, and we were determined that it would not be known as the New Women's Prison or Mountjoy Women's Prison. Suggestions for a name for the new center were sought from all members of the community, and eventually the name "Dóchas Center" was agreed—"Dóchas" is the Irish word for "hope."

Prior to the opening of the Dóchas Center, a working group made up of the heads of services and other staff members, in consultation with the women prisoners, drew up a vision statement for the center. This vision statement is on display in the main entrance hall and underpins the whole ethos of the center. The vision statement is as follows:

We are a community that embraces people's respect
and dignity. We encourage personal growth and
development in a caring and safe environment. We
are committed to addressing the needs of each person
in a healing and holistic way. We actively promote
close interaction with the wider community.

The Dóchas Center was officially opened by Mr. John
O'Donoghue, member of the Irish "House of Commons,"
Minister for Justice, Equality, and Law Reform in September
1999, and the old prison closed on Christmas Eve 1999.

There is a sad story attached to the closing of the old prison. A
young woman in her mid-twenties approached me one day in
December 1999 and asked me if she could lock the gate for the
last time on the day the prison was closing. When I joked with
her that I was going to do it, she responded by saying, "I'm
entitled to do it." When I asked her why she felt that she was
entitled to do it, she told me, "Well, my grandmother served time
in this prison, my mother served time in this prison, most of my
sisters served time here, and most of my brothers served time in
the men's prison." She concluded, "I think I am entitled to do it."
And I agreed. She duly locked the gate for the final time on the
evening of Christmas Eve 1999. A photograph was taken on the
occasion. Sadly, it was her only claim to fame.

Long before the new prison was built, many progressive
improvements took place in the women's prison. For example, in
1984 the women were allowed to wear their own clothes for the
first time. This was a most significant development, as it allowed
the women to hold on to a big part of their own identity. They
were also allowed to have makeup. Again, this was of huge
importance to the women, as it helped them to feel better about
themselves and their self-esteem improved. People who feel
good about themselves are much easier to help, and they are also
much more cooperative. In addition, the role of education
became much more central, with the "school" providing a wide
variety of subjects which enabled many of the women to reenter
the formal educational system. The school operated an adult
education model of teaching, and this proved to be very popular
with most of the women. The school played an important role in
the development of a more modern and progressive regime. The
concept of a community was now beginning to materialize, with

more and more emphasis being placed on caring for the women rather than containing them.

In 1995 a multidisciplinary group was established in the women's prison to identify the values and principles on which a progressive regime should be based. The group produced a most useful document, one that greatly influenced the design and development of the Dóchas Center.

Another progressive change introduced around this time was the elimination of the routine handcuffing of all women prisoners. One morning on my way into work, I saw a woman prisoner being escorted out to the hospital in handcuffs. The previous day she had been out of the prison on home leave. Yet she was going to the hospital handcuffed. So I began reflecting, were we handcuffing people because of a risk that they might run away, or because they were a security danger if they escaped, or to reinforce the belief that they were bad or dangerous people? Handcuffing people in public is humiliating and should not be done unless it is absolutely essential.

When the issue was initially discussed with the staff, questions about authority, control, power, and the repercussions, should the women escape, were raised. Eventually it was accepted that handcuffing was solely an operational issue and all decisions in relation to their use should be based on security and safety factors. For many years now this has become the established practice. The results have proved to be outstandingly successful, with an obvious improvement in relationships between staff and the women. So for the last number of years most women go out of the women's prison to hospitals or courts without handcuffs. It has made a huge difference to the whole atmosphere in the center. In a community, trust is a key dynamic; but unfortunately the whole philosophy of prison is based on mistrust, thus the bars on windows, the constant checking on people, the handcuffing. People cannot grow and develop in an atmosphere of mistrust.

The Dóchas Center is unique in design, and it certainly does not have the normal institutionalized atmosphere or appearance. It was designed to facilitate community-style living. We moved away from the idea of cellblocks and opted instead for house-style units. This was to ensure that the new center reflected normal living facilities, as in the wider community. So each house was designed with a communal kitchen and a communal dining room. There are six houses accommodating seventy-five women in single rooms all with integral sanitation and showering facilities. The houses face onto small courtyards. All the gates in the women's prison are open except for the main external one. The women can move around freely within the center, and they are not shackled. They experience a sense of trust and freedom even within the constraints of an institution. As they feel happier within themselves, they are more open to education, counseling, and other opportunities.

Just inside the main entrance there is a water fountain with running water. Shortly after the opening of the center in 1999, Marian Finucane did a live radio broadcast inside the center for her morning program on RTÉ (Radio Telefís Éireann, the Irish National Public Service Broadcasting Organization). She mentioned the fountain, and a listener phoned in saying it was a disgrace to have a fountain in a prison. Marian asked one of the women, "What do you think about that? She seems critical of the fountain." The woman's response was, "She doesn't understand that the fountain costs very little, and she doesn't appreciate what running water means to us. When I pass that pump, the running water signifies freedom to me. That's my dream—to be free again. I can see that in the water as it runs freely." It just proves that little things can truly make a difference.

We have also worked hard to eliminate some of the old institutionalized culture, like the excessive noise, the rattling of keys, the banging of gates, the shouting and roaring at each other. Initially, when the women wanted something, they shouted at each other and at staff. But they have learned that they can get things a lot easier by just speaking normally. Of course, we still have the disputes and arguments over things that one has in any community, but we are now able to resolve most of them without aggression or abusive language.

In addition, we regularly have community occasions—different events to promote the concept of community. For example, at the end of the school year the community assembles and the women who have sat examinations are presented with certificates. The evening closes with a barbecue. We also stage drama productions in both the women's and the men's prisons where the entire cast is drawn from within the prisoner population. People actually pay to get into prison to see these plays.

Just recently, in November 2002, we staged *The Factory Girls* by Frank McGuinness, produced by Marie Louise O'Donnell. More than twelve hundred people attended the production and they gave the cast a standing ovation every night. Midnight Mass on Christmas Eve 2002 was broadcast live on national television.

Also, every year at Christmas a communal dinner is held involving staff, befrienders, and the women. Shortly before Christmas we arrange for the women's children to be brought in to have a special celebration. Although there is joy and happiness, there is also a huge amount of sadness when the children are leaving their mothers. It is on occasions like this that the punishment element of prison really strikes home. People on the outside don't realize that sadness is another reality of prison, but it is. The women are often very sad about the hurt they have caused others, their own loss of freedom, their separation from their children, and, above all, their lives of misery.

Most of the women come from the two lowest socioeconomic groups. They are not just financially and materialistically disadvantaged; they are also poverty-stricken in many other ways, such as in education, their emotional and psychological development, and their mental state. A large number of the women have been abused emotionally, psychologically, physically, and sexually, both as children and as adults. Society doesn't fully understand how damaging some environments and cultures are for those who are forced to live in them. A high percentage of our women are addicted to drugs and alcohol. They are often very insecure people; they have very low self-esteem, and many are unaware of their talents and potential.

To build up the women's motivation and self-esteem and to support them in their personal development, the center provides a variety of programs and activities. The education unit delivers a wide range of courses; various workshops provide work-training programs; the probation and welfare service supports and encourages the women to address many of their personal and family problems; a comprehensive health-care service is provided; chaplaincy provides a spiritual and supportive service; custodial staff are caring and compassionate; befrienders drawn from the outside community visit on a regular basis to befriend the women; a high-quality catering service provides a good, balanced diet; and family visits are facilitated in a modern and homey visiting area. The basic philosophy for all those who work in the Dóchas Center is to accept the women as they are, to support and encourage them to use their time in the Dóchas Center as positively as possible, and to assist them in achieving their full potential.

All too often, society generalizes and labels prisoners as being dangerous, useless, "no-hopers," and "all the same." Of course, they are all different and unique individuals, and I can truly say that I've never met anyone in prison who was totally bad. I've always found a redeeming feature, some element of humanity, of goodness. They may have been overwhelmed with their dark side and the demons within them, but there was always a little light somewhere.

As Governor of Mountjoy, I believe that, fundamentally, I am no better or worse than any other man or woman. We are all human beings with the potential to do good and bad. Perhaps some of us are better able to manage and control our dark side, but it is there. Here at Dóchas our philosophy is based on promoting the good in people, giving them an opportunity to do something positive, and supporting them in that. In the process, we help them develop their humanity. If we only emphasize the bad in people, we will get more badness out of them. So, while people are here, we treat them as human beings and try to bring out the good in them.

Another significant element in restoration is respect. Unfortunately, the poor, the homeless, the addicted, and the imprisoned rarely experience respect, and, not surprisingly, they are the people who need it the most. But usually they are rejected, alienated, and ostracized. We try to help our staff understand that people who end up in prison are in a very vulnerable position. I once compared it to how people feel while on their way to the operating room in a hospital. Before they nod off under anesthetic, they feel very vulnerable. Why? Because they are no longer in charge. It's like that in prison too; people are afraid because they are no longer in control. At that point they need somebody who cares about them.

Prisoners need to experience basic human respect simply because they are human beings. By being locked up in prison, prisoners have already been judged by the courts. They have already been punished for their crimes. Therefore, it is important for us to leave the judging outside the gate. By doing that, we can respond to them in a more helpful and normal way, and they may feel an element of forgiveness because they are not constantly being reminded of their wrongdoing. Most people in prison actually feel badly about what they have done. They may appear to be hardhearted and uncaring, but that's not often true.

The changes we are making at the Dóchas Center are positive, progressive, and empowering for the women, but they are not always popular with the media or general public. My belief is that what is right is seldom popular, and what is popular is seldom right. Trying to do the right thing in prison is usually unpopular. Some politicians, the public, and the media will hound you. Nevertheless, that doesn't change the fact that it's the right thing to do. The popular notion is that prisoners should be treated like "scum," but that most certainly isn't the right thing. If we want prison to help prisoners change and move away from their lives of crime, we must treat them as human beings. Above all, we must be human ourselves.

Recently I attended a talk given by well-known author Charles Handy. He was once an executive with Shell, the multinational oil company, but he became dissatisfied with his life and left the company to concentrate on his writing. He felt that, in such a big organization, there was little recognition for the individual. During his talk someone asked him to define happiness. He responded by saying that he thought the Chinese have a good theory on it. They believe that happiness has three elements—to have something to work for, to have something to dream for, to have somebody to love. If you experience all three at the same time, you are on the road to happiness. We are trying to promote this at the Dóchas Center.

The transition from the old regime to a new progressive model is moving along slowly but surely. However, many issues still remain to be fully resolved. The roles of various staff members; cohesive multidisciplinary working; and involving the women in a genuine consultative process, team development, and cohesion are all areas requiring ongoing attention. Change is a slow process—tradition, culture, personal attitudes, and fear of the unknown are all inhibiting factors.

Has the Dóchas Center made a difference? Of course it has. Catholic chaplain Father Eamon Crosson, who worked here for several years, described the changes that had taken place during his time here as a miracle. When it opened, the cynics knocked it and a lot of destructive things were written about it. Some predicted it would be burned down within a week. But it has lasted, and it has developed. In the past, the prison system always dominated and decided for the prisoners. It never consulted them. There was an assumption that if you were a prisoner, the system told you what to do. The old system never really got to know the prisoner as a human being. Indeed, the prisoner was nothing but a number. In the Dóchas Center we try to understand the individual prisoner, we refuse to judge or condemn them, we involve them in decisions that affect their lives, we encourage them to be positive about themselves, and we treat them as fellow human beings. They are responding positively, and many have already done themselves proud. We hope that they will never end up in prison again, but if they do, it does not give us the right to write them off.

Every day is a new opportunity for us and for them. If we can help people to understand themselves, that is a major achievement. Every human being, young or old, rich or poor, needs to be loved and accepted as they are, warts and all. We are determined that the women in the Dóchas Center will not be regarded as the Least, the Last, and the Lost.

Kathleen McMahon, Deputy Governor of Mountjoy's Dóchas Center

I joined the Prison Service in 1976 and was assigned to the staff of the women's prison at Mountjoy. In those days the emphasis was almost totally on control, discipline, and rules; there was a rule for everything. Personally, I hated this regime, and in 1977 I jumped at the opportunity to work in Loughan House in county Cavan, when it was designated as a special school for boys aged between twelve and sixteen.

I really enjoyed my time there; the regime allowed me to work closely with the boys, and as a result, I got to know, and understand them much better. Many of them had never really experienced a normal childhood, and they were crying out for attention and acceptance. I soon discovered that they responded positively when they were treated with respect, kindness, and compassion. Indeed, I have always believed that to get the best out of a person you must concentrate on their positive side. It worked in Loughan House in the seventies, and it works today in the Dóchas Center.

I returned to the women's prison in 1981 and was appointed Chief Officer in 1993. I was promoted to the grade of Deputy Governor in 2002. I have overall responsibility for the day-to-day management of the center, and I love my job here.

I came to the Dóchas Center in early 1999 to prepare for its official opening in September of that year. I was delighted to be given the opportunity to have an input from the very beginning. I organized a small team of staff and women prisoners, and collectively we set about creating the infrastructure and services to develop a modern and progressive regime for the new center.

As well as finding an appropriate name for the center, we also looked at naming the six houses that make up the residential section of the center. In the prison system living areas are commonly known as wings, cellblocks, or divisions and are usually called "A Wing" or "B Wing," etc. Again, we moved away from this institutionalized approach, and, after much debate, it was decided to name each house after well-known trees. Accordingly, we have names such as Hazel House, Elm House, Cedar House, Laurel House, and so on. These were small details, but crucial if you want to change a culture. Labeling and prison jargon were also tackled. We felt that the term "prisoner" was a most negative label, and we all agreed that this term would not be used and the prisoners would be referred to collectively as "the women" and individually by their names. This is a much more positive approach, and it is now well established at the center.

Above all, we decided that each person would be treated as an individual human being with a clear emphasis on supporting and encouraging each one to use their time in the Dóchas Center in a productive and positive way. We decided that a most important first step was for the staff to get to know the women individually. This would only happen if we all spent time listening to and hearing one another. Of all the developments and practices in the Dóchas Center, this has proven to be the most significant. We hear so many stories about loss, grief, abuse, rejection, poverty, and despair. "Mary" comes to mind. I know her well; she lost her mother at the age of thirteen, was homeless, pregnant, and involved with a violent partner by the age of fifteen. Shortly afterward she became addicted to drugs and alcohol. Today, at the age of thirty, she is still a regular resident here, and recently she told me that the only comfort, security, and acceptance she experiences in her life is while she is here at the Dóchas Center. Mary is typical of so many of the women that we meet here each day.

Most of the women in the Center are in ongoing pain. It may be physical, emotional, or psychological, but all too often it is a combination of all three. This is why we use the expression "healing" in our vision statement. We have worked very hard at creating a healing environment here. The secret is to build up trust between ourselves and the women. This takes time and effort, but as trust develops, the individual woman feels more secure and safe to talk about her real feelings. In the center we believe that until such time as the individual woman is confident that she can trust the system here, no real progress can be made.

As we get to know the women, we realize that often their wrongdoings pale in significance in comparison with the neglect they have suffered throughout their lives. Poverty is nearly always the main cause of their downfall and their suffering. For example, approximately twenty of the women in the Dóchas Center are homeless, more than fifty are chronic heroin addicts, and many suffer from serious psychiatric disorders. The prospects for many of these women after release are gloomy. What hope have they in life? During the recent festive season, one woman, who I have known for years and who was approved for release at Christmas, asked me privately if she could stay in the Dóchas Center for Christmas. At least she would have company and friends there, because last year she spent Christmas alone, hungry, and depressed in a bed-and-breakfast accommodation. I have met so many such cases during my working life, and it is nothing short of a miracle that they survive at all.

Our overriding philosophy in the Dóchas Center is that the women are not judged, condemned, or demonized. They are accepted as human beings with their strengths and weaknesses. Each person is treated with respect and compassion, and we try hard to give them hope for the future. So much depends on the staff, and in the Dóchas Center I am proud of their efforts and commitment. They really go out of their way to help and support the women. We have made great progress here in three short years, but it is a never-ending journey. There is always more to be done.

My own priority during a woman's stay here is that she is empowered to take more control over her own life. To help achieve this, the women are involved directly in all decisions that affect their lives. They really appreciate being consulted, and at a recent planning meeting to organize Christmas activities one of the women shared her joy with the group on how good she felt to be sitting at the conference table as a full participant.

Finally, I want to share this little story with you. When we were preparing for the official opening of the Dóchas Center, I asked a young woman—"Nicola"—to read out the vision statement during the official opening ceremony. A short time later she came to my office and asked me why I had chosen her to do it. When I told her that it was on the basis that she had worked hard in preparation for the opening and that she deserved this honor, she responded by saying, "This is the first time ever in my life that I have been selected for anything." My hope is that we will continue to empower such women in the future. It is the small things that often matter most in life.

❖ ❖ ❖ ❖ ❖ ❖ ❖ ❖

*When you cannot forgive, you are a prisoner of the
hurt done to you. If you are really disappointed in
someone and you become embittered, you become
incarcerated inside that feeling. Only the grace of
forgiveness can break the straight logic of hurt and
embitterment.*
—John O'Donohue

I will always remember my day at Mountjoy Prison in the Dóchas Center—a special place of hope. After spending time with the women inside the center, I felt like I had been given a priceless gift. I learned a great deal about the importance of believing in people's innate goodness, about not making snap judgments regarding those who are considered to be "unworthy criminals," about valuing and treating all people with kindness and respect.

As I left the women in the Dóchas Center, I heard the heavy metal door slide open that allowed me to leave the prison. As I listened to that sound, it occurred to me that just by accident of birth I was not staying behind as one of the prisoners. Because I had been born into a privileged class and culture, I will probably always have the freedom to step from one world into another—something the women and men in Mountjoy Prison don't have and may never have. As the door banged shut behind me, I vowed to join Governor Lonergan in his crusade to educate the world about the value of treating all people with dignity and respect—especially those who have been disadvantaged by the misfortunes of poverty, cruelty, and abuse.

We usually don't like to think about what it would be like to be "imprisoned." Yet it might be worthwhile to do that. Like the women in the Dóchas Center, many of us are locked in our own personal prisons. We don't want to be stereotyped or labeled or abused. We desperately want to be trusted and embraced in a place of hope. And we, too, yearn to be treated as though we are valuable people with great worth.

There are many things worth contemplating from this story, and it might be useful for us to take the time to do that right now.

Northern Ireland

INTRODUCTION

Violence is impractical because it is a descending spiral ending in destruction for all. It is immoral because it seeks to humiliate the opponent rather than win understanding; it seeks to annihilate rather than convert; it thrives on hatred rather than love. Violence ends by defeating itself.
—Dr. Martin Luther King, Jr.

The teachings and writings of Dr. Martin Luther King, Jr., are often quoted by John Hume, who is regarded internationally as the "architect of peace" in Northern Ireland. Somehow Dr. King's words have the potential to cut across cultural, religious, racial, and ethnic situations because they are filled with wisdom and deep insight for any situation of violence in any country in the world. They are particularly appropriate for the tragedies of violence that have taken place in Northern Ireland's history.

If you ask almost any person in the world about Northern Ireland, he or she will have an opinion and a judgment about what happened in the more than thirty years of what has been known as "the Troubles." To most outsiders, the dilemmas and issues of Northern Ireland just seem irreconcilable, divisive, bitter, and endlessly violent. Many people, however, do not know much about why things are so bad. They likely do not know about the history of the area, how it was partitioned by the Anglo-Irish Treaty of 1921, or that Northern Ireland is a part of Great Britain politically although attached to the island of Ireland. Nor will they know that the problems in Northern Ireland will not be easily resolved, partly because of what John Hume called the "systematic discrimination and official injustice aimed at the minority Catholic Nationalist population by the Protestant Unionists who continued to hold absolute political and economic power through a system of apartheid, gerrymandering, and vote-rigging."4

For those who are interested in having a better understanding of this complex situation, Hume's book *A New Ireland: Politics, Peace, and Reconciliation* is very helpful. Hume has written about the problems in

Northern Ireland and how they were provoked by a conflict between the struggles and dreams of ordinary people—900,000 Unionists and 600,000 Nationalists—rather than by religious conflicts. These two communities lived in fear and in competition with each other in one small corner of the island of Ireland. In 1968, at a civil rights march in Derry, things turned violent. That violence marked the beginning of the Troubles.

The more than thirty years of violence of the Troubles has caused enormous human loss. Perhaps the most tragic outcome has been the needless deaths of more than 3,600 men, women, and children in a country that has a population of only 1.6 million. In the United States, that would translate as the equivalent of approximately 350,000 people. Almost 91 percent of those who died were male, 53 percent were civilians with no affiliation to any security or paramilitary organization, and 74 percent were under the age of thirty-nine.

In addition to the violent deaths, nearly 25,000 people have been wounded or maimed. Thousands suffer from psychological stress that has been caused by tension and fear—a direct consequence of intimidation, security countermeasures, bombing, and murder. The living victims of the Troubles are people whose lives have been harmed by horrendous events, a lower standard of life, mental agony, and ongoing trauma. The overall impact of this has been devastating to Northern Ireland's society.

Certainly, the chapters in this section give witness to the long-term negative and devastating effects of violence and trauma. Not a single person who lived in Northern Ireland during this difficult period was able to escape without some kind of emotional, spiritual, or physical damage. Even though many people escaped death or injury, they were exposed to serious danger and threats of hostility and cruelty. Many of the people lived in areas where they experienced an enormous amount of tension and peril. Without a doubt, their social, physical, and emotional well-being has been inhibited and constrained. Many were wounded with the secondary effects of guilt, grief, depression, and paralyzing fear.

Yet in these chapters are stories of courageous and spirited people, who not only survived the Troubles, but who made a tremendous contribution to their communities. As you read their stories, I ask you to set aside your preconceived ideas, opinions, and judgments about Northern Ireland. I invite you to walk in the shoes of these people and to try to understand a little of what they have experienced. If we are able to open ourselves to fresh or different concepts and ideas about people whom we might have stereotyped or judged, we may be surprised to find that we will see our own problems and difficult situations more clearly or in a new light. And we may just open ourselves to new knowledge, wisdom, and healing possibilities for our own lives and for our own communities.

SURVIVORS OF TRAUMA:
YEARNING FOR WHOLENESS

As told by Brendan, Mary, David, Lillian, Marie, and Rosemary

. . . I realized that the first person I had to learn how to forgive was myself. At times I thought I might have brought these tragedies onto our family. I wondered if it was God's way of paying back my family for all the things that I blamed myself for doing. I was the hardest person to forgive. But after I did, it was easier to forgive others.
—Brendan

[The Survivors of Trauma Center] has served as a vessel to help me. . . . A few years ago I wouldn't have even spoken to you, I wouldn't have sat in the same room with you unless I knew you. Today I feel a lot better, and I'm able to . . . speak and listen and help other people as well as myself.
—Mary

Certainly [my brother's] death was a terrible thing,
but. . . . I'm grateful I'm able to channel some of the
lessons I've learned from . . . his death back into the
community. Like many people [at the center], I'm both
in my own healing process and in the process of
helping others. . . .
—*David*

On a very rainy Friday afternoon in the middle of rush hour in Belfast, I was scheduled to visit the Survivors of Trauma Center to learn about the self-help grass-roots organization that had been established in north Belfast in 1995. As I stood drenched on a street corner in the blustery wind waiting for a ride to the center, I watched my umbrella as it flipped inside out. It was then that the traffic came to a dead stop. I later learned that a large bomb had been found in a bread van. It seemed to illustrate that Northern Ireland's troubles, unlike the traffic, had not yet come to a complete halt.

Hours later I arrived at the Survivors Center, where a group of people was sitting in an old church that had been beautifully renovated. They were having tea as they waited patiently for me. Within a matter of minutes, these hospitable people had offered me food, tea, dry clothes, a warm welcome, and a willingness to share their stories with me. They openly embraced me into their center and into their lives as they told me the story of the Survivors of Trauma Center.

The organization originally developed because people were worried about the effects of years of horrendous violence and trauma on themselves, their children, and their children's children. Tired of waiting for the unfulfilled promise of help from others, they decided to respond to the deep losses, grief, anger, and despair that people in their community had experienced over the years. They took matters into their own hands, formed a community organization, and reached out to each other with understanding and compassion.

As we sat around a large table and I listened to their stories, filled with almost unbearable pain and suffering, there were moments when I felt my heart would break with sadness for them. But I also found my soul soaring with hope as this courageous community talked about how they were transforming themselves from "victims" to "survivors." Although this may be one of the most pain-filled chapters in the book, I encourage each one of us to take this journey with these brave people. We may find their story to be filled with hope.

❖ ❖ ❖ ❖ ❖ ❖ ❖ ❖

Brendan

After the cease-fires of 1984, people who lived in communities badly affected by the Troubles felt they could begin to speak about the problems of those years. However, there were very few facilities for them to come together in those communities. In Ardoyne, where I come from, many people were killed during the conflicts, but it rarely made the headlines. Everyone knows about big incidents like the Enniskillen and Omagh bombings. Although our community had the equivalent of three Omagh bombings, nobody spoke about it. People weren't killed all at the same time, so it was death by a million cuts—a slow and painful death that tore the community apart.

In 1984, representatives from the European Union (EU) started talking about a peace package for Northern Ireland, with possible support for peace and reconciliation programs for damaged communities and victims of the Troubles. At a meeting to learn how this money was to be spent, many people talked about who needed the resources. Someone said the universities should receive the money so people could be well educated and get good jobs. However, only about 1 percent of those who live in the peace line areas go on to third-level education. So if the money went there, 99 percent of the people from my area would have been excluded. A banker said the money should go to banks to kick-start the economy with small loans to businesses. Lots of people asked for the money. When I looked around, I saw that people from the communities most affected weren't there. I left the meeting feeling a wee bit despondent.

I went back to my community and started knocking on people's doors. I told them there were a lot of "sharks" out there that were going to eat up the resources and possibly victimize us again. Although this was money designated to help us, we were not going to be asked how it should be spent. They were going to spend it the way they wanted. A few weeks later, a meeting was called by one of the "sharks," who informed us that there were three counseling services within our community. But we knew there were no counseling facilities.

There was a lot of hurt, anger, and frustration at the meeting. People were emotionally charged, so we were asked to leave and come back with a solution. About sixty people went to a community center and talked about what to do. To be honest, nobody knew. This was new for all of us. As we sat around a table, someone said, "This is what happened to me." And then another person said, "And this is what happened to me." So we came with our own baggage and left with fifteen other people's baggage. That went on for months. Eventually we got a facilitator who helped us design a strategy and write a proposal, which was funded by the EU peace and reconciliation money. So that's how Survivors of Trauma got started.

Today people who come in for our services soon learn that they too have a role to play at the center. The people who staff the place are all victim-survivors who have moved up through the ranks. Marie Close, who runs the place, lost her husband. She started here at the bottom, and now she's the manager. That's progress.

Mary

My brother Brendan was very involved in setting up Survivors of Trauma. When I first came to the center, I wanted to help other people, but I completely forgot about me. From the beginning, I volunteered by knocking on people's doors and bringing them to the center. But I felt lost because I wasn't looking after myself or handling my own grief. One of Brendan's and my brothers was killed in 1975, and a sister in 1982. Then two of our nephews were killed soon after that. All I did was live with my bereavement, day in and day out.

When our brother was killed, his body was taken out of our house in a black bag and put into a van. Our mother was standing there sobbing and crying out to her son. It was an awful thing to see. To this day I see that black bag in my mind more than anything else. Now whenever I see a van go by, I remember that terrible night.

My neighbors have told me that I often walked right past them on the street without speaking to them. Looking back, I think I was like a zombie, because I didn't have any interest in anything. When I went out, I didn't see anybody, or I saw them, but they seemed very far away. Often I didn't want to speak to anyone, because I was afraid they'd start talking about what had happened. I was in another world, trapped in grief and trauma. I knew I had to get up and move on.

The thing that really helped open me up was seeing other people coming in here who were changing. Although I was telling people to use the center, I wasn't using it myself. I was still stuck in a rut. I knew I needed to look into my own trauma; I realized I couldn't start to get better until I began to heal myself. Finally, I decided to try some of the things at Survivors. I wanted to get some counseling and to further my education. I ended up taking a diploma course to become a reflexologist—I knew it would be beneficial for me, and I could use it to help others too. After I finished that, I started offering reflexology to the community.

This place has served as a vessel to help me move on. A few years ago I wouldn't have even spoken to you, I wouldn't have sat in the same room with you unless I knew you. Today I feel a lot better, and I'm able to sit and speak and listen and help other people as well as myself. I'm not saying I'm completely healed, but I'm in the process and am much better.

David

My brother, Brian, was murdered in 1988. I came to work for Survivors because they needed a therapist and I was trained in complementary therapies—Reiki, reflexology, aromatherapy, and massage. They have helped me a great deal on my own healing journey, and I'm also helping others by using these techniques.

Everyone in this place is a victim, so when new people come to Survivors, they don't need to go into any great depth about their past traumas. A few words can be spoken, but generally we understand what the other person is suffering because we too have been on that journey. Some people are in the early stages of healing; others are further down the road. I'm four years down the road. Our pain doesn't really go away, but we learn how to manage it better. Sometimes, even now, when I try to talk about my brother, I get a lump in my throat. For men it's difficult, because we're supposed to put up a façade, a macho image that we're strong. At least here we can be open and get a clearer insight into what we're going through.

Certainly Brian's death was a terrible thing, but it has taught me how to help people get respite from their pain. I'm grateful I'm able to channel some of the lessons I've learned from the trauma of his death back into the community. Like many people here, I'm both in my own healing process and in the process of helping others with theirs.

Brendan

People come here for many reasons: the place is beautiful, and they feel welcome; they want somebody to talk with who will let them tell their story; they are looking for someone warm and trusting, someone they can feel at home with. We try to create a space for people to take time out from the day-to-day chores of life and from their grief. This center is a place where they can spend some healing time for themselves and feel safe, comfortable, and unafraid.

Although the center was set up for people in north Belfast, we also get people from Armagh, Derry, and other places. They come for lots of different reasons. If they want a political or religious fix, they shouldn't come here, because we're not political or religious. However, if they want something practical or healing for themselves, they might find it here. We have an open-door policy, and our literature is sent out to all the communities around here, but about 95 percent of the people who come here are Catholics who live in Ardoyne. One woman rang us from Glenbrinn, which is at loggerheads with Ardoyne, and she said, "I have a twelve-year-old son, and I need somebody to talk to him, but I can't go near your place. Do you know somebody he could talk with?" We gave her a list of people.

About 350 people come here each week to take classes or have therapy. Some people just come to sit and have a cup of tea or talk with someone. That's all they want. Nobody tells people what they need. We don't have a monopoly on wisdom and good sense. People have to find themselves at their own pace, not ours. We try to allow them to be who they really are. We offer both day and night classes, so people who work are also accommodated. We have cultural and heritage classes, music classes, arts and crafts.

We also offer different educational classes. Recent reports from the Social Services Trust have indicated that the average reading age of those leaving school in north and west Belfast is that of an eight-year-old. Many people living around these areas can't read or write, and the kids don't take the transfer test from primary to secondary school, so they're judged as failures by the age of eleven. We offer tutoring for young people to take the transfer test and to help them pass it or at least get a better score. We also have a class called "Second Chance" where people can achieve three credits, which entitles them to attend a technical school.

Lillian

I started coming to Survivors about three years ago. I had friends who came here, and I also received leaflets about it. The first time I walked into the center there was a feeling of great warmth about the place that made me like going to it. I felt as if I could leave something outside, like I was away from everything. I felt an inner peace, as though somebody cared about me and welcomed me.

My brother was shot dead in 1991. I started coming to the center for reflexology treatments. They were wonderful, because they brought me out of myself a bit and gave me a good lift. During the first couple of years after a terrible trauma, people don't really realize that they're not really in touch with what's going on, that they're having awful dreams that keep coming back to haunt them. It takes a long time for people to begin to recover and heal. Sometimes it takes years to really feel better.

Brendan

The first time death rapped at the door for Mary and me was in 1975, when our younger brother was killed. Somebody came to our house and told our parents that their son was dead. As an eighteen-year-old, I didn't know what I was supposed to do. I wasn't in touch with my feelings, because they hadn't yet been formulated. Nothing could get through my sadness and grief. I kept wondering, "Why him?" He was the quietest and youngest of all of us. It wasn't the first funeral we had gone to, but it was the first one for our family. Many people in our community had gone up that road before. We had watched from a distance and pondered how it would feel to lose someone. When it came, it was a terrible blow. It was years later when we really got in touch with our feelings. For a year or two, the grief process didn't let anything else in.

People who have passed are constantly with you; their faces are in front of yours. Sometimes you can't even see past them. It's only when we are able to get in touch with all our feelings, think about other things, and let other people in that we start to move on. During the sixties, seventies, and eighties, there was no counseling or therapy; nothing was offered to anybody. People just closed their doors. That's how they dealt with their grief and trauma. And there was no money to bury our loved ones. The local community often had to raise money to help families.

It would have been easy for us to have hatred toward the people we thought were responsible for making such terrible things happen to us. But at the end of the day, I realized that the first person I had to learn how to forgive was myself. At times I thought I might have brought these tragedies onto our family. I wondered if it was God's way of paying back my family for all the things that I blamed myself for doing. I was the hardest person to forgive. But after I did, it was easier to forgive others.

A lot of us have had to swallow some very big pills, especially when we learned that people who had murdered our loved ones were being released from jail. For the sake of peace, we had to accept that. After the discussions regarding the Good Friday Agreement, we all agreed that for the betterment of society we needed to draw a line in the sand, not necessarily to forget, but to let other people and other concepts in and to move on. The bad days are starting to roll back a little now. Yet whenever we look at the empty chairs, we know this wasn't just a bad dream. For our own sanity we have to try to make sense out of things, but we also have to be willing to live and let live.

Many people's lives have been changed because of the center's work. A woman whose son had been murdered came here every day dressed in black. In our discussions she talked about her hatred for "every person on the other side of the road." She thought they were all involved in the murder of her son. After the Shankhill bombing, I went to a conference where a man whose wife had died at that bombing spoke. He was saying terrible things about the person who had set off the bomb. He was sure the mother and father of this "devil" were devils as well. At one point I told him I would be happy to introduce him to the parents, that they were probably some of the gentlest people he'd ever meet. The man talked about the guy being educationally subnormal and manipulated by others, I told him I agreed with him, but I asked him whose fault this was. I said, "If we live in a society that allows someone to fall through the net and not be educated, it's my fault and your fault as well, because we're both a part of that society." The woman in black was listening very intently to what this man said. At the end she took his hand and said, "Don't let hatred eat away at you. It's like a cancer that will eat from the inside out." I don't think she was saying that for him; she was saying it for herself.

A day later she came into the center and the black gear was off. Two weeks later she was gone, and we never saw her again. But I think she had changed by hearing about the pain and hurt of somebody from "the other side of the road" who had the same pain as she did. She was able to let go of something that she had been carrying around for a long time. These two people may have been miles apart, and their heads might never agree, but in her heart they were very close.

One of the first casualties of terrorism or war is truth. Although people hear half-truths and downright lies, they often accept them as truths. When people first come into the center, they're usually at the beginning of their healing process. They often have a story to tell, and some of that story might not be the truth. It might not be the truth they end up with, but it's their truth at the time and we accept that.

David

One of the most difficult things for me to live with is that my brother died on the street after he left my house. I was lying in my bed all night not knowing that he was already dead on the street. At a quarter past seven the next morning, I had a phone call from my mother screaming that my brother had been killed. I went into automatic pilot. I thought about how my mother and father were going to cope with this, how I had to be strong for them, how I would take control of the situation, how I would do my grieving quietly.

But I had to deal with my own guilt. When Brian left me that night, I couldn't protect him. I couldn't put my arms around him when he was lying on the street and dying. I thought I should have insisted that he take a taxi so it wouldn't have happened. Later I was told there were two boys on the street that night and one of them put his arms around my brother and said a prayer for him. The other fellow ran to ring for the ambulance. I still live with a lot of that, but I'm beginning to accept that there was nothing I could do about the situation. Brian was in control of his own life, and he wanted to go home that night.

I have a wife and kids, so when Brian died I couldn't forget about them. I had to focus my life on them and that helped me on my healing journey. Also, I have an inner belief that this is only part of a journey that continues on with another one, that Brian left this world to go to another one, that he's probably watching over me now as we're talking. Sometimes I get information from him in my dreams. They're like wee telephone connections to him. It may be my emotions taking over, but it feels like he's sent messages to me, that he's fine. I think that's why I haven't held on to the hatred for the killers who shot him.

I'm confident that Brian will always play a part in my life. I think of him as being in the big coffee shop up above, because whenever he came into our house the first thing he'd say was, "Put the coffee on." He's looking after our whole family, especially my mother and father and my younger brother. I'm sure he'll be at my daughter's wedding. I talk to him regularly, and that's one of the ways I've dealt with his death. I will always long to be with Brian, and I miss the friendship we had that I can never get back, but I'm definitely making progress on my healing journey.

Marie

I heard about Survivors of Trauma through my sister. She comes here because it helps her relax. She wanted me to come to the center because I haven't really talked with anyone about our father's death. He was murdered in 1991. My sister was with daddy when he was killed.

I understand what David said about how difficult it is to forgive ourselves. I feel something like that myself. I left my parents' house at about twenty past six that night. It was still bright outside. I can't forgive myself because I left the front door slightly open. Five minutes later friends came to tell me that my daddy had been murdered. To this day I think if only I hadn't left him, or if I had really closed the door that night, they might not have gone in and killed him. It's hard to get past those feelings. A couple of months ago, I had a dream about my dad. My whole family was together—my mammy, my daddy, all of us—just like we used to be. Then I woke up and realized it was just a dream, but it was wonderful.

This is my first time at Survivors, and I hope to come back and try some of the classes. Maybe they might help me a bit. This place seems good for people. When I walked into the center, I felt comfortable. Although I had never met most of the people, I felt like I knew some of their faces.

Rosemary

My husband was killed in 1979. I had been married for only four and a half months, and I was two months pregnant. I know many people find it difficult to understand how and why people can get involved in paramilitary groups. Here in Ardoyne, we went through a lot of bad things and my husband didn't think it was right. He was a good fellow, and he came from a very fine family. He believed in what he was doing. Unfortunately, he lost his life. I feel my grief deeply, but I think it must be worse for people who lost innocent family members, like the way David lost his brother. My husband knew what he was doing, that his life was in danger, so I have to accept it, although it doesn't make my grief any easier.

When I talk to people who didn't know my husband, I feel I have to justify things and make them think he was a good person. Then I feel guilty because I'm justifying who he was. I'm an only child, and my daughter is an only child. At the time of his death, I felt very isolated, because I had nobody to talk to who would understand. My mammy and daddy are older, and my friends have their own husbands and families, so I often feel very isolated and lonely. Sometimes I cry for my husband, because he's not here any more. He should have had a life and experienced the birth of his daughter. And then I cry for myself and for my daughter, because she's growing up and I realize what she's missed. Next year she'll be exactly the same age as her daddy was when he died.

My daughter wasn't yet born when my husband died, so she never knew him, but I have pictures of him everywhere—I have even superimposed photos of the two of them together. She's the absolute image of her daddy. Every now and then she sees him in her dreams. Maybe it's because we talk about him so much and I involve her in trying to see what he was like, or maybe he has revealed himself to her, too. In my dreams, I get letters from my husband. He's in the south, telling me he's been there for years. I'm angry with him because he didn't tell me that he had been taken away. Now he's coming back, and I'm upset because he's never even seen his daughter. Maybe I have these dreams because I never saw his body and so haven't really accepted that he died. One morning he left the house and I never saw him again. Maybe if I'd seen his body in the coffin, it would be easier. To this day, I see him as a living person.

Brendan

Rosemary's husband was a decent man who lived in our community and got caught up in some of the things that were going on then in Ardoyne. That could have been any one of us. Lots of young men did exactly the same thing. There are many roads in front of us, and each one of us chooses our own path.

Seeing the body of a loved one is a kind of verification of their death. I often think my brother is away, that I'll see him again someday. Perhaps we feel that way because we want so much to have the person back. It may be a way of coping. When we admit to ourselves that they'll never come back, it's very final and difficult.

I know a young woman whose mother was killed when she was only two or three weeks old. The family often sits around recalling stories about her mother, but she doesn't remember her mother, or any of the stories. In her dreams, she often sees someone walking away from her. Although she can't see her face or any features, she knows it's her mother. She can never catch up with her, so she continues to chase after her endlessly.

Here at Survivors, we try to help everyone who is trying to cope with their loss. It doesn't matter what the circumstances of the death were or how their loved one died. That's irrelevant. Rosemary's grief is as significant as David's or anyone else's around this table. Each person's grief is of equal importance.

Mary

Two years ago, when our sister's eldest daughter got married, her heart was breaking the whole day because she kept looking for her mammy. Even when she was up at the altar, I could see her looking among the guests. At the reception, her new husband stood up and made a toast to the two people who weren't there that day—his father and her mother, my sister. Just as he did that, there was a loud roar of thunder. I said, "Oh, my God, she's moving the furniture up there. She's letting us know that she can see us." We recorded the event on video, and when my niece watched it later, she said, "Yeah, that sure was mammy doing her thing."

Brendan

Our sister planned to visit us the week before she died, but something came up, so she changed her plans. It takes about two seconds to fire four shots from a rifle. In those two seconds, my sister had to be in a particular place at a particular time and the person doing the shooting had to be in a particular place at a particular time. The guy he was aiming for also had to be in that place at that time. All those things had to come together, and they did when my sister was there.

There have been a lot of tragedies in our family, and we have learned how important it is to focus our attention on positive things after something bad has happened. Ten weeks after our sister was killed, I was told that one of our nephews had been shot on the Crumlin Road. He was a very sweet and gentle young man. He had just walked into his sister's house, picked up her child and put him on his shoulders. Right then somebody walked in the door and shot him as he stood in the living room with his nephew on his shoulders. His sister, who was preparing dinner, thought the cooker had exploded. So when she turned around and saw a man firing a gun at her brother, she couldn't connect with the traumatic event that was happening. She kept thinking it was the cooker blowing up, not a man shooting her innocent brother with her two-year-old son on his shoulders.

After our nephew's death, we tried to remember the things he did that made us smile, like the time he reversed my car and drove it into a telegraph pole. Our big family has a great deal of love, which sees us through lots of heartache and pain. We always have a wake, and try to sit and laugh and cry together for the three days the person is lying there in the coffin. That's what keeps us together. The crying is the pain coming out of our bodies, but the laughter is healing our souls.

David

Sometimes I think it must be quite overwhelming for people who don't live here to hear all of our pain-filled stories. Because we've had the Troubles going on for more than thirty years, we've heard so many stories, and we have likely developed a thick skin. Whenever somebody dies tragically, empathy naturally goes out to the family. But in a way each one of us says to ourselves, "Thank God, it didn't happened to me and my family." Even though we share a certain amount of understanding about their pain, it's not until tragedy comes to our own door that we realize what other families have been suffering.

Brendan

We all know that we're going to die; we just don't know how or when. Here at Survivors we have learned that we can't experience deep joy without experiencing pain. Sometimes when the pain is so horrible for us, we are surprised to find that our joy can be tenfold—especially the joy of seeing other people getting well.

Since what happened on September 11, we've often thought about the people in New York City. Their loved ones were taken away from them so savagely that day. We feel a special connection with them. We hope we can exchange ideas and feelings with each other. Certainly, no one can ever give them back their loved ones. In the past we've always asked people to come and help us. Now we've started to turn the corner, and we may have something we can offer to help others. People in Northern Ireland have suffered so much over the years. We have gone through a process of healing without much help, and we have learned a lot. There may be a real connection between the people who have suffered so much since 9/11 and us. We believe the hearts of the people of Northern Ireland and the United States could definitely meet and bond with one another.

❖   ❖   ❖   ❖   ❖   ❖   ❖   ❖

We work on ourselves then in order to help others.
And we help others as a vehicle for working
on ourselves.

—*Ram Dass*

This story of grass-roots transformation can teach us so much about getting involved in our own healing process by jumping in and joining forces to take charge of changing terrible situations. These courageous people, living in areas of poverty that lack economic and educational opportunities, have suffered almost beyond belief from endless loss, trauma, and violence for far too many years. They were the so-called little people who were caught up in isolated incidents of shocking violence that made them slowly bleed to death through "a million cuts." Their situation was not on a grand scale and therefore did not catch the world's attention.

During the three decades of the Troubles, these people did not have adequate opportunities to voice their feelings or to be represented in the plans for reconciliation. Yet in the midst of unbelievably terrible situations, these extraordinary people were able to claim their role and responsibility within society, to find humor and positive aspects in their pain and anguish, and to help create a space for themselves where they could heal one another.

Like the Survivors of Trauma, we, too, can refuse to allow ourselves to be "victims." We, too, can transform ourselves into "survivors" by joining forces with others in our communities, trying to find some positive aspects within our difficult situations, and focusing our efforts on our healing process.

Perhaps one of the most important lessons to remember from this story is what Brendan has learned: we need to forgive ourselves in order to forgive others and to truly heal ourselves. That's not always easy to do. At times we may think that we are responsible for the tragedies in our communities or in our families. We may blame ourselves for things that have happened. Indeed, we may be the most difficult people to forgive. But once we do, the rest will be easier.

POLITICAL PRISONERS IN THE MAZE PRISON:

EMBRACING OUR MOTHERS' SONS

As told by Father John Friel

A sizable number of political ex-prisoners are . . .
making very serious and positive contributions within
the community at every level. That is impressive and
should be applauded. . . . The peace process has
brought people to see that political violence is not
where they want to be or to go.
                                    —Father John Friel

Mention the H-Block at the Maze and all kinds of images and memories come to mind: paramilitary prisoners, mass breakouts, riots, the "dirty protest," and the hunger strikes when eleven republican prisoners starved to death, including Bobby Sands, the twenty-seven-year-old Provisional IRA prisoner who won an election while in prison. The effects of those events echoed far beyond the walls of the prison and served as strong symbols of the years of political and paramilitary conflict in Northern Ireland.

The Maze began its life as a symptom of Northern Ireland's Troubles. It soon became a place of political protests and death. For more than a quarter of a century, the Maze housed up to seventeen hundred prisoners. They were considered to be some of the most dangerous men in Europe, those convicted for killings and bombings committed during the thirty years of violence. The Maze was a fundamental part of the Troubles and, in the end, was crucial to the Good Friday Agreement of 1998.

In 2000, despite misgivings from some politicians and victims, paramilitary-linked parties demanded the release of prisoners, because it was believed that they had been driven to violence by a condition of war. Following the agreement, the prisoners were released or transferred to other units. Today the Maze is closed.

In Belfast, I met Father John Friel, who had served as a chaplain and counselor inside the Maze. I was certain he would tell me stories about cold-blooded political prisoners and paramilitaries who casually killed people and did horrendous things. I expected to hear stereotypical descriptions of these terrible people. I was surprised when Father John told me stories about sensitive people who suffered from depression and sorrow, who worried about their families, who took care of each other inside their cells, who played musical instruments to lift their spirits. As Father John said, "There were no monsters in the prison. . . . There were people's brothers, husbands, and sons in that prison."

Somehow, even the community within the Maze served as a "healing" community.

❖ ❖ ❖ ❖ ❖ ❖ ❖ ❖

I was stationed in Scotland for six years, training people for youth ministry and working with young offenders in an establishment for underage offenders. After that, I was asked to set up a project for young people in the Ardoyne area, a Catholic enclave within north Belfast. Of all the districts in north Belfast, Ardoyne has had one of the highest percentages of killings related to the Troubles. So there is a lot of bereavement and loss and many absent fathers and brothers due to death, assassinations, or removal by the authorities for political activities and violence.

Soon after I started my work in Ardoyne, I was invited to celebrate Mass at weekends in Long Kesh, or the Maze, as it's officially known. I was also invited to do some part-time counseling with prisoners. I worked in the Maze from 1991 until it closed in 1998.

One of my most interesting experiences happened on my first day at the Maze. I met some prisoners who asked me who I was and where I was from. When I said I was from Derry, they told me there were some Derry men in the wing, men whom I had known when I was young. When we had last met, we were children playing in the streets of Derry. Now we were grown men whose paths had taken very different turns; I had returned home to Ireland as a prison chaplain, and they were incarcerated as republican paramilitary prisoners. To be honest, I sometimes wonder if I had stayed in Derry if I would have been in prison too. These men and their families were ordinary, decent human beings. Who knows? If I had not left and gone to the seminary, perhaps I too would have ended up in the Maze. There were many good people who ended up in prison for paramilitary activity.

The famous H-Block was built like an H; the staff lived in the middle part of the H, and the prisoners were in the rest of it. Generally, staff didn't interact very much with prisoners in the wings. Within the actual blocks, the prisoners had a great deal of freedom. It hadn't always been that way, but by the 1990s the prisoners had a fair bit of freedom, and teachers and other people came into those areas and gave classes. The authorities controlled the overall security and administration of the prison, but each block had its own structure and one of the prisoners was given the role as the commanding officer. They basically ran their own regime.

Initially my work was very much that of a young chaplain, doing religious services and working on compassionate parole issues for the prisoners. If a parent or close family member was sick, the prisoner could petition the Northern Ireland Office for home leave. Often chaplains were asked to support the application by speaking on behalf of the prisoner's family. In some cases, prisoners were released into my care or I was asked to accompany them on certain occasions. No one ever tried to escape from me.

One of the things that always struck me as I worked with the prisoners in the Maze was how republican prisoners had a strong moral code by which they lived. They lived in a community. Those who were struggling were supported. Prisoners encouraged each other to set educational goals. Many completed Open University programs, and some of them graduated with doctorates.

After a while, I began to notice that some of the prisoners' psychological needs were not being met. The prison authorities provided doctors and nurses and other resources; however, prisoners didn't talk about their lives. There was an unspoken rule that they didn't access official therapists or official people in the medical profession for fear that the security of the organization might be compromised or jeopardized. Anyone who was not part of their organization was seen as a potential risk to them. However, when individuals and leaders within the group approached me and asked to take referrals for therapy, I agreed to do that.

So, almost by default, other religious therapists and I began to work at meeting some of the psychological needs of the prisoners. I began working with Nano Cluskey, who is trained in teaching the Enneagram, a personality-type indicator. By using this tool, we tried to help prisoners appreciate their own personality type and to understand the differences in other people in less contentious ways. It helped the prisoners develop tolerance in their community lives and a more compassionate and realistic view of themselves. It also had additional benefits for them in how they related to their wives, their partners, and their children in a broader, more compassionate way.

Recently I came across a short evaluation that the prisoners wrote following the completion of an Enneagram course. It indicates how receptive they were to the insights they gained from the work and how meaningful it had been for them. They wrote:

> The overall and constant attendance of the group was the best indicator of just how well the Enneagram was received by us. The group was evidently committed to undertaking the journey and making the most of the experience. While some had difficulty in accepting the feedback they received from others

and others were initially skeptical of the process and the motivation for it, all who participated benefited from the experience.

Deeper and valuable insights were gained into ourselves and others as we proceeded on this challenging journey of self-discovery. For some the experience helped to reinforce their experience of themselves. It enabled them to make sense of who they are and to identify the motivating traits that often underpin their lives. We learned how our core motivation sometimes enhanced, and at other times inhibited, our relationship with self and others.

People were encouraged to open-up; this in turn built up people's confidence and encouraged development of the group. To confront one's self is difficult, but the facilitating skills and patience of Nano and John ensured that the experience was a positive, interesting, and enlightening one.

As the course progressed, almost all the group, with the exception of the two young people who may have been just too young to fully benefit from the experience, discovered their personality type. All things considered, the Enneagram was a valuable experience and one that any of us who participated are unlikely to forget.

Thank you for the experience.

H3 C/D wings, Long Kesh

A prison sentence does not only affect the prisoner; his or her family will also "do time." Children are denied a parent's attention, so they "do time" at a period in their life when their parent's presence and influence are very crucial. That's an enormous issue for families. Sometimes prisoners' families gathered together to bond and support each other. Within the community, families learned to adapt to their situation and they came together in support groups. In Belfast and Derry alone, ten organizations were created to support prisoners' families. It is often said that Irish generosity extends not just to visitors who come to see our country but to people in need within the community, such as the families of prisoners. When families needed practical assistance, like traveling to prison for visits, these support groups organized transport. It was a compassionate feature of local communities, which occurred consistently through the roughest times. There were a lot of people who helped contribute to the resilience of people, and ultimately to the healing of people, by bolstering them and providing them with little acts of kindness.

I was very moved by some of the healing and generosity that took place inside the prison. A prisoner would often stay in the same cell as another prisoner who couldn't sleep or was depressed. Sometimes prisoners took turns sitting up with someone who was suicidal. There was a deep compassion within these men, who are often stereotypically viewed from the outside as being hard and violent. I marveled at the ability of these people to reach out to each other. I developed much respect for the prisoners when I witnessed this.

One of the drawbacks of doing therapy in a prison setting is that eventually everyone knows if a prisoner is being treated on a regular basis. There's not a lot of privacy there. Prisoners who came to me might feel that they were being spotlighted as having mental health problems. That was a serious drawback. Therefore, not everyone who needed help came forward. There were a number of people who did not come to me for therapy while they were in prison, but did so as soon as they got out. They didn't want to risk the exposure while they were inside. It's a reminder that people need confidentiality and to feel safe—especially in prison.

Some political prisoners worked very hard at maintaining strong relationships with their families while they were in prison. Their wives and children came regularly to visit them. But for many prisoners, being released was very difficult. They had to go back to a completely different life and setting outside prison and to a family they had not lived with for a long time. Suddenly they were back in the family, thinking of themselves in the traditional role, but the traditional family of father, mother, and children no longer existed. They very much wanted to fit in, to take their place within the traditional family setting, but the family had compensated and adapted to their long absence. The mother had taken on the role of father and mother, or one of the siblings had become father. Of course, that caused a lot of marital and family issues.

If prisoners had a reasonably fulfilling job fairly quickly after release, they generally adapted quite well. Sometimes family members and contacts helped them get a job before they left prison. Many ex-prisoners drove taxis when they first got out; others went into mainstream and neighborhood community work; some worked as volunteers and then got jobs from that; others went into counseling. Being able to get a meaningful job that gave them a reasonable salary and that was worth getting up for in the morning significantly contributed to their adjustment to the outside world.

There are a significant number of ex-prisoners who have had a hard time adjusting. Coming out of prison is like the swing of a pendulum. While they were in prison, there was a certain status that went with that: they were political prisoners. They were not just criminals. When they first came out, the community tended to treat them very well and held them up as an example or as someone to admire. They got a lot of attention, but that type of attention could not be sustained. It lasted for a while. But then suddenly it disappeared—almost overnight. Sometimes people on the outside made promises to the prisoners when they first came out. Many of those promises were well meaning but not really very realistic. Often prisoners felt a sense of rejection. Sometimes they felt isolated and discarded by the community they had risked life and limb for.

Some ex-prisoners were overwhelmed by the challenges they faced adjusting to life outside. This led to problems such as alcoholism, drug addiction, intimacy problems, domestic violence, depression, anxiety, and even feelings of suicide. A lot of it has to do with personal isolation.

Another problem for political prisoners is that of paranoia. When they were engaged in paramilitary activity, paranoia helped keep them safe from capture. It was a heightened state of alert to the fact that they were in danger and that people were out to capture them or kill them. Back then paranoia served a real purpose in their lives. Unfortunately, some ex-prisoners continue to have symptoms of paranoia. This suspiciousness and fear is no longer appropriate, because the danger has been primarily removed. This intrusive condition can disturb and disrupt their attempts to reengage in society.

If prisoners' families and communities were supportive and adaptable, there was a good possibility that things would fall into place for them. There are a sizable number of political ex-prisoners who are making very serious and positive contributions within the community at every level. That is impressive and should be applauded. Many of these prisoners had consciences and real commitments to their local neighborhoods as well as to "their side." In the time of peace, it manifests itself in community work.

I believe the peace process has brought people to see that political violence is not where they want to be or to go. It's been a few years now since the political prisoners have begun to settle back into their communities. The majority seem to have moved into healthy relationships and roles within their communities. I'm struck by the number of ex-prisoners who are now community leaders. Prisoners put a big emphasis on political education and on community politics when they were incarcerated. They made a real effort to try and understand the meaningfulness of their being in prison. This actually served them well on their release.

What really struck me over the years of working with the prisoners was their ability to be in a difficult place in a difficult situation and to make the best of it. On Friday nights in the H-block, there was a kind of céilí, where prisoners with musical instruments came together to play. I joined in on occasion. It was a bit of a human moment, and I think a lot of healing went on in such ordinary and simple ways. It didn't have the word "healing" attached to it, but giving the prisoners a bit of hope even when the situation looked hopeless had such a profound effect on them.

When I first went into the Maze, I had a stereotypical view of prisoners. But I discovered every different personality that you could imagine, the whole range of individuals. But there were no monsters in the prison. I think that was my conclusion and my overriding lesson from the whole experience. There were people's brothers, husbands, and sons in that prison.

Certainly, there are lessons to be learned from the political prisoners on both sides in Northern Ireland. In many ways the men and women who end up in prison are motivated by the same feelings of loyalty and patriotic vision, albeit to different causes. It's sad when we realize that both sides look the same and sound the same. There are very few differences between them. One set of young people gets equally as passionate about the issues of their tribe as the other does, and young people on both sides are willing to risk life and limb in the same way.

There are so many parallels where we think similarly, but we haven't yet chosen to be in each other's company long enough to trust each other, or to hear each other's perspective, or to feel what it's like from each other's position. Small groups are doing it, but we have a fair distance to go.

The political prisoners and the people of Northern Ireland are beginning to emerge from the pain and suffering of this period. Now we need to learn how to use the freedom even within our own communities to be able to analyze what we have experienced and learned. Maybe one of the most important lessons that we've learned is that Protestant pain is the same as Catholic pain. Protestant prisoners' wives and children have the same loss as Catholic prisoners' wives and children. One side's pain is not more significant or more meaningful than the other side's pain. Hopefully, this is what we are learning at this moment in our history.

❖ ❖ ❖ ❖ ❖ ❖ ❖ ❖

We all have to have the moral courage to seize this opportunity. No instant package will wipe away the damage done over the centuries. The healing process must begin. The old prejudices and hatreds progressively will dissolve.

—*John Hume*

Somehow a story like this has the power to wipe away some of the stereotypical ideas and biases we have about people—especially those who we think are not as good as we are, such as the prisoners who have served in paramilitary groups. Just thinking about a paramilitary doing an Enneagram personality test so that he can understand how he might better interact with his family can blow away some of our judgmental thoughts and can touch us deeply. It can also make us pause for a moment to think about how and why people do what they do. Father John pointed out that the prisoners whom he had known when they were all children playing in the streets of Derry were ordinary, decent human beings, as were their parents. But because of luck or fate, their paths had taken different turns and Father John was not in the Maze.

As we leave this story, we should remember that every person is some mother's child, no matter what they have done or who they are. And if Father John is right about Protestant pain being the same as Catholic pain, then Jewish pain, Muslim pain, Christian pain, and Hindu pain are the same too. None is more significant or more meaningful than any other is.

Maybe the lesson learned here is not to make judgments about people, to stop throwing rocks when we live in glass houses. We certainly have some fine role models who looked deep inside people and saw beyond the surface and who treated all people with kindness no matter who they were, Their names were Mahatma Gandhi, Dr. Martin Luther King, Jr., Archbishop Desmond Tutu, Buddha, Jesus. "Judge not that you be not judged"—yes, that sounds like a good principle for all of us to follow.

The Corrymeela Community:
Welcoming to All

As told by Mary Catney, Trevor Williams, and Billy Kane

An inclusive community is a community that is not divided against other people but is welcoming to all. It's a very important ingredient of a healing community.
—Trevor Williams

People have said to me, "It's not normal at Corrymeela." And my answer is that what happens at Corrymeela is normal. To live in segregated communities and housing and to hate each other because of our differences is not normal.
—Billy Kane

Why can't we just be together as one people in the North of Ireland? We don't need to sacrifice our different beliefs or our unique expressions of faith. . . .
—Mary Catney

The Corrymeela Community has been a shining light of healing, forgiveness, and reconciliation in Northern Ireland for more than thirty-seven years. A sign near the entrance to the residential center in Ballycastle boldly announces that "Corrymeela is people of all ages and Christian traditions who individually and together are committed to the healing of social, religious, and political divisions in Northern Ireland and throughout the world."

Corrymeela was founded by Ray Davey, a World War II chaplain and prisoner of war, who experienced firsthand the effects of "man's inhumanity to man." In the prison camps he realized that close up the enemy is also a victim of hatred and war and a part of tortured humanity. In 1965, Davey and a small group of dedicated people decided to help world peace by setting their own house in order. So they opened Corrymeela. They understood that religious affiliations, cultural commitments, and political perspectives had all added to the hostility and divisions in the past, so their first major activity was a joint Protestant and Roman Catholic conference—a unique event at the time.

When the political situation began to deteriorate in 1968 and fierce fighting broke out, Corrymeela offered alternatives to violence and encouraged cooperation that focused on justice, peace, and forgiveness. Both Catholic and Protestant families torn apart by violence have found respite at Corrymeela. Many neighboring towns followed Corrymeela's lead and opened their school kitchens and gymnasiums to care for children who were orphaned or at risk.

On a lovely sunny day, I sat with members of the Corrymeela Community and listened to them tell the stories of their lives, of their work, and of their hopes and dreams. I felt honored to be sitting with a community that had been such an important part of peacemaking in Northern Ireland.

❖ ❖ ❖ ❖ ❖ ❖ ❖ ❖

Mary Catney

I'm from Andersonstown in west Belfast. I was eleven years old when the Troubles first started in 1969. It's difficult to talk about that time. As a child I observed violence that grew from nowhere and erupted from nowhere. One day I saw on television that there was a civil rights march in Derry and things were happening all over Belfast. Before I knew it, there were concerns in the community where I lived.

In our street there were Protestant and Catholic neighbors. To be honest, I never really knew the difference between a Protestant and a Catholic. I thought everyone was of the same faith. We got up every morning and went to Mass at 6:30 or 7:30 before we went to school or to do our day's work. Our next-door neighbors were Protestants on either side of us, but we didn't know that until the Troubles broke out. Then there was chaos and sheer violence.

The policemen were supposed to be protecting us. I remember standing at the corner of the street and thinking, "If these are our police who are supposed to be protecting us, what's going to happen if they don't protect us? Or if they're not really interested in protecting us?" Within a few months, the British Army had been brought in to protect Catholics. At first it was terrifying, but then it was a great relief, thinking that we were safe because the British Army was on our streets and we were going to be protected. Everyone was making tea and coffee for them and giving them cigarettes. After all, they were just young men doing a job.

But within a space of four or five weeks, it became a real war situation and the tanks and guns began coming out bigtime. Initially we thought the army was there to protect us, and suddenly it seemed they were there to crucify us. As a child I thought, "If I live through this, I certainly will make sure that my children will never experience or be exposed to the kinds of violence that I witnessed on these streets." There were attacks on Catholic homes from the Protestant communities. The vast majority of homes destroyed were Catholic, but there were Protestant homes burned as well.

My dad had sisters who lived in Ballymurphy, so we moved there because we thought it was a safe place. Many other families did the same thing. In one house there might be as many as four or five families, each with five or six people. One day eight or ten people were shot dead in the avenue. We weren't allowed out of the area because of the constant violence and shooting going on and we were really afraid. It seemed we had moved from a bad situation to a worse one. Eventually we went back to our old neighborhood of Clonard. People were using their furniture to block both ends of the streets, but then the army came and brought in huge barbed-wire barricades, tanks, and guns.

Shortly after that there were lots of bombs and horrific violence spreading right down to the bottom of the Falls Road. So much aggression was directed against people who really didn't have any way to defend themselves—no guns or bombs, just their hands and their furniture. Then we moved to the outskirts of Belfast, to Twinbrook, a Protestant/Catholic estate that was designed strategically to stand trial against conflict and sectarianism. It was beautifully laid out. Many of the Protestant families moved out because there was such a big influx of families moving in from the Catholic areas that had been burned out. Today a few Protestant and mixed-marriage families are still living there.

As I was growing up in Twinbrook, Billy Kane was a youth worker at Corrymeela. I was attending the local Catholic youth club when Sister Evelyn and Billy did a training course there. One weekend I went with them to Corrymeela in Ballycastle, where there were young people and youth workers from both sides. The youth workers seemed to get on well with each other. So we looked at each other and said, "If they can get on, surely we can too." They led us in a program of looking at our families, our family trees, our histories, our religions, and our faith. Then we looked at our personalities and our relationships with one another in the group. It was a tough experience, because we'd never been put in such a position before. I had never been asked questions like why I believed in the Virgin Mary, why I prayed to her, why we had holy water in our chapel. It felt like my faith was being challenged. I was a bit miffed by what I thought were these rather ignorant Protestant people who didn't know me.

Then I started to ask questions about them. Why were they running such a regime here? Why weren't Catholics entitled to fairness, justice, and equality? We came together for about six to eight weekends over eighteen months; each weekend we looked at a different topic and subject from history to politics to our relationship with each other. I was sixteen or seventeen at the time, and it was a real turning point for me. If I hadn't had the opportunity to question, to be challenged, to be questioned about the issues around me and my upbringing, then I think I wouldn't be here today. Watching my own community, my family, my neighbors growing up in a vacuum, there seemed to be no hope.

The only thing that got people's attention was violence; that's when people listened.

In the early days, people in the Catholic Church saw Corrymeela as a very affluent, Protestant, middle-class community that was trying to convert us. There were people at the church who really didn't want us to mix with those people. However, Sister Evelyn continued to encourage me to become involved in the Corrymeela community.

When I was eighteen, I left school with no qualifications. I was the second eldest of eleven children, and our priority was about safety—not about being in school. During the Troubles, education was not a big issue for any of my family. Access to quality education was really not available unless you had resources and money. I went to work part-time, and I also did some volunteer work. Meanwhile, in our community we were blockaded and sealed off every day, every week, every month. Corrymeela was a place where I felt safe and I could say what I wanted to say without feeling that I was going to get shot dead or blown up. Through my exposure there, I had opportunities to explore some of my own experiences.

Then Billy started encouraging me to get involved in other youth organizations like the Northern Ireland Association Youth Club and the Nationalist Association Youth Club in England. I went to England with young people from many different backgrounds. Meeting English people was a whole different dimension, because they saw Protestants and Catholics as Irish people, not as British people. That was a new thing for me. I was also exposed to Scottish and Welsh people, black and Indian people, lesbians and gay men, religious people and atheists. These people were living in a totally different world from me. It made me wonder where I was living because I was constantly kept in a ghetto, physically, mentally, and emotionally.

Not long after that, I met Ray Davey. After Ray sat and listened to me tell my story, he told me his, about how he wanted to create a place for people to have a sense of belonging without sacrificing their own identity or their faith, where they would be enriched. He and Billy Kane gave people like me opportunities to express ourselves in a way that we never would have had anywhere else. Ray told me it would be lovely if I became a member of the community, but I felt I didn't really have anything to offer—a job or money or special skills. And I was from west

Belfast, where things weren't very good. Ray told me, "It's not about those things; it's about the love you have to give in your work here."

I decided to join Corrymeela because if I didn't, I was probably going to be dead in a couple of years anyway. I worried a bit that it was a predominantly middle-class Protestant community. Yet the essence of the community was about Christianity in practice. It demonstrated the ethos of Christianity that I had been brought up with in my home. It was really God's law being implemented and practiced. Corrymeela's main emphasis is not on religion; it's about the challenging work on justice and access to equality of opportunity. It's about our Christian faith that welcomes other faiths to experience our way of life.

In my neighborhood, we were asked to take sides and we were caught in the backing of sectarianism in schools, institutions, and the environment in which we lived. If we are to have healing, it has to come from the Protestant and Catholic churches acknowledging that true Christianity is about putting aside their differences and doing what Billy and Ray did for me: putting Christ's teachings into practice, accepting me for who I was, and allowing me to grow where I was. The Catholic Church claims to be Christian, and the Protestant churches claim to be Christian. So we're all Christians, and if we do what Christ told us to do, what's the big problem? Why can't we just be together as one people in the North of Ireland? We don't need to sacrifice our different beliefs or our unique expressions of faith, but we have to walk hand in hand together and stand firm for the betterment of all the people on this small island.

Trevor Williams

Corrymeela exists as a healing community created out of a need to learn what it means to follow in the steps of the Christ in Northern Ireland during these times. We've been working here since 1965. Since the beginning, our vision was to do something about the violence in Northern Ireland. We've been inspired by visits to the Taizé community in France, the Iona community in Scotland, and the Agape community in northern Italy. All were places of reconciliation in different ways and had a powerful influence as witnesses to peace and reconciliation. They demonstrated a new way of being church that had something dynamic and prophetic to say to the world. After visiting those places, we knew we needed something like that in Northern Ireland. We found our center in Ballycastle, and we were able to raise enough money to buy it.

Our community was formed by working with connections people had made in social service projects, youth clubs, and other organizations. We often brought people we knew to Ballycastle on the weekends. Starting in a very informal way, we developed and shaped a program as we began to understand what we were about and what we needed to do. We started our work in 1965, and the Troubles broke out in 1968, 1969. There were huge dislocations of people who were intimidated out of mixed areas, so in time housing estates became either Protestant or Catholic. We were involved in helping people find temporary accommodations. Gradually our work evolved from family work to youth work into schoolwork, church-related work, and community work.

At the center of our work are the Corrymeela community and its members. What's really important is that in a country divided by politics and religion we are a community of diversity, of Catholics and Protestants who consciously come together across political and religious divides. We walk together and find what it means to follow in the footsteps of the Christ. We live in a contested society where there's no simple answer as to who we are. Each fragmented part has a different answer along with different aspirations as to where we should go as a community. Two things tend to happen: there's underlying fear of the other community, and a large part of one's identity tends to be against the other community. In other words, I know who I am because I'm opposed to what you stand for. That happens in politics, but also in religion. Personally speaking, the only way I can discover what it means to be a Protestant Christian in Northern Ireland is to do that in the company of Catholics. Together we can challenge one another's assumptions.

When two communities are divided against each other, each one knows "the truth." But usually the two truths are in conflict with each other. And the truth as we hold it within our communities, what we take as "normal," is what we think everyone else should know. If it's "normal," we don't ask questions or challenge it. That's why we need Catholics, because all the things we think are normal as Protestants are not necessarily normal to them. They are only Protestant perspectives, but we're not even aware of that because they seem so natural and comfortable to us. Therefore, we need other people to tell us this isn't the only way, and we have to hear the other half of the story to accompany us on our journey.

When Jesus talked about loving our enemies, he didn't say it would get us out of riots and troubles. Rather, we were to hear the enemies' viewpoint. In that way we might learn something important about ourselves. Perhaps we need our enemies for our personal growth, and we may need to be in a relationship with them.

In the Northern Ireland situation we might be too polite to say that Catholics are the enemies of Protestants and Protestants are the enemies of Catholics. Unfortunately, our fears put us into a feeling of defensiveness and hostility toward the other tradition. I've come to believe that we desperately need interaction with those whom we fear to enable us to know how we might change and how we might grow.

An inclusive community is a community that is not divided against other people but is welcoming to all. It's a very important ingredient of a healing community. In healing and inclusive communities, we can't just say we're open to everybody. We have to strive to have permeable boundaries and welcome diversity and change. Most communities are like-minded, and there is something in common which draws the people together. But there should be an equal effort to encourage difference and variety. We have learned that the more we embrace diversity, the richer we become. So we try to create a safe place where there is respect for listening and honoring of differences.

In a divided and contested society, there are very few safe spaces around where people can actually feel it's okay for them to be who they are, to think what they think and to say what they believe. Through our experiences, we realize just how important it is that people have opportunities to find such a space. And we've come to appreciate and understand the power of sharing stories as a way of opening up a deep human relationship with someone, even though the other person may be totally different.

The experiences of Ray Davey's life as a chaplain in a prisoner - of-war camp in Italy validate the power of sharing stories. Some of the soldiers took to their beds due to depression, not because the German guards were so terrible—they were a mixture of people just like the rest of us, some were great and some had to be avoided—it was the endless routine and boredom of everyday life in a prisoner-of-war camp for months and months that caused the men to be depressed. Ray and other chaplains started getting people together in the evenings just to meet. They began by telling jokes, but after a couple of meetings they ran out of jokes. Even those who made up jokes on the spur of the moment got tired of doing that. So people began to talk about what really mattered to them. They talked about their childhood, about the people who were important to them, incidents that had happened, their home and who was there, who they really missed. These people were quite transformed by hearing each other talk this way, by hearing one another's story. They learned not only that they were friends but that they became a community through the sharing of their stories.

A community is an extension of people who hold and share a story or set of stories in common. That's certainly true of faith communities. I believe that's what happened in the prisoner-of-war camp. People found new meaning and a new importance in their lives. They started a bed-watch patrol to help people who were taking to their beds and refusing to eat because of their depression. They saved people from despair.

Our experiences in Corrymeela are very similar. We are often asked how we bring people together who have such huge differences—social, educational, religious, and political. We try to provide people with the gift of a safe and secure place where they can feel protected and can make contact with each other in an open and honest way. Then it's okay for them to be who they are, to say who they really are, and it's relatively easy to develop new relationships and connections.

We ask people not to speak about what they think or what their views are about other people. They are simply to tell their own story: "This is what happened to me, and this is how it felt." Our experience is that even between people of very different views a connection can be made. People may not agree on the final outcome of the many contentious issues in Northern Ireland, but they can make a connection with someone who has a totally different view. We don't need to learn how to solve all our problems; rather, we need to learn how to live with differences, with various opinions, with people who don't agree with us or who may never agree with us. To feel safe in that kind of company is what Corrymeela is about. With all the pain and messiness of our lives, it's about trying to create a refuge, a shelter, a place of safety for all people.

Billy Kane

I grew up in Greencastle in north Belfast, one of the problem areas where both Protestants and Catholics lived. I was very involved in the Methodist Church. In fact it was my whole life for a long time, and I was somewhat sheltered by it. Although I had a Catholic friend, we never talked about politics or religion. When election time came, I was curious why his family didn't support the Unionists. It felt like their vote was against us, but we just left it there.

Then I went through a rebellious stage, when I disappeared from the church and went dancing and did all sorts of things people do at eighteen or nineteen. I had a whole new set of friends. Eventually, I returned to the church and started a youth club with some other people. I got a job running a youth club in the east of the city. I started meeting youth workers from the other side of town and learned that they had the same problems as me. Kids were involved with paramilitaries and were getting put in jail.

One day a guy told me about a job with Corrymeela that would suit me down to the ground. So I met with Ray Davey, the leader, and was hired. The job description had two pages—it looked like a big job. I was based in Belfast but was responsible for the youth groups that went to the Corrymeela Center in Ballycastle. When I came in, I created a bit of a monster, because I brought along my youth program with lots of activities and about six thousand young people a year. The kids mostly came from working-class backgrounds, and I wanted them to be involved in programs that would keep them from going to jail. To a certain extent the youth groups nearly pushed all the middle-class young people out of Corrymeela, but I thought they would be all right, because they had the qualifications, went to university, got good jobs, and wouldn't have a lot of problems. The kids I worked with went to jail or got killed, and they definitely needed help.

We started something called the "resource group." The idea behind these groups was that people were to look at the things that affected them as they grew up: their family, relationships, education, sexuality, politics, history, faith. The groups brought together many different types of young people: male, female, Protestant, Catholic, people from the North and the Republic, rural, city, unemployed, employed, students. The more mixed the group, the more the young people liked it, and the more they expanded their horizons. By the end of six months they had a better understanding of who they were and who others were, and they were better able to face up to whatever they might meet in life.

Most of the young people weren't very interested in religion and politics. To them the Troubles started before they were born: they didn't know how it started: they didn't really care why it started; they just wanted out of it. Many didn't feel that they were part of it. It was something that happened before them, and they had to live with it. Regarding religion, they knew the Protestant/Catholic stuff, and they knew all the bad things about each other, but they didn't really know much about themselves. So whenever we talked about the two views of Christianity, in Protestantism and Catholicism, we tried to put forward the viewpoint that they are two ways of expressing one religion.

I've always had a strong faith, almost a simple belief. At Corrymeela I felt that there was a deep spiritual dimension to the place that always worked in spite of the people. Things happened that couldn't be explained. I don't believe you can help people; when you try to do that, you actually make them worse. People can only help themselves. My work ethos at Corrymeela was to challenge people or give them opportunities that they could build on. Sometimes I think I was bit of a fraud as a youth worker because I didn't do much. I tried to provide them with new experiences that they wouldn't have had. And I believed in them even when they didn't believe in themselves. Maybe that's what we have to do. If we trust people, it will come back to us. A substantial number of young people I worked with went on to full-time education and are now professional workers. In fact one of them is now a Corrymeela youth worker.

Recently, one of the kids who came to the program who is now an adult said to me, "You took us to London and let us wander about. You trusted us." And I replied, "Well, you never let me down." I've gotten such a buzz out of watching these young people develop. When I think back over my life, there were certain adults who trusted in me or listened to me, which changed the direction of my life.

Although I grew up in the Methodist Church and was impressed by the work of the church, I don't believe the "big miracle thing" is about everybody being the same. I think it's about everybody being different. I bring what I know as a Methodist, Mary brings what she knows as a Catholic, we share with each other, and that's where we get our strength. Maybe together we can grow into being some sort of world church, which would be more healing for everyone.

We have a song that one of our members wrote called "The Pollen of Peace." The chorus has a line: "Let us spread the pollen of peace throughout our land." People used to say to me, "Corrymeela's an ostrich farm. You people have your heads buried in the sand. You're not facing reality. It's a waste of time what you're doing, because people come back and they're just the same." But I don't believe that. People have said to me, "It's not normal at Corrymeela." And my answer is that what happens at Corrymeela is normal. To live in segregated communities and housing and to hate each other because of our differences is not normal.

Mary Catney

Ray's story about his experience in the prisoner-of-war camp is very helpful. There are enemies, and there are friends, but all people, including our enemies, can become strong friends through sharing their humanity. Love is really precious, especially love that is without condition, that is accepting of you as you are, that is understanding of where you're at and where you're coming from, and that is not wanting you to be somewhere else. We need that kind of love. It's the biggest gift we can ever give to each other.

❖ ❖ ❖ ❖ ❖ ❖ ❖ ❖

Don't waste any time dividing the world into good
guys and bad guys. Hold them both together in your

own soul—where they are anyway—and you will
have held together the whole world.
—Richard Rohr

As I listened to the Corrymeela Community members talk, I felt a sense of pride in their accomplishments over the years. These good people have been around in Northern Ireland for a long time, even before the Troubles. And they have a track record that proves that being a community of diversity is truly the way to go. So many groups of people have passed through their doors who have been touched by their hospitality, their openness to differences and variety. All people who go to Corrymeela are allowed and encouraged to be just who they are, and it is believed that they have something to offer that is uniquely theirs.

Corrymeela's philosophy and practice of welcoming all and of opening doors to friends and enemies is well known throughout the country and across the globe. What sets this community apart is their willingness not only to open their doors to their enemies, but to hear and be open to their enemies' viewpoints as well. If we want to meet this challenge, we need to open the doors of our hearts, which may have been closed to others' viewpoints. And that's strong stuff.

As individuals, or as groups, it would be good if we could remember what Trevor said about two groups or communities that are divided against each other. Each one thinks they have the "truth" or the "answer," even though the two "truths" or "answers" are in conflict. As communities, we need people who have opposite viewpoints from us, who don't believe what we believe, because they can challenge us about what we think is normal. Then we can listen to the other half of the story, so that it too will accompany us on our journey.

RESTORATION MINISTRIES:
INTERLOCKING OUR JOURNEYS

As told by the Reverend Ruth Patterson

Looking back, there's been so much heartache, trauma,
and trouble for people, but not unlike the experiences
of 9/11 there have also been many good things. . . .
Many people who were closed . . . have opened up.
There's been the discovery of new horizons, and there's
been so many named and unnamed acts of generosity,
forgiveness, and bigness of spirit.
—the Reverend Ruth Patterson

It seems very fitting to end this section on Northern Ireland with a story of a community that believes in reconciliation and restoration and approaches it with great courage and hope. During a recent visit to Belfast, I had the opportunity to meet with the Reverend Ruth Patterson, the Director of Restoration Ministries, a very special healing community.

On a lovely sunny day, Ruth and I visited together in the Restoration Ministries' retreat center. As we sat in a cozy sitting room overlooking a beautiful garden filled with enormous, colorful dahlias, we reflected on the many lessons we have learned from the devastating years of the Troubles in Northern Ireland and from the tragedy of 9/11 in the United

States. In her gentle but prophetic voice, Ruth talked about the options and choices that lie ahead for communities and countries, and the many possibilities that could emerge from the ashes and devastation of these tragic events—one of more than three decades, the other of 102 minutes. She holds firmly to the belief that it is possible to make positive changes from what we have learned from the violent Troubles and from the trauma of 9/11.

I was deeply touched by this woman's faith, courage, and strong beliefs, which are reflected in the convictions and work of this community. In her book, *A Farther Shore*, Ruth writes about the vision for the healing work of Restoration Ministries:

> Our calling in this organization is to healing and reconciliation . . . to those who have been in any way diminished or trapped or victimized in their own personal lives or through their communal history. . . . In all humility, we feel called to be restorers, seeking to revitalize and renew people in the community and church. . . . We promote the work, not in order to become a big organization, but rather to seek to get the message across that everyone can be a restorer, everyone is needed, everyone has a part to play.[5]

Yes, Ruth, let us listen to you now, let us all play our parts and let us have faith and courage to be restorers on our journey.

❖ ❖ ❖ ❖ ❖ ❖ ❖ ❖

My father was a clergyman, and I was brought up in a church family. I did the usual things: an arts degree and a social work diploma at Queens University in Belfast. Then I went to the University of Toronto to do a master's degree in social work and to get training in community work. In the autumn of 1968, I came back to Belfast to work at Queens University with Chaplain Ray Davey, the founder of Corrymeela. It was the autumn of the civil rights marches.

For a very short period, we thought we were working for a better Ireland and there seemed to be a great sense of togetherness. But as history now tells us, it was the beginning of a period of violence that we've lived with for the last thirty-plus years; some young people have never known another way of life. Certainly, it has shaped our lives to a great degree.

Near the end of my time at Queens, I felt compelled to study theology. I knew it would make sense of everything I had done before, and I thought there was a need for people in Northern Ireland to be trained in both community work and theology. But when I went off to Edinburgh to study, I felt like a rat deserting a sinking ship. I didn't want to leave.

As the first woman to be ordained as a minister in Ireland, in 1976, I knew the biggest test would be if a Presbyterian congregation would be brave or foolish enough to invite me to be their minister. In the end there was a congregation in a large housing estate on the outskirts of south Belfast that was 99.9 percent loyalist working class. I went there in 1977 and was their pastor for fourteen years. It was both challenging and rewarding, and I loved the people. There was no "put on" about them, as we say. They were very real. As people began to trust me with bits of their lives, it was possible to take them further along the road of reconciliation. There is a lot of what I call "secondhand religion" in Ireland. As people began to move from that "secondhand religion" to more of a "living faith," they no longer had to label people as much and they were willing to get involved in more cross-community things. After people shared and prayed together, they could no longer knife each other in the back.

Over time a number of us began to be interested in the prayer healing ministry. We began gently to pray with people about hurts and wounds of the past. We found that people, including myself, were being freed up to move further on the journey of life and of faith. As that happened, we began to do more bridge-building work, not only in the local community, but also regarding North-South concerns. There were many people here who had never been South, and many in the South who had never been North.

I had connections in the South with a Carmelite community in Dublin. Whenever I needed to get out for a day or two, I stayed with them. Eventually I issued an invitation for some of the Carmelites to visit us in the North, and five of them came for a weekend to join in the life of our congregation. It was a bit mind-blowing that five priests from Dublin came to establish relationships in the very Presbyterian, Protestant, loyalist area where I worked. That began a friendship that grew over the years. In the late eighties, all of the elders went to Dublin to stay in the Carmelite monastery for a weekend.

That weekend we also visited some of my friends who are enclosed Carmelite sisters. One of the elders was an Orangeman, and I didn't know if he would go, but he did. The groups exchanged thoughts about how the Presbyterian Church operated and what it was like to be enclosed sisters. Then we had a short worship together and sang some songs. When I looked around, I was surprised to see that some of the men were in tears.

Afterward we had an informal time for chatting and tea. There was a wire grill down the center of the room with the sisters on one side and us on the other. At the end of the room the Orangeman was talking away, with his nose tight up against the wire, with a sister on the other side. It turned out that they had been born in the same town in the North. Everything else fell away as they made this discovery. I felt like I was witnessing a little miracle of reconciliation. Whatever might happen to them in the future, their lives would never be the same because of that encounter.

That example of the building of relationships is our hope for the future. Certainly, it doesn't happen overnight. It can take years of hard work, of creating opportunities and safe spaces where people can meet and build relationships. But when people start to move from just a nodding acquaintance to a relationship to a friendship of trust, many preconceived myths are blown away. Then people begin to see the human being and their common humanity, and they can build from there. Much of our work is about helping people get to know each other in a safe place and then to take those experiences out to where they live.

In 1988 our work was growing very fast. People from different denominations of the Christian faith came to the church because we ran various conferences and they heard about our healing ministry. A small interdenominational group got together to talk and pray about our future. As we did, the words of the Twenty-third Psalm, "He restores my soul," kept coming to us, so we felt guided to call ourselves "Restoration Ministries" and to establish a charity.

My responsibilities and duties to my parish were always first for me. But in the late eighties, I had a feeling that the work of reconciliation and of prayer ministry was what I was supposed to do. It was growing a great deal and was using up all of my spare time. Finally it came to a point where I knew I had to make a decision whether or not to move out of the parish. But, I thought, if people had had a problem with ordained women, how in heaven's name would they understand my doing such a thing? It had cost me so much to get into the system that I didn't really want to think about leaving it. I said to God, "If you find me a place from which to work, something to live on, and if you clear the debt on our church roof, I'll take those three things as signs that I should go." I sat back and thought, "Okay, God, work that one out if you can."

A couple of months later, I realized that I'd been bargaining with God. I also knew he was saying, "No, you go, and I'll see to the rest." So I told the congregation that I was leaving. One week before I left, a gift of ten thousand pounds came through for the church roof. Then when I didn't know where I would live, the congregation told me, "We're going to sell the manse. We can't afford to repair it, so you can stay on as caretaker until we sell it." So that solved the problem of a place to live. And four months later, someone in England funded the work for three years. So God took care of everything. That was 1991.

When I left the parish ministry, I had to apply to the Presbyterian Church to have a recognized ministry standing. I am under the Inter-Church Relations Board, but we are not funded by the church. We're totally interdenominational, with a board of trustees, a management team, and forty wonderful volunteers from different denominations.

In the early years we stumbled along on our journey, but over the last six to eight years we've risen from our knees and are really moving forward. We focus much more on reconciliation, and at the base of our work is prayer, which is central to everything we do. Every day at noon we stop and gather around the kitchen table and pray for peace in Ireland, in the world, and for whoever has asked us to pray. We have a prayer ministry team, and people come to see them and to tell their story. Once a week we have a drop-in prayer time in our conference room. Prayer is the real strength behind everything we do.

Because we aren't a breakaway church, we don't do a weekly meeting. We're about restoring the church and the community. We do some spiritual direction and have a monthly gathering. For the last two years we have been working in partnership with an organization called ECONI (Evangelical Contribution in

Northern Ireland), which has been very courageous in addressing some of the sectarianism on the loyalist side. People from every denomination come from all over the country to participate. We also run courses such as a joint Catholic-Protestant Bible study and hospitality evenings where all our speakers come from the South of Ireland—another opportunity to build relationships.

Hospitality is at the core of the gospel, and everything we do could be called hospitality. We've tried several pilot projects to encourage people to take the concept of hospitality further. We have to push out the boundaries and recognize that God is calling us not to uniformity but to unity in diversity and an acceptance of our differences. Everybody has something to offer the other.

In 1998 we launched a hand of friendship project. It was the two hundredth anniversary of the 1798 rebellion, perhaps the last time when Presbyterians and Catholics stood together, the rebellion of the United Irishmen. We encouraged people to invite a family from another tradition into their home for a simple meal. We encouraged people to refind a friendship that had existed in times of adversity. People phoned the office saying they wanted to do it, but they didn't know any Catholics or Protestants, and could we put them in touch with someone. It's very sad that in such a small place people had to ask for that.

During the Troubles, most of the violence was not very intimate; people didn't have to be very close to be shot or bombed. But now we see more intimate violence like stabbing and kicking. There's something bizarre and frightening about that. Part of it is drug related. During the thirty years, we had no drug problem, because security was so tight. Shortly after the Good Friday Agreement was signed, we caught up with the rest of Europe. But I think part of the problem is that people feel lost, a fear, a lack of identity, a not knowing who they are anymore now that the thirty years are over. So they lash out into a nothingness. The loyalist side may have a bigger sense of fear or loss of identity. If they could only see that building relationships and moving forward together is the solution.

Many people cope relatively well while they are going through trauma or a crisis, but once that is over, the weariness and other problems they didn't allow themselves to feel during the crisis start to come to the surface. Some fall apart; others become exceedingly weary. That hasn't just happened to individuals; it's happened to the whole country. The feet of the peacemakers are weary. We desperately need to be reenergized. The question is who's going to do it for us. The work of reconciliation is much more difficult now than it was just a year ago because of the exhaustion and because a sizable number of people are saying, "We've got peace now. Let those responsible for doing it get on with it. We'll get on with living our lives." That is what happened in Eastern Europe. After a year of the new freedom, people began to look out for "number one," and the insidious selfishness just crept through everything. That's what seems to be happening here as well. It's very hard to motivate people.

I continue to believe the answer is a spiritual one. I don't mean by using a magic wand or some supernatural energy of people finding themselves again. Within everybody there's a God-shaped soul, and there's a homesickness for wholeness and community within them. Once they begin to recognize that, there's a sign of hope. We who call ourselves "church" should not try to provide answers but rather be "accompaniers" on the journey. However, many in the church today are weary, or they don't understand there's a journey to make, or they're too scared. Joan Chittister, OSB, a Benedictine sister and author, talks about the raw and radical call of the gospel in today's world, that it's important to discover who we really are. That means our identity is not that we are male or female or Protestant or Catholic. It's who we are in relationship with God, which is a bigger identity than any label anyone can stick on us. The problem is how to introduce people to that concept who have been so "churched" that their minds are closed or who have been so turned off by organized religion. How do we break through all those preconceived notions?

In Ireland it's as if we are living with a modern paganism that still has a religious vocabulary. People know the words, but they don't necessarily have an understanding of the meaning behind the words. So there's a lot of unlearning that has to be done. People are very caught up in allegiances to lesser things, like putting Presbyterianism or Catholicism or political allegiance or anything else in the place of God. In this country, many people see their own tribe or their own particular political or denominational allegiance as what is important to them. It's very hard to break through that. Maybe we simply have to recognize that we are fellow human beings and start from there.

As I look back over the past thirty-three years, I realize that many people gave so much. Now we all need to restore ourselves. When we get too weary, we run on reserve tanks. Then there's nothing left to offer people, and what we say becomes dull. Perhaps we've been driven to that point because of the needs of all those years. Some of the people who worked very hard are now old, are forgotten, are exhausted. We who are still going must seek them out, encourage them, thank them, and let them know they are not forgotten. That might provide a little lever for some new energy to flow. There's a tremendous healing power in gratitude, both for the one who says thank-you and for the one who receives it. During these times, we need to be generous with our gratitude. We also need to be generous to ourselves. Certainly, Northern Ireland Protestants can be very guilt-ridden and defensive. We don't know what it means to really celebrate. But we're called to celebrate, and it's probably more crucial now than during some of the years at the heart of the violence.

There's the possibility that things could go backward. But I have faith that we will get there, although we may have several major blips before we do. The sad thing is that we don't need to have them, but it could happen because of our weariness or because of unaddressed causes of aggression. Perhaps our political and church leadership is also weary and people have lost confidence in them. There's a tremendous need for prophetic voices, but we haven't had too many of them here.

At some stage I would like to gather together people in an informal way who are recognized as prophetic voices. Jean Vanier, who founded the L'Arche communities for people with learning disabilities, has a prophetic voice for the world. He believes that the poor, the little, and the broken of the world are God's gift to us, that they reveal the truth to us about ourselves. In terms of Ireland, we are little and broken and we have a learning disability because we've never learned from our history. We are also beloved. If something can happen here that is of God and in the form of hospitality, then Ireland still has a chance to say something to the world.

In Ireland one of the most important messages from the Bible is when Jesus tells people to love their neighbor as they love themselves. Maybe we're in such difficulty because we don't love ourselves. If the way we love our neighbors reflects the way we love ourselves, then we're in big trouble. Many of us don't even know what it means to love ourselves. In a Protestant background, we might confuse loving ourselves with patting ourselves on the back and therefore never even embark on the journey. Others get it really twisted, and it ends up being self-righteousness. With that, they cannot hear the truth because they believe they *have* the truth and therefore don't need to listen. Without listening, how can they hear anything that will smash their self-righteous bubble? So it's a vicious circle in a descending spiral.

Perhaps people hit out and become violent and aggressive because they do not know that they are loved. When we know we're loved, we have a sense of security, and we don't need to hit out. We can be generous and be open to the other.

A very liberating thing for us has been the realization that Restoration Ministries doesn't belong to any human being. It belongs to God. There is enormous freedom in that. If one door is closed, another opens. We're not funded by any church or any government agency, so when we feel optimistic it's faith building and when we're not it's downright scary. We are called to trust at a deeper level. It's all about a journey.

We're not really an organization that people join. Different representatives from communities of reconciliation and Christian communities often use this place as a venue just to retell their stories to one another. Apart from a solid core body of volunteers, we're very fluid, and people come and receive from us as they need. They may associate with us for a year or two, and after they've received what they need, they go back to where they're meant to be. That's great, and that's what we're about.

At times it can be lonely, because people are always coming and going. Most of the people who come to Restoration Ministries are on a journey. One wonderful woman who comes here suffered greatly during the Troubles. She said, "I like coming here because nobody asks you who you are or where you've come from. Everybody's treated the same." A woman who works with us says that over the years her view of the people who've come to this place has changed by building relationships with them. Even though she still can't agree with some of the things that they express or do, she's come to love them and she can embrace their differences as well.

Our secretary is from Nigeria, and she's lived here for twenty years. She's from the Ibo people, and their language is beautiful. One day she told me that their word for love is *ifunanya*, which means "the way I see you through my eyes." So when we say that God loves us, it's the way he sees us through his eyes. When somebody loves us, they are seeing us through eyes that have the scales taken from them. That *ifunanya* needs to happen here. We need to see one another and ourselves through different eyes.

A woman who is a deaconess in her church came here for some time. One day she said publicly that she had really been very afraid of Catholics. The job she had, prior to being a deaconess, took her in and out of areas that were mixed. She had been brought up with a view that Catholics weren't Christian, but by coming here, attending courses, and building a relationship with Catholics, she reached a whole new understanding of what the family of God means and has grown to love Catholics as Christians.

There's still a possibility that Ireland could be recognized as a place where there is room enough for all. For years we've had a nostalgia about Ireland as the land of a hundred thousand welcomes. Unfortunately, that's no more than a folk memory, if it ever really existed. When you scratch the surface, we're really quite a racist society. One of our challenges is to make that folk memory into a reality in terms of nationalist and loyalist, Protestant and Catholic, North and South. If the peace process progresses, many more people from other countries will be coming here. We can demonstrate something different because of what we've been through for the last thirty-three years. We have a chance to show the world something, but time may be running out for us, and the world may no longer want to listen to us. We've had so many opportunities given to us, and we should have our act together by now.

In the past, we have not been prophetic or courageous. Part of that is quite understandable because we're such a small community. Often churches and the leadership of churches are themselves prisoners of their own communities. In the past there have been far too many words said. Now we need to move into the phase of actions, where people see by what we do that we mean it, that our future lies together, and that we belong to each other. Whether that future will be a political unity in Ireland is not so important. The most important thing is that we live together with justice, in peace, and with a deep respect for one another.

We're in the day of small things. If little acts are done with love, we could turn this island upside down. If we reach out to somebody who's different and invite them to have a cup of coffee and start a conversation, that's building relationships. Or if we say, "Can I come with you to your church?" or "Will you come with me to my church?" It's seeking to learn about the culture of another group, or it's daring to speak up for something when in the past we might have been silent, or it's being silent when we could have said something that was detrimental. It's being brave enough to do that. And once we've done that, we get the courage to do it again.

We have a new magazine called *Let the Broken Places Sing*. Kathy Galloway, the current director of the Iona Community, in Scotland, wrote that it's not so much a question of mending as a willingness to let the broken places sing. When we do that, then other people can join in and recognize that we are all a community of the broken and of the violent.

Looking back, there's been so much heartache, trauma, and trouble for people, but not unlike the experiences of 9/11 there have also been many good things that have happened. There's a verse, Isaiah 45:3, where God says through the prophet, "I will give you the treasures of darkness, riches stored in secret places, so that you will know that I am the Lord, the God of Israel, the one who calls you by name." When I look back, I can see many treasures of darkness. Many people who were closed because of what was happening have opened up. There's been the discovery of new horizons, and there's been so many named and unnamed acts of generosity, forgiveness, and bigness of spirit. We have many unsung acts of heroism.

The real meaning of encouragement is to give courage to one another. People are given courage by stories of hope or by actions of hope. There are so many little communities and groups doing the reconciliation work, doing the acts of hospitality, being good neighbors in situations of great difficulty. That's feeding into the positive side. Bad news makes news, so much of this good stuff has never been told. I feel that healing stories need to be shouted from the rooftop. This is the time to spread our good news.

Maybe we can encourage the rest of the world if they hear our good stories, our stories of courage, of hope, of forgiveness, of coming together, of new life.

❖ ❖ ❖ ❖ ❖ ❖ ❖ ❖

When we have developed a heart of generosity, a heart that wishes well to all beings, not just a few, when we've come close to suffering in the world, the heart moves to alleviate suffering.
—*Joseph Goldstein*

Accompaniers on the journey! Perhaps that's what every community needs to think about having for itself and being for someone else. When major changes are made in our communities, as they are right now in Northern Ireland, we naturally have a fear of the loss of our identity, of our familiar roles—even though they may not necessarily be healthy ones. In these fast-moving times, we know there will be many big changes made for all of us and for our communities in this very precarious world we live in. That's why we need to turn to accompaniers on our journey. They can encourage us to rest when we are weary, to carry on when we have enough energy to proceed, to move with caution when things need to slow down, and to cheer up when we think we can't go another step.

The Restoration Ministries understands that the work of healing is a very slow process, but it doesn't mean we can give up hope when we don't see progress or we think all is lost. We just have to keep plugging away at it, bit by bit, step by step, piece by piece. We have to try to create safe, nonthreatening places for people to interact with one another. Who would have ever expected that an Orangeman and a cloistered Carmelite nun could have connected in such a beautiful way in a convent? That's progress.

Yes, Ruth, you are absolutely right that it is time for us to be generous with ourselves. Even though there is much more to do and miles to go before we sleep, we have worked hard, we have come a long way already, and we have accomplished much. We need to tell each other that, to remind ourselves that we deserve a good pat on the back now and then, to say "job well done." And we need to celebrate and shout our healing stories from every rooftop. Everyone is tired of hearing bad news, so let's change the picture. Maybe positive healing stories will give people the courage to face times that are very difficult, such as thirty years of the Troubles or a 9/11 tragedy.

Finally, it's a great place to end this chapter by thinking about love— for ourselves and for our neighbors. If we don't love ourselves, it will be very hard to love our neighbors, our communities, or our enemies. So let's start right now learning how to love ourselves. Yes, right now.

AFTERWORD

For while the tale of how we suffer, and how we are
delighted, and how we may triumph is never new, it
always must be heard. . . . It's the only light we've got
in all this darkness.

—*James Baldwin*

What an astonishing world we live in! Although it is full of pain, anxiety, trauma, insecurity, and instability, at the same time it is filled with surprises, great moments, wonder, joy, and healing. Just when we think that the challenges of the universe are extremely difficult for us, that there is just too much suffering and confusion, that what we face is almost impossible to bear, we unexpectedly meet up with an act of kindness, something miraculous that takes our breath away, a caring community full of courage.

Certainly, when we think about all the problems and difficulties in today's world—poverty, discrimination, injustice, hatred, terrorism, war, uncertainty—we can feel absolutely overwhelmed and feel that life is almost without hope. Unquestionably, the tragedies of 9/11 in the United States or the thirty years of the Troubles in Northern Ireland seemed like they could not have been worse. Huge numbers of people and communities have been deeply wounded and affected by these enormous catastrophes.

Yet, as the powerful stories of these *journeys of courage* have shown, adversity and tribulation can also serve in positive ways. They have the potential to help us find deeper meaning in our being, to transform our lives of mediocrity and apathy to lives of passion and caring, to discover some wonderful unexpected gifts of wisdom and service within ourselves and our communities, even to catapult us into newfound roles of bravery and courage.

The communities in this book have given us some admirable portrayals of how we can choose to change the focus of our burdens and pain away from apprehension, hostility, mistrust, cynicism, bitterness, and self-pity to a sense of security, peace, goodwill, faith, confidence, and compassion.

❖ ❖ ❖ ❖ ❖ ❖ ❖ ❖

*I am convinced that the truest act of courage, the
strongest act of humanity is to sacrifice ourselves for
something higher—that which we believe in and love deeply.*
                                              —Cesar Chavez

Listening to these communities tell their stories of healing, it is apparent that there were many different ways that they were "healed" or helped others to "heal." There are some important elements that we see repeated in these stories. Perhaps they can teach us some valuable lessons for our own dilemmas and limitations and provide us with encouragement to pursue our dreams and goals.

As we take a closer look at some of the key themes in these stories, we can turn them into questions to ask ourselves. In the process, we may find that they can help us face our own issues, problems, and needs for healing with candidness and clarity. If we undertake this process, we too may bring to light some understandings and unforeseen wisdom and guidance for our own growth, transformation, and courage.

- **Can we be patient** in understanding that the work of healing is often a very slow process, one that needs perseverance and optimism? We need to bear in mind that healing can take a long time and that we have to keep plugging away at it, especially when we don't see progress. During very tough times we have to be especially generous and give ourselves credit for working hard and for any of our accomplishments—even the smallest ones.

- **Are we able to hold on to a thread of hope** when we are traumatized during volatile times and realize that good things can grow out of adversity? When we are overwhelmed with afflictions and pain—both our own and others', it's helpful if we can believe that there is always the possibility for improvement and healing, that what we are doing does make a difference. When we want to walk away, it's important to remember that someone might still need us to do just what we are doing. Then we may find the courage not to give up hope, even when we feel exhausted and depleted.

Occasionally we may be surprised to learn that someone has responded to our needs with compassion.

- **Are we willing to acknowledge our pain and suffering** and take time to go through a healing process with others? When we gather with others and share our stories of adversity, we are able to experience each other's support. This can serve as a part of our healing process, empowering us to rid our minds and bodies of anguish and anxiety. And if we take the time to come together around a "kitchen table," we can cry over our losses, laugh at our mistakes, learn from each other, and find some healing together.

- **Can we reach out to one another with sensitivity and compassion** at times of tragedy and loss, whether we are the ones able to help others or the ones deeply wounded? When a catastrophe occurs, we need one another's compassion and support to move beyond the paralysis of despair. Often when we have been wounded, we think we are only capable of receiving support. But at times we may find that we are strong enough to reach out and assist others, which may intensify our own healing process.

- **Are we willing to attempt to "do something,"** especially when we feel powerless? Sometimes we think we are completely vulnerable and useless and unable to do anything for ourselves or for others. We will likely feel better if we make an effort to do something rather than merely groveling in the awful feeling of uselessness. Surprisingly, our actions will likely have a positive effect, even if they seem modest or inconsequential.

- **Are we willing to pull together and become a "community"** to get a tough job done without receiving any credit or honor for doing it? When terrible events happen or we find ourselves facing a monumental job, it's easy to become discouraged, especially if we work "behind the scenes" without seeing the results of our efforts. But when we work as a team and approach difficult tasks with confidence and perseverance, we may be surprised at how easily we can achieve our goals. In a true community we can inspire and encourage each other to muster up the strength to do almost any job.

- **Can we let go of some of our needs to control** and, instead, be open to every person's gifts and contributions? Sometimes we have to understand that it's important to appreciate and utilize the skills of all the members of a community, no matter how diverse or unusual they might be. If we trust that people will do their best and let them do it, they will feel empowered, will work with a passion, and will likely do the job well.

- **Are we open to what may be our true purpose in life** or what we were created to be? Sometimes a terrible event can cause us to discover our authentic identity or our real direction in life. It may be revealed to us if we are receptive and allow it to happen. If we don't try too hard to find it, we may be surprised to learn what our genuine mission in life is.

- **Can we encourage forgiveness and reconciliation** within our communities and serve as forgiving role models to others? All of us make endless blunders and mistakes. If we acknowledge our shadow sides, we will likely be more understanding and forgiving of others and appreciate that everyone has both good and bad qualities—just like us. Within each one of us there is sacredness.

- **Are we working against the causes of discrimination?** If we value every person, including those who are different from us and who have been disadvantaged by the misfortunes of poverty, cruelty, and abuse, we can help arrest biases, prejudices, judgments, and acts of discrimination. As we value and treat all people with kindness, dignity, and respect, we may experience our own healing in the process.

- **Do we believe in and practice being a "community of diversity"?** By opening ourselves to those who are different and even those who are considered to be our "enemies," we may learn some new and important viewpoints that are different from our own. In the process we may discover that there is truth, accuracy, and uprightness in every person.

- **Do we believe that even our "smallest dreams" can grow** into something positive and significant? If as "ordinary people" we are open to possibilities and willing to try, our tiny ideas, our seeds of hope, can grow and multiply. We just might find that we can make a huge difference in the world.

- **Are we able to face horrendous situations and transform ourselves** into "survivors" and "winners" even when we have been the "victims"? This is very difficult to do, but if we are willing to try, we may find that it is possible to pull ourselves out of the paralyzing role of "victim." In the process, we may discover some positive aspects, some unexpected joys that come out of the most difficult of circumstances. And if we can learn to forgive ourselves, it will be easier to leave our victim role behind and move toward healing.

- **Are we open to having "accompaniers" on our journey** to help in the healing process? When major tragedies or changes occur in communities, we naturally have fears about dangers to our health and safety. If we allow someone to accompany us, he or she can encourage us to carry on, to move through our anguish and to be cheerful when we feel unable to go another step.

- **Do we have a sense of the Divine in our lives?** Even through horrible grief, disappointments, and sadness, we can find comfort in the belief that there is a Higher Power. According to scientific research, faith is an important factor in good mental and physical health, which can help people come to terms with loss and trauma.

- **Are we remembering to do what is best for future generations?** During difficult times, it's very important to remember our children and to treat them with gentleness and respect. Their concerns and fears need to be dealt with in a thoughtful manner to ensure that their development is protected and nurtured. We must show tenderness toward our children's special needs. By reaching out and encouraging children, we can give them hope, lift their spirits, and heal their wounds.

- **Do we take care of ourselves and take respites and retreats?**
  If we care for ourselves, we can care for our families and our
  communities. To be effective in our work, we need safe places
  where we can heal our wounds, take time out to restore our
  souls, and gear ourselves up to serve others. We need to recognize and deal with our own feelings of anger, depression,
  sorrow, grief, and pain. Without these safety measures, we are
  in danger of burning out.

❖ ❖ ❖ ❖ ❖ ❖ ❖ ❖

Whenever we exhibit courage, we demonstrate the
healing power of paying attention to what has heart
and meaning for us.
—*Angeles Arrien*

When I first started doing the research for *Journeys of Courage*, I
had no idea of the extraordinary gifts that were in store for me.
By entering into these wonderful peoples' lives and listening to
their stories, my own perspectives, attitudes, biases, and
stereotypes changed. Interestingly, I too underwent a healing
process as I heard each of them describe what had happened to
them, their suffering and pain, their healing. It felt like I gained
something almost tangible from every interaction and interview
with these communities: inspiration, fresh hope and courage,
new understandings, feelings of forgiveness and reconciliation.

As I listened, I found my mind and heart being opened by these
remarkable people, by the stories of their journeys of courage. I
felt a deep sense of wonder and awe when I discovered that there
was a great deal of harmony and synchronicity among each and
every one of them. It didn't seem to matter whether their story
was about the healing of a community in New York City
following the disaster of September 11, 2001, or a group of
prisoners in the Dóchas Center of Mountjoy Prison in Dublin, or
survivors in a trauma center in Belfast. Something of openness,
rejuvenation, reconciliation, compassion, and "community"
crossed all the boundaries and made them somehow connected
to each other like kindred spirits. It was as if they were merging

into a greater community reaching out across differences, issues, pain, suffering, and distance.

The process of listening to these stories and writing this book has been a transforming experience for me. It has led me into new undertakings, new beliefs, new communities, and a new mission in life. As I connected with each one of them, I felt I was embraced into their stories, their lives, their pain, and their healing. I was deeply honored to be considered part of their communities.

As you read the last words of this book of courageous, healing stories, I invite you to reflect on your own life, your mission, and your community. And I encourage you to allow these stories to inspire you, to uplift you, to transform you, and to help you consider new options and possibilities on your *journeys of courage*.

NOTES

1. All rights reserved. No reproduction or performance without permission of the author. Copyright September 16, 2002, by John van Amerongen, 11529 Vashon Hwy. SW, Vashon, WA 98070.
2. Reproduced by permission of the Killaloe Diocesan Office, Ennis, Ireland.
3. Tim Carey, *Mountjoy: The Story of a Prison* (Cork: The Collins Press, 2000), 243-44.
4. John Hume, *A New Ireland: Politics, Peace, and Reconciliation* (Boulder, CO: Roberts Rinehart Publishers, 1996), 15.
5. Ruth Patterson, *A Farther Shore* (Dublin: Veritas Publications, 2002), 41.

**JOY CAROL** is a spiritual director, counselor, and author. She leads retreats and workshops for medical schools, seminaries, retreat centers, churches, and other groups on a wide range of topics, including spirituality, healing, prayer, caregiving, and death and dying.

Carol has worked for the Ford Foundation, Save the Children, and Christian Children's Fund. She has been honored nationally as an outstanding educator and holds an honorary doctorate from Nebraska Wesleyan University and master's degrees from the New York's General Theological Seminary and from the University of Maryland. Carol's previous book, *Towers of Hope: Stories to Help Us Heal*, has enjoyed wide acclaim.